Praise for Blood in the Water

"*Blood in the Water* is utterly immersive. Casey Sherman is a master true crime storyteller. Like always, he brings characters to life which makes it hard to tear yourself away from the page!"

—Zibby Owens, host of *Moms Don't Have Time to Read Books*, bestselling author of *Blank*

"Right from the opening pages, Casey Sherman's *Blood in the Water* establishes a sense of foreboding. All signs point in one direction, but—even if you know the Nathan Carman case—you can't help but think, and perhaps even hope, that there will be surprises, something to make you believe there is more than darkness in the tale of a family mired in tragedy, accusation, and intrigue. As each thread of the story is pulled and facts are revealed, the reader is offered chances to examine their own thoughts, feelings, and beliefs about human behavior, and how we decide what the truth is when there are few clear guideposts."

—Holly Frey, creator *Criminalia* and co-host of *Stuff You Missed in History Class*

"What I most admire about Casey Sherman is that he's more than a writer. He's also an outstanding investigative journalist, and he uses these skills to great effect in bringing this mind-boggling case to life. *Blood in the Water* is a twisty true crime narrative of greed, suspicion, and revenge, taking us from the high seas to the mansion of an enormously wealthy family. Compelling and cinematic, it keeps you guessing about the complicated family at the heart of this saga until the very last page. And it shows us that no matter how sophisticated our technology becomes, we can never have all the answers about what happens behind closed doors."

—Shawn Cohen, *New York Times* bestselling author of *College Girl, Missing*

"*Blood in the Water* is a book for every true crime fan's 'to be read' pile…though you won't want to wait to read it! The tautly woven narrative showcases Sherman's lyrical writing style and formidable research skills, guaranteeing a deep dive into family drama and depravity that's nearly impossible to turn away from. Sherman is at the top of his game!"

—Kristin Dilley, co-host, *Mind Over Murder* podcast

"In *Blood in the Water,* Casey Sherman digs behind the headlines to create a vivid and absorbing account of a fascinating true crime story. Immersive and compelling, this Capote-esque narrative skillfully takes the reader through its many shocking twists and turns while unfolding a disturbing mystery as to what really happened on that little boat in the icy North Atlantic, when two went out and only one came back."

—Paul Tamasy and Eric Johnson, Oscar-nominated screen-writers of *The Fighter, The Finest Hours, Patriots Day, The Outpost,* and *The Ministry of Ungentlemanly Warfare*

PRAISE FOR A MURDER IN HOLLYWOOD

"A wild ride beneath the glitz and glamour of 1950s Hollywood, proving once again that Casey Sherman is a master of the genre. Riveting, eye-opening, and impeccably researched, *A Murder in Hollywood* is a cinematic tour de force that pulls back the curtain on one of Tinseltown's darkest moments, reinventing our understanding of Lana Turner as an enduring icon of feminine power. Casey Sherman's research is revelatory—a game changer that shifts the spotlight from scandal to the strength and resilience of a woman fighting for her life and her legacy."

—Ben Mezrich, *New York Times* bestselling author of *Dumb Money, Bringing Down the House,* and *The Accidental Billionaires*

"If you like a lively Hollywood yarn or crave a good gangster tale—or both—*A Murder in Hollywood* is the book for you. Casey Sherman turns his sharp eye to the famed Lana Turner murder case, and he delivers the liveliest, grittiest, juiciest page-turner of the year, a true story that reads like Harold Robbins on steroids. Lovely Lana, the bottle-blonde heart-throb, gets top billing. Surrounding her is a fantastic cast of featured players, hoods like Bugsy Siegel, Mickey Cohen, and Johnny Stompanato, Hollywood giants like Clark Gable, Joan Crawford, and even Sean Connery. It's the kind of book that's just plain fun to read, but when you're done, you'll wonder at the toxic effects of ambition, greed, and unfulfilled dreams of love…even in the land where dreams are supposed to come true."

—William Martin, *New York Times* bestselling author of *Back Bay* and *December '41*

"A must read for fans of true crime and Hollywood history, *A Murder in Hollywood* never disappoints! Casey Sherman deftly serves just the right mix of glamour, glitz, and grit to keep the reader turning pages. It's a stunner from start to finish."

—Kristin Dilley, cohost, *Mind over Murder* podcast

"In his stunning new book, *A Murder in Hollywood*, Casey Sherman takes us behind the glitz and glamour of 1950s Technicolor to a front row seat at a real-life film noir, the story of Lana Turner and her terrifying love affair with LA gangster Johnny Stompanato. It's a violent and harrowing tale of female empowerment, a page-turner more gripping than any film in which she ever starred."

—Terence Winter, executive producer of *The Sopranos*, creator of *Boardwalk Empire*

"Casey Sherman's *A Murder in Hollywood* is a riveting page-turner. This book shines a much-needed light on sexism and overt violence against women in Hollywood during the twentieth century. Bravo to Sherman for exposing a toxic Hollywood culture against the backdrop of one of Tinseltown's most famous crimes."

—Tamara Leitner, bestselling author of *Don't Say a Thing*

"A well-researched and new take on one of Hollywood's most notorious mysteries. True-crime fans and celebrity mavens will enjoy."

—*Library Journal*

PRAISE FOR HELLTOWN

"With *Helltown*, Casey Sherman delivers the kind of true crime that keeps eyes glued to the pages—smart, impeccably researched, and utterly absorbing. Destined to be on all the year-end best nonfiction lists, this is an unqualified triumph by a writer at the top of his game!"

—Gregg Olsen, #1 *New York Times* bestselling author of *If You Tell*

"Searing and important, *Helltown* is an immaculately researched and rivetingly propulsive chronicle illustrating a pivotal part of our history. Brilliantly weaving together true crime, a grotesque criminal, the political landscape, and the brilliant minds who wrote about it—Casey Sherman is a master at bringing history alive. Compelling, complex, and revealing—do not miss this!"

—Hank Phillippi Ryan, *USA Today* bestselling author of *Her Perfect Life*

"Master storyteller Casey Sherman takes us back in time to the 1960s and into the dark mind of a charismatic killer. Set against the idyllic backdrop of Cape Cod, *Helltown* is a riveting, often spine-tingling true crime story."

—Terence Winter, executive producer of *The Sopranos*, creator of *Boardwalk Empire*

"*Helltown* is an immersive and captivating journey into the mind of a serial killer."

—Associated Press

"*Helltown* will render even the calmest reader unsettled when the book has been concluded. Author Casey Sherman continues his excellent work in the true crime realm with his latest effort. The narrative relayed by Sherman is engrossing and never wavers in its intensity."

—*Seattle Book Review*

PRAISE FOR *THE LAST DAYS* OF JOHN LENNON

"Incredibly tense and thriller-like… I totally recommend it."
—Lee Child, #1 bestselling author of the Jack Reacher series

"A must read for music fans, true crime aficionados, or anyone looking for a deep, insightful dive into a dark chapter of American history."

—*Town & Country*

"A first-rate book…a winner."

—*Baltimore Post Examiner*

ALSO BY CASEY SHERMAN

A Rose for Mary: The Hunt for the Real Boston Strangler

Black Irish

Black Dragon

Bad Blood: Freedom & Death in the White Mountains

The Finest Hours

Animal: The Bloody Rise and Fall of the Mob's Most Feared Assassin

Boston Strong: A City's Triumph Over Terror

*Above & Beyond: John F. Kennedy and America's
Most Dangerous Cold War Spy Mission*

12: The Inside Story of Tom Brady's Fight for Redemption

The Ice Bucket Challenge: Pete Frates and the Fight Against ALS

*Hunting Whitey: The Inside Story of the Capture &
Killing of America's Most Wanted Crime Boss*

The Last Days of John Lennon with James Patterson

Helltown: The Untold Story of a Serial Killer on Cape Cod

*A Murder in Hollywood: The Untold Story of
Tinseltown's Most Shocking Crime*

BLOOD

IN THE

WATER

THE UNTOLD STORY
OF A FAMILY TRAGEDY

CASEY SHERMAN

Published by Sourcebooks
P.O. Box 4410, Naperville, Illinois 60567-4410
(630) 961-3900
sourcebooks.com

Cataloging-in-Publication Data is on file with the Library of Congress.

Printed and bound in the United States of America.
LB 10 9 8 7 6 5 4 3 2 1

For Kristin

A beautiful soul, a caring partner, and the love of my life.

*Land and sea, weakness and decline, are great
separators, but death is the great divorcer for ever.*
—*John Keats*

Chapter One

The sun's reflection danced atop the cold, choppy waters 115 nautical miles south of Martha's Vineyard as the Chinese supermax cargo ship *Orient Lucky* powered its way like a slow-moving freight train through the turbulent waves. The *Orient Lucky* had just departed from Providence, Rhode Island, and was in the process of shifting its ballast, moving it from one side of the vessel to the other before making its way north to Boston, Massachusetts, for refueling. From there, it would continue on to Canada and the Bay of Fundy in New Brunswick to pick up tons of scrap metals at the American Iron and Metal terminal in the port city of Saint John, over 1500 nautical miles from its current location.

The *Orient Lucky* would then sail to Turkey and make several more stops before eventually heading home to mainland China, where crew members looked forward to planting their feet on terra firma and enjoying the warm embrace of their loved ones after nine long months at sea. The journey had been uneventful thus far, no different from countless other scrap metal runs along the East Coast of the United States, continental Europe, and beyond. Forecasters were keeping a watchful eye on a giant storm that was forming off the Lesser Antilles and would later wreak deadly havoc on the people of Haiti as Hurricane Matthew. But the *Orient Lucky* was hundreds of miles outside the danger zone and was expected to reach port in Boston in two days' time.

To stave off boredom, one young crew member stretched his legs and took a stroll on the sun-splashed deck, which was the length of more than two football fields. The temperature had reached the low sixties by midafternoon, but a gusty wind made it feel much colder, especially on the open deck of the *Orient Lucky.* The sailor lit a cigarette and blew smoke on his hands to keep them warm. The crew had just turned over the watch, which meant that the ship's captain, Zhao Hengdong, was back on the bridge. The sailor knew that he could not dawdle for long. Captain Hengdong was known as a good and fair captain, but he was also one to lean hard on his merchant mariners if he saw that they were not actively engaged in their duties.

The crew member stared out at the vast emptiness of the ocean while he enjoyed another puff from his cigarette. The endless view reminded him of the ancient idiom that appeared in black ink on a small frame outside the ship's mess hall: *Between heaven and earth, I am nothing but a small particle in the middle of the vast lands. Even the seven seas together are nothing but a small grain of dust in the universe. I am far from being vast.*

Suddenly, the sailor saw an orange ball bobbing up and down in the sea about one nautical mile away. He then heard the shouts of his fellow sailors and quickly turned toward the commotion as a group of men lined up in rescue formation. He flicked the cigarette into the choppy water and joined them.

On the bridge, Captain Hengdong could hardly believe what he was seeing. After clocking in, the captain had inspected the ship's ECDIS, the electronic chart display and information system, which displayed the cargo carrier's speed log, GPS position, and NAVTEX receiver. Everything appeared to be normal, and there were no meteorological or navigational issues facing the crew on the short run from Providence to Boston. But Captain Hengdong had been married to the sea for sixteen years, and he never completely relied on his computer screens. He grabbed a pair of binoculars and swept the ocean from port to starboard. The sea was a minefield of whitecaps, which may have made conditions difficult for pleasure boaters or day fishermen but posed no threat for the 33,547-ton freighter.

Captain Hengdong peered through the eyepiece of the binoculars and spotted a flash of red off the right side of the ship. *Was it flotsam, some kind of debris?* he asked himself. The captain turned the focus wheel on his binoculars and the image became clearer. It appeared to be a red-and-yellow life raft, and standing in the middle of it was a tall, scraggly-haired young man trying to maintain his balance while desperately waving a flag in the air with both arms to attract attention.

The captain had never taken part in a sea rescue before. He had only read about such things. He would have to rely on his training and common sense now. Captain Hengdong sounded the rescue horn on the bridge. A high-pitched wail echoed throughout the tanker, sending crew members topside. The waves were too rough for Hengdong to deploy a dinghy, so the captain carefully maneuvered the hulking freighter close enough for his crew to lower the ship's accommodation ladder and throw a life ring to the stranded man.

The orange flotation device landed with a splash several yards away from the drifting life raft. The castaway dove from the small inflatable into the cold, unforgiving sea and swam toward his salvation. Watching the rescue unfold through his binoculars on the bridge, Captain Hengdong held his breath as the man performed the breaststroke, trying desperately to cut through the strong ocean current. The captain lost sight of the swimmer as a frothy whitecap crashed over his head. Hengdong prayed that the man would return to the surface. After a few seconds, an arm pushed its way out of the water, followed by the man's head as he gasped for air. The castaway was alive but still caught about fifteen feet away from the life ring, which was attached to a nylon rope line. The swimmer plunged forward, spitting out salt water while working his arms and kicking his legs feverishly to close the distance.

Nathan Carman swims from his life raft toward the Orient Lucky *during his rescue at sea in 2016. (United States Coast Guard Handout)*

Captain Hengdong feared that the man was overexerting himself and might not have the strength for one final push. In that case, one or two of Hengdong's crew would have to dive into the water themselves, and the situation could get even more dangerous. After several more strokes, the swimmer finally extended his long body and reached for the life ring. The flotation device was just beyond his grasp. Another wave knocked the castaway back a few yards. Crew members pulled the ring out of the water and tossed it back twice more before the man grabbed hold of it, slipped it over his head, and tucked it under one of his arms. Waves knocked the man against the freighter's giant hull. He used his right arm to push himself off the ship's starboard side while rescuers got into position to pluck him from the sea.

The swimmer was lifted onto the

The crew of the Orient Lucky *toss Carman a life ring in the Atlantic Ocean. (United States Coast Guard Handout)*

platform of the accommodation ladder and handed a thick brown blanket, which he immediately wrapped around his narrow shoulders. The ship's doctor was among the first to meet the rescued boater on the platform. The man's teeth were chattering, but the physician was surprised yet relieved to see that he could stand on his own. The rescuers then led the castaway up the accommodation ladder and onto the deck of the *Orient Lucky*. The ladder was steep, but the castaway climbed it with ease. Captain Hengdong continued to watch through his binoculars from the bridge. At that moment, the captain felt that his ship had lived up to its promising name.

The young man was escorted from the deck to a private, spacious cabin where the ship's doctor offered to examine him more closely. The doctor looked

into the man's eyes. They were clear yet distant. His breathing was normal. He was neither hypothermic nor dehydrated. To the physician and to the crew, it looked like the stranded sailor had been floating in the

Nathan Carman greeted by Orient Lucky *crew members, including the ship's doctor. (United States Coast Guard Handout)*

ocean for just a matter of hours. All were startled when, through a translator, the young man told them that he had been trapped on the life raft for seven long days. The young man refused any more medical attention at that point.

The captain of the *Orient Lucky* could see that the rescued castaway was distressed. The young man spoke very little and avoided eye contact with his rescuers. It was as if his mind was someplace else, far away from the trauma of the Atlantic Ocean.

The stranded boater identified himself as twenty-two-year-old Nathan Carman, and he was soon given a bowl of hot soup and a bottle of water along with a white crew jumpsuit to replace his drenched long-sleeved shirt and blue jeans. Captain Hengdong then invited Nathan into his private quarters and radioed for assistance.

The skipper reached Coast Guard Search and Rescue controller Richard Arsenault at the U.S. Coast Guard's First District in Boston. Arsenault grew up close to the ocean in New Bedford, Massachusetts, which was immortalized in Herman Melville's 1851 classic novel, *Moby Dick*. But Arsenault did not live off dreams of Captain Ahab, Starbuck, and the *Pequod*. He really had no interest in life at sea. He joined the Coast Guard by chance. "I hung around with some guys in the neighborhood who worked at a convenience store, and they had an attached liquor store. The Coast Guard recruiter worked there as a side hustle. So I said, let me try the service," Arsenault recalled.

He imagined that he would enlist only for four years. Instead, Arsenault was in the middle of his tenth year as a Coastie and had performed hundreds of search and rescue missions over the course of

Nathan Carman is given dry clothes and hot soup aboard the Orient Lucky. *(United States Coast Guard Handout)*

his career in the service. Now, he was in command of the watch floor, leading a massive team in a search and rescue case with an overdue boat that had two people on board. After seven frustrating days with no results, the Coast Guard had suspended its search.

Arsenault was surprised to get a call from Captain Hengdong. He listened intently while the Chinese ship captain described the scene in near-perfect English. Hengdong relayed the coordinates of the rescue near Block Canyon, a spot that had conflicted with Arsenault's search models. When asked about the physical condition of the rescued boater, Hengdong added, "His health looks normal."

Arsenault did not want to relay any more information through the captain. He needed to hear from the castaway himself.

"Can I speak with him?"

Hengdong handed the receiver to Nathan.

"Hello, this is Nathan Carman."

"Nathan, this is the United States Coast Guard Boston," replied Arsenault. Base Boston was the touch point for the Coast Guard's First District and managed all other Coast Guard units stationed throughout New England, New York, and northern New Jersey. The year 2016 had already been a busy one for the U.S. Coast Guard, as the maritime service had responded to over forty-five hundred accidents at sea that had resulted in more than seven hundred deaths.

"Hello?" Nathan repeated.

There was a moment of inaudible chatter on the radio before the connection became clear.

"Yes, I hear you." Nathan said.

"Yes, sir," replied Arsenault. "I need to understand what happened. Over."

Nathan took a deep breath and began to speak. His thoughts were jumbled. *Where should he begin?* He decided to cut right to the heart of the matter.

"Mom and I, two people, myself and my mom, were fishing at Block Canyon, and there was a funny noise in the engine compartment. I looked and saw a lot of water."

Arsenault listened closely to the inflection and energy in Nathan's voice. *He doesn't seem lethargic,* the Coastie thought to himself. *He doesn't sound like someone who's been in a life raft for several days without moving their body. It takes a while to get your body moving.*

Nathan continued. "I was bringing [in] the lines. As my mom [brought] in the reels, I brought the safety stuff forward. And I was bringing one of the safety bags forward, and the boat just dropped out from under my feet. Ah, when I saw the life raft, I did not see my mom. Have you found her?"

"No," Arsenault replied. "We haven't been able to find her yet."

Nathan paused for a moment before continuing with his story. "So I got to the life raft after I got my bearings, and I was whistling and calling and looking around, and I didn't see her."

"Understood. Okay."

"So we're fishing around Block Canyon," Nathan repeated.

"Right, and when did that happen?" Arsenault asked. "Do you remember the day?"

"I don't know the exact correlation."

"Do you remember the day?"

"Yes," Nathan responded. "It was a week ago today, around midday."

Arsenault glanced over at a calendar pinned up on the watch floor and quickly counted the days. "Okay, so last Sunday?"

"Yes," Nathan confirmed.

Unbeknownst to Nathan Carman, the U.S. Coast Guard had already searched over sixty thousand square miles for both him and his mother, Linda Carman.

After speaking with Arsenault, Nathan was escorted to a cabin, where he collapsed on a bunk and slept. He did not open the door until the next morning. On the second day, Nathan asked for a tour of the bridge and had a conversation with Captain Hengdong.

"How much distance do you need before you can spot someone like me in the ocean?"

The captain gave it some thought. "About three nautical miles."

The young man left the bridge and walked alone on the deck.

"He just stood and looked out at the ocean," Captain Hengdong said later. "I got a feeling that he was looking for his mother."

For the next two hours, Nathan stood virtually still on the deck, staring out at the sea. It was a miracle that the Chinese freighter had stumbled upon his life raft. It would take another miracle to find Linda Carman.

CHAPTER TWO

Randy Beach was puttering around his quaint New Haven, Connecticut, home when he heard a news flash on local television about a dramatic rescue at sea off the coast of Rhode Island. The female news reporter mentioned the name of the stranded boater, and Beach's head spun around.

Did she just say Nathan Carman? he asked himself.

Beach was familiar with the name but could not immediately place it. He had covered thousands of stories during his long career as a print journalist and celebrated columnist, and the narratives all seemed to blur together over the decades. He ran a hand through a long lock of his silver hair and racked his brain a moment before recognizing the connection. Beach had covered a story years before about a boy with the same name who went missing from his home in the town of Middletown, Connecticut.

Beach poured himself a cup of coffee and walked from the kitchen to his writing office where he kept an archive of his work. He had been a reporter since 1975 after landing a job at the *Morning Record* in Wallingford, Connecticut, about twenty-six miles south of Hartford. He grew up in Westchester County, New York, and vacationed along the Connecticut shoreline with his family when he was a kid. He loved the region and jumped at the chance to join the fledgling community newspaper while in his early twenties. Like most small-town reporters, Beach covered mundane news stories like town and school committee meetings along with occasionally exciting assignments such as a five-alarm fire or a nor'easter that would pull down trees and knock out power around town. He had strong instincts about what made for a good news story and had a particular gift for person-to-person journalism, where a story's characters were given as much importance as the news he covered.

Beach quickly caught the eye of an editor at the *New Haven Register*, which was established in 1812, making it one of the oldest continuously run daily newspapers in America. He arrived in New Haven as a cub reporter and music critic in 1977. To Beach, the newsroom on Orange Street appeared to be something straight out of *The Front Page*, "filled with the rat-a-tats of typewriter keys and animated telephone conversations of reporters working on their stories."

Randy Beach had found a home there, and a few years later, he found himself reporting on two of the biggest stories in the world.

"I covered the vigil at Central Park after John Lennon was assassinated in December 1980," Beach recalled. "I was also there at the courthouse when Mark David Chapman, Lennon's assassin, rolled in and opened up a copy of *The Catcher in the Rye* and read a passage."

Beach also wrote about the assassination attempt on President Ronald Reagan by John Hinckley Jr. Much of the intense media attention surrounding the assassination attempt focused on the campus of Yale University, in the heart of New Haven, where actress Jodie Foster attended classes as a sophomore student. Hinckley told investigators that he shot the president in an attempt to impress the eighteen-year-old Foster and had called her dorm room at least five times and even had conversations with her.

"I got involved in covering that case," Beach said. "She [Foster] was just trying to go about her business being a Yale student, and this guy was stalking her. Foster performed in a Yale theater production in the middle of all that, and I wrote about it for the *Register*."

The news articles about John Lennon and Jodie Foster helped the reporter gather a following of dedicated readers in the New Haven area, offering him a chance to move from general assignment reporter to the lofty position as the *Register*'s star columnist. He became so popular that the newspaper splashed his handsome, smiling face on giant billboards across the city under the banner *Beach, Beach, Beach* [as in bitch, bitch, bitch], *Randall Beach speaks his mind Tuesdays, Thursdays and Sundays.*

Mementos from Beach's prominent news career were scattered throughout his office, along with a clipping from August 18, 2011. The headline read, "Middletown Parents Just Thankful Runaway Son Is Home Again." The reporter turned columnist knew that he had heard the name Nathan Carman before.

In early August 2011, Nathan woke up one bright, sunny morning and told his mother, Linda, that he planned to go on a bike ride for the day. The seventeen-year-old did not have a summer job, and the start of the school year was still more than three weeks away. Linda did not ask her son whether he had planned the trip with a friend; he did not have any. Nathan told her that he was going to take his black mountain bike and pedal thirty miles north to the town of Westbrook where he could cast off from the town dock or Pier 76 along the Patchogue River for rainbow trout and smallmouth bass. He had been fishing those waters for a while, and the long bike ride was nothing new.

Nathan got dressed and headed out to the garage to grab his mountain bike and his fishing pole. He placed the fishing rod in a black backpack and strapped on a silver bike helmet. He walked the bike out of the garage and hopped on. The mountain bike was heavy. It had a rack on the back and two saddlebags. Nathan balanced the weight as he pedaled down the street. He did not look back.

Linda Carman thought the excursion might do him some good. She had been worried for her son more than usual for the past several months, since his horse, Cruise, died from colic and other health-related problems in December 2010. The Irish horse with the light gray coat had been a lifeline for the teenager, who was diagnosed with autism spectrum disorder when he was a child.

"He had no other friends. Cruise was his only friend," said Nathan's father, Clark Carman, who had been divorced from Linda Carman since their son was a toddler. "We tried basketball and other team sports, but Nathan could not connect to other kids and instead gravitated toward individual sports and hobbies."

Horseback riding was one of the only social outlets that Nathan had. His maternal grandfather, John Chakalos, a wealthy real estate developer, doted on him and bought the horse for Nathan and paid for riding lessons and expensive boarding fees. The teenager had spent countless hours with Cruise at Fox Ledge Farm, a sprawling horse training center in nearby East Haddam, Connecticut, under the watchful eye of farm owner Ann Guptill, a world-class equestrian.

Guptill trained Nathan on basic horsemanship, including riding lessons and grooming. It did not take long for her to see the strong connection being formed between the teenager and the animal.

"Nathan and Cruise definitely had a special bond," the trainer recalled. "Even before Nathan got to his stall, he [Cruise] knew he was there."

Unlike many of Nathan's classmates at Middletown High School, the horse did not judge the boy, who had always had trouble connecting with his peers. Cruise offered Nathan unconditional love.

The horse did not respond the same way toward others. When Nathan's parents walked around the barn, Cruise was ambivalent to their presence, but as soon as Nathan drew near, he would start pawing at the stall.

"Stop pawing," Linda Carman scolded the horse.

Nathan quickly corrected his mother. "He's not pawing; he's hoofing."

When the sixteen-year-old horse became ill with colic, Nathan's grandfather paid for his transport and treatment at a nearby equine clinic. Cruise was suffering from major gastrointestinal problems and had no appetite. Nathan visited the sick horse every day. Veterinarians spread alfalfa around the horse's stall to increase the animal's protein and fiber, but Cruise would not touch it. At that point, the normally shy and quiet teenager spoke up.

"He wants the hay wet and he wants it hung up," Nathan told them.

The veterinarians took his advice and sprayed down the alfalfa with a hose and then hung it up in a slow feed hay net tied to the stall. Cruise responded immediately and devoured the feed. The horse's health improved soon after, and he was allowed to return to Fox Ledge Farm. Nathan and his mother drove out to the equine clinic to manage the horse's transport. As the teenager lent a hand guiding Cruise into the large aluminum horse trailer, the veterinarian pulled Linda Carman aside.

"We didn't think the horse was going to pull through," he told her.

Linda believed that her son's constant presence at the clinic and comfort for his horse had allowed Cruise to regain his strength. The teen's grandfather continued to pay for the horse's care, which caused tension with some family members who complained about high veterinary costs and urged him to euthanize the sick animal.

Once back at Fox Ledge Farm, Cruise's medical problems returned, and Nathan watched helplessly as the horse withered away and eventually died.

"After the death of his horse, Nathan personally thanked all of the veterinarians for all of their help in trying to save Cruise's life," his father recalled. "That's how close he was to that horse. Cruise's death had a major effect on him."

At that point, the teenager became inconsolable. His grandfather purchased another horse for Nathan, but the emotional connection was not there. Eventually, he quit his riding lessons under Ann Guptill and stopped going to Fox Ledge Farm.

Nathan turned his attention to fishing that summer, and Linda hoped that her son might strike up a friendship with another angler while casting a line in the Patchogue River.

The day that Nathan told her he planned to pedal his mountain bike to Westbrook, Linda expected to see her son again before nightfall. Nathan had a self-imposed curfew and rarely went out after dark. When he rode his bike to visit Cruise, he would always call for a ride home when night fell.

Linda waited anxiously for her son to walk through the front door with his fish tales from the day, but he did not return home that night.

Linda told Clark Carman that their son had not come home, and both surmised that he had probably found a safe place to spend the night and would ride his bike home at daybreak. This idea may have briefly comforted Nathan's parents, but they were not going to sit idly by, hoping that he would turn up the next day. At dusk, Linda and Clark sounded the alarm bells. At first, the Carmans were apprehensive, as they believed they had to wait a full twenty-four hours before reporting their son as missing. But panic soon took over, and they called the Middletown police station and spoke to Officer Jeffrey Laskowski, who went right to work on their case.

Linda told Laskowski that she never had any indication that her son would run away but that he was still grieving the loss of his horse. Linda and Clark also described the teen's diagnosis and why it might be hard to find him. "Social interaction is very difficult for him," they told Laskowski. The officer typed up a report and spoke to reporters about a statewide search that was getting underway. Technically, Nathan was not considered to be a "youth in crisis," as he did not have a history of running away from home. Until any evidence suggested otherwise, the teen was simply considered "lost," a designation indicating that he had strayed away and that his whereabouts were unknown.

But the boy's autism spectrum disorder added a complicated wrinkle to the search. Laskowski had to be careful when asking for the public's help in finding Nathan.

"[Nathan] may come off as extremely rude, but he's not violent," Laskowski told members of the press. "Nathan will use passive resistance instead and will likely go limp. If anyone comes across Nathan, it is better to just calmly talk with him, but don't touch him because that will cause him to shut down."

Laskowski spoke to his police counterparts across Connecticut and provided them with a description and a photo of the boy. "He has light brown hair and brown eyes," Laskowski said. "He's tall, six foot three, but slight. The boy weighs about one hundred and forty-five pounds."

It was also standard procedure for the officer to upload Nathan's information into the National Crime Information Center, which was maintained by the FBI.

Two days went by with no sign of Nathan Carman. No one remembered seeing him fishing anywhere in Westbrook, and he had not turned up at his grandfather's home in the town of Windsor, just north of Hartford. There was a suspicion that he might return to Cruise's old stall at Fox Ledge Farm, but the staff there told police that he had not come around in months. FBI agents visited Linda and Clark Carman and were given access to Nathan's computer, hoping that the search engine would offer some digital breadcrumbs leading to his location. Agents discovered that the teenager had recently conducted searches for pornography and motorcycles, but the computer yielded no other clues.

Nathan's family members also discussed their suspicions that he may have been corresponding with members of a right-wing militia group somewhere down south. His grandfather had ordered the caretaker at his second home, a large, sprawling estate in New Hampshire, to keep the doors unlocked just in case the teenager traveled north for shelter.

Finally, on Saturday, August 13, 2011, investigators caught a break. Someone fitting Nathan's description had been captured on a surveillance camera getting off a bus at the corner of Chapel and Temple Streets in New

Haven, near the historic town green. The young man was carrying a brief-case, and he had a bag strapped across his chest. He was wearing a long-sleeved shirt and khaki pants. When shown the image by police, Nathan's parents confirmed that it was their son in the photo. An employee at the Middletown Area Transit Station in downtown Middletown also remem-bered selling him a bus ticket.

Clark Carman jumped in his car and drove twenty-seven miles south to New Haven, where he rode around the city with a police officer, checking the Amtrak train terminal at Union Station for any sign of his son and also scouring the city's homeless shelters. They found no trace of Nathan.

The following day, while Linda monitored the telephone at home in case her son decided to call, her best friend, Sharon Hartstein, gathered twenty-five volunteers and drove down to New Haven to help police with their search.

"We have a cold trail and no leads," Hartstein told reporters as the group of volunteers gathered inside the police substation at New Haven city hall. "We're beside ourselves. We have nowhere else to turn."

Clark spoke about his son's love for his horse and his deepening depres-sion since his death. "The special partner he had died. [Nathan] had [Cruise] for five or six years, but they were like this," he said, folding his pointer over his middle finger. "So for him, that was his friend. He has no friends. He loved that horse. That was a bond. It's like the horse whisperer."

Clark then made a desperate, teary-eyed plea directly to his son.

"Come home," he said, his voice cracking. "Don't be afraid to contact us or the police. I'll come get you anywhere."

Clark went on to say that his ex-wife, Linda, was not handling the situa-tion well after days without any word of their son's whereabouts. Linda's friend Sharon Hartstein passed out flyers with a picture of Nathan Carman under the words *Urgent Missing*. In three paragraphs, the flyers explained that the teenager had "a disorder under the umbrella of autism which leaves him vulnerable" and offered specific instructions for anyone who saw him. "He may appear to be extremely agitated or may make statements that those who may encounter him may find as odd or offensive," the flyer read. "Please talk to him calmly, if approachable, and most importantly keep him in your sight and contact the Middletown police at 860-347-2541, or phone 9-1-1 immediately."

Hartstein informed reporters and news photographers that the teen did not carry any identification and did not own a cell phone. She also stressed that the family had created a Facebook page for tipsters to share information. "[The Facebook page] is where we need people to post, repost, ask your friends and family to post, share the information," Hartstein said. "We need this to go viral, to go nationwide as soon as possible. Chances are he's still here [in Connecticut], but we're not sure. We have to go beyond this because we have no substantial leads that I am aware of since Thursday. The sooner and wider and nationwide we can get this, the more people that know about it, the more in the forefront of people's minds this will be."

Friends and strangers flooded the Facebook page with twenty-eight hundred comments and likes, with new posts coming every five minutes.

With flyers in hand, the group of volunteers, which included family members and friends, then began canvassing the area around the Ivy League campus of Yale University, wondering if Nathan had found shelter in one of the school's nineteenth-century Gothic Revival buildings, where he would appear to be just another college student taking a quick cat nap between classes and exams.

Randy Beach was working that Sunday morning for the *New Haven Register* as reporters and columnists rotated their weekend shifts. The newsroom was quiet, and there was a skeleton crew of editors and reporters prepared to chase whatever stories broke from late Friday night through late Sunday evening. Beach's editor learned that a group of volunteers had arrived in town to aid in the search for a missing teenager. Since Beach had two daughters around the same age as Nathan, his editor felt that he was best suited to work on the story. While other reporters might focus solely on the facts of the case, Beach would drill deeper into the heart of the story. This was an opportunity to perform the kind of person-to-person journalism that he so relished.

When Beach arrived at city hall, he spoke with a volunteer who had driven more than an hour to help with the search. The volunteer, named Jeannette Brodeur, said she was compelled to assist because she also had two children living with disabilities. "It must be very frightening for him [Nathan]," she told Beach.

Brodeur had learned about the case through her friend Sharon Hartstein.

"When you're a mom, all I could think of was, what if those were my kids?" Brodeur remembered. "I couldn't say no. I just wanted to help."

She tried to imagine the anguish that Linda was experiencing while her teenage son was missing. Brodeur asked Hartstein if there was anything she could bring Linda at home. They decided on a hot meal from Boston Market, a fast-food, homestyle chicken take-out restaurant. Brodeur drove to Middletown and knocked on the door with her eleven-year-old autistic son, Aaron, in tow. Linda opened the door and welcomed them both inside. She thanked the kind stranger for the hot meal and doted on her son.

"As soon as I met her, I thought I had known her my whole life," Brodeur recalled. "And the attention she showed to my son while her own son was lost was amazing."

Back at the search site in New Haven, volunteers appeared confident that they would be successful in finding Nathan. "We're going to find him," one volunteer said. "We're going to bring him home. Somebody has seen him. They need to step forward."

It was inconceivable to all that Nathan could have vanished without a trace.

When Beach finally spotted Clark Carman at city hall, he thought he was staring into a mirror. Both men were middle-aged, and both liked to wear worn-out baseball caps. The stark difference between them was that one of their children was now missing. Beach approached the distraught dad as he handed out flyers to strangers on the street.

"I'm trying to find my son," Clark said. "He's missing."

Clark told Beach that Nathan was a considerate teenager who volunteered at a local soup kitchen. He said that a few people dismissed his son as being odd simply because he walked in an erect manner, always staring straight

Nathan Carman and his mother Linda on one of their many mother-son trips. (Facebook photo)

ahead, but that narrow-minded people only saw Nathan's disorder and never took the time to see him as a person.

Since Clark was not too familiar with downtown New Haven, Beach offered to show him a few places where his son might have gone. After learning that Nathan owned a mountain bike, Beach suggested they go to the Devil's Gear Bike Shop on nearby Orange Street. They entered the storefront under three decorative old-style penny-farthing bicycles and made their way to the cash register. If Nathan was interested in the local bike culture, this was the place that he would most likely go. Dozens of mountain bike frames hung from the ceiling and jutted out from the walls.

Clark spoke with store employees about his son and handed them a few flyers. The staffers at the bike shop looked closely at the photo on the flyer and told Clark that they had not seen his son but that they would ask around.

"Okay, thanks," Clark replied. "But if you see him, don't touch him."

"It's like *The Twilight Zone*," he told Beach as they exited the bike shop. "A person steps off the bus and disappears."

The morning's light drizzle expanded into a heavy rain that fell vertically on the father and the reporter as they continued to fan out across the city. During the walk, Clark expressed his fear that his son was not equipped to get himself around a place like New Haven because he did not like noise or crowds.

"The problem is, he doesn't function well in the city," he told Beach. "He can be taken advantage of."

Clark said that he would have felt less anxious if Nathan had been spotted in Sleeping Giant State Park in nearby Hamden, Connecticut, instead of downtown New Haven, where police were grappling with a spike in the murder rate. Homicides had climbed from eighteen in 2010 to twenty-six in 2011. The numbers are jarring considering that the average murder rate in the state of Connecticut was just 3.60.

"[Nathan's] a nature kid. He's skilled in the woods," Clark told Beach.

Clark said that his son, who was an honors student, began to have problems at school over the loss of Cruise and that he had missed several classes that spring.

They headed next for Union Station, where Clark once again approached security guards and employees manning the ticket booths. Their answer was the same as the previous day. No one had seen Nathan Carman.

Randy Beach felt tremendous empathy for the father of the missing teen. He wasn't just working on a story for the newspaper anymore. Beach was consoling a fellow parent who was losing all hope. "I have a seventeen-year-old too, and I can't imagine what you're going through," he told the distraught dad.

The reporter's words were not hollow. They meant something to Clark Carman. A brief smile crossed his face before his lips began to tremble.

Clark gazed up at a large digital sign displaying destinations and departure times. He fought back tears. "It's frustrating, nerve-racking. I just want some sort of direction," he told Beach. "Even though he's not a little toddler, he's still my son."

As the day's search ended without any new clues as to the whereabouts of Nathan Carman, Beach wondered if he would ever see the man again, and if so, would it be at the funeral for his son or at a criminal trial if the boy had been abducted? Each scenario made the reporter sick to his stomach.

Beach returned to the newsroom and typed up his story, which would make the front page of Monday's newspaper. He then drove home and hugged his children.

CHAPTER THREE

The call came in to the Sussex County Sheriff's Department in Stony Creek, Virginia, some time before 7:00 p.m. A man named Martin Harrell had noticed a suspicious person loitering around his family's general store on a remote road in the nearby town of Jarratt, about thirty miles north of the North Carolina border. Harrell spoke to Sussex County Deputy John Ogburn and said that he saw a teenager with a motorized scooter hanging around the small building. The J. B. Harrell Store, which was named after an old relative of Martin Harrell's, had closed its door promptly at 5:00 p.m. The Esso gas pump was turned off for the day, but the front porch light remained on. Harrell was worried that the loiterer was looking to break in and rob the store and take whatever cash was left in the register that day. The evening was quiet, and teens did not normally hang around the general store after sunset. There were only five hundred or so residents in the sleepy town, and there wasn't a heck of a lot for young people to do other than drink beer or smoke pot outside Fritz's Diner on Main Street or hang out along the muddy banks of the Nottoway River. If someone was milling about the general store after closing time, it meant they were probably up to no good.

Deputy Ogburn climbed into his squad car and drove to take a look. He arrived a few minutes later and saw the familiar faded Pepsi sign painted on the side of the building, which itself was in need of a paint job. The building was narrow in the front and long in the rear. The structure bowed like an old donkey's back in the middle. Ogburn pulled over and stepped out of his vehicle with a flashlight in his hand. He flicked it on and ran a beam of light across the front of the store. He noticed a moped parked next to a set of train tracks that had been abandoned long ago. The deputy then shone his flashlight onto the porch and saw a young man sitting on a metal chair, which he had tilted back against the store's front window. Ogburn approached slowly and asked the teenager to show some identification.

"I have a Social Security card," the teen said as he fished the laminated card from the pocket of his pants.

Ogburn noticed a large wad of cash inside the pocket.

"My name's Nathan Carman, and I'm from Maryland."

"What are you doing here?" Ogburn asked.

"My mom kicked me out of the house," Nathan responded. "I caught a bus to Richmond and then bought the scooter."

"Where are you headed?"

"Florida."

Ogburn looked at the moped, scratched his head, and wondered how the teenager would make it riding over five hundred miles to the Florida state line. The deputy took a pair of handcuffs off his belt and approached the teenager. Nathan did not resist and held out his hands. Once he was cuffed, Ogburn led him to the back of his police cruiser. The officer got in the front seat, opened his laptop, and typed the teenager's name and the date of birth Nathan had given him into the computer. A quick search of Nathan's record came back empty.

"Wanna tell me who you really are?" Ogburn asked.

"Okay. My name is Nathan Carman. That's my real name. But I did not get kicked out of my house. I ran away from home. I live in Connecticut."

Nathan was concerned about his scooter, so Ogburn got Martin

Harrell's permission to park it in one of the sheds on his property until they could figure out the teen's status. The deputy then drove the teenager to the sheriff's office for further questioning.

Back at the police station, Ogburn fed Nathan's information into the National Crime Information Center and learned that the boy was missing. He then called a Connecticut state trooper at the Connecticut State Police, who asked that Nathan continue to be held until his parents picked him up. Ogburn asked Nathan to take the wad of cash from his pocket and count it on a table. The bills totaled $4,220.00.

"Where did you get all this money?" the deputy asked.

"I earned it from working at my job," Nathan lied.

Ogburn copied the serial numbers of all the dollar bills in his possession in case they were stolen.

While checking his pockets, the police officer also came across a small ziplock plastic bag.

"Please do not throw it away," Nathan begged. "It contains some hair from my horse that died."

Ogburn found two photos of the teen and Cruise in his belongings.

Investigators in Connecticut called Linda Carman at home and informed her that Nathan had been found safe in Virginia. She was overjoyed by the news but somewhat befuddled. Why would her son travel so far south? For much of the day, police had been tracking down a lead in northern Connecticut after someone fitting the boy's description was spotted at the Mystic Aquarium, which made sense to the family because Nathan was familiar with the area and liked animals.

Linda got into her car with her ex-husband, Clark, and together they drove through the night to Virginia to pick up their son. The trip would take nine hours, and each took turns at the wheel with no stops for rest. Family friend Sharon Hartstein announced on Facebook that the teenager had been found safe in rural Virginia.

Best news all day, wrote one well-wisher.

Oh, thank goodness, wrote another. **Too many people go missing and are never found. Glad you are safe Nathan.**

The reunion at the Sussex County sheriff's office was tearful but led to more questions. Nathan was reluctant to share much information with his parents about his decision to run away from home. Linda and Clark were told about the photos in their son's possession and the ziplock bag containing hair from the teen's dead horse. They also learned about the wad of cash the boy had with him to fund his journey to Florida. They believed the money came from Nathan's rich grandfather, John Chakalos.

When Randy Beach heard the news of the teenager's safe return home, he placed a telephone call to Clark Carman in Middletown.

"He did not want to be found," the exhausted father told Beach. "Apparently, he wanted to be on his own."

"How did the reunion go?" Beach asked.

"Fair," Clark replied. He told Beach that his son was not really "keen" on reuniting with his parents or explaining his bizarre disappearance. "This was totally out of character," Clark added. "I don't know the exact reasons. We probably won't know for a while."

Linda Carman attempted to put the puzzle pieces together when she had her own conversation with a local reporter. "I don't know what his final plan was," she said. "He's so typically level-headed. The only thing we can think of is that he's so big into fishing and there's horses in Ocala, so Florida has both of those things."

Linda stressed that she and her ex-husband would need to work on methods to improve their communication with their son. "It's a matter of where his outlet is. That's where our work as parents continues."

She also made sure to thank the volunteers who took time out of their own lives in the search for Nathan. "The gratitude and the appreciation of the entire Carman family is immeasurable," she said. "To all those who helped in any way, even just thoughts and prayers, we are forever grateful."

Nathan later told his father that he ran away to Florida hoping to get a job at a horse farm because that was the only place he felt normal.

CHAPTER FOUR

Brandon Downer lifted his heavy backpack off his shoulder and tucked it under his desk. It was the first day of school in Middletown, Connecticut, and the high school senior looked forward to reconnecting with Nathan Carman after the long summer. Hallways and lockers were decorated with banners and balloons the color of Columbia blue in advance of the Middletown Blue Dragons' upcoming gridiron matchup against nearby Enrico Fermi High.

Downer, like most people in town, had followed the news of his classmate's mysterious odyssey down south. Downer promised himself that he wouldn't ask Nathan for answers as to why he ran away from home, and he doubted that his classmate would offer any insight about his brief disappearance. But Downer was convinced that Nathan's choice to run away from home was not a spur-of-the-moment decision. "He was intelligent and very calculated. He would not do anything that he did not want to do," Downer later observed.

The two students had met during their junior year in AP history class and had bonded over their mutual disdain for their teacher, who Downer claimed never missed an opportunity to praise President Barack Obama's record or other progressive ideals. The year 2011 had been tumultuous thus far. The Arab Spring had taken hold in Egypt in late January and had spread across the Middle East. In April, WikiLeaks had released 779 formerly secret documents from Guantanamo Bay that revealed that 150 Afghans and Pakistanis had been held for years without charges, and in May 2011, Osama Bin Laden was dead, killed in his compound by members of SEAL Team Six. No matter if the class was learning about the American Revolution or the factors that led to the U.S. Civil War, the teacher would routinely share his opinions about current news events. "Our teacher had a very clear left-leaning attitude toward things, so there were a lot of back-and-forths, and not always the nicest back-and-forths," Downer recalled. "Nathan is very opinionated, and if the teacher didn't agree with his opinion, Nathan was not happy about it. If the teacher tried to cut him off in class, you could see the frustration on Nathan's face."

Downer shared Nathan's conservative views, and the two formed an "us against them" kinship in the class. At first, Nathan would raise his hand to speak if he had a point to share on a particular subject. But the dialogue became so contentious that the teacher soon refused to call on him anymore in class. Instead of staying quiet, though, the teen would shout out his opinions, oftentimes drowning out the teacher or another student in an effort to make his point. If he felt that no one was listening to him, Nathan would swipe his arm across the desk and knock his books to the floor. He would be ordered out of the classroom as the teacher followed and tried to calm him down in the hallway. Students would fidget nervously at their desks while Nathan hollered at the teacher.

"He was very loud, but he was also very proper," Downer recalled. "Nathan never used swear words. He reminded me of someone from another era. If someone cursed around him in class, Nathan would try to correct them."

Still, some classmates thought Nathan's behavior was rude, but he did attempt to explain his disorder to them.

"I have Asperger's syndrome," he told kids in his AP history class, using an outdated term to describe his condition. "It's a neurological disorder on the autism spectrum. I have difficulty in social situations, and sometimes I may say things that can be seen as inappropriate. I don't really have a filter."

For the most part, Middletown high schoolers took Nathan's explanation at face value, but there were other students who thought he was weird and picked on him mercilessly for his ramrod-straight walk; his monotone, unique speech pattern, where he often repeated phrases and spoke very fast; his habit of wearing only fishing shirts, hiking boots, and cargo pants to class; and his avoidance of any eye contact with others. In gym class, he was the kid who no one wanted on their team.

While Middletown High School warned of disciplinary actions against students who showed "bullying behavior," Nathan's teenage tormentors often went unpunished. He tried to limit his time in the hallways between classes in an effort to avoid getting picked on, laughed at, and even shoved by other students.

"There was no small talk after class," Downer remembered. "He would book it to his next class as soon as the bell rang."

But Nathan also created several school disruptions of his own. One day, during an argument with school administrators, he called the vice principal "Satan" and a secretary "an agent of the devil."

He also got into trouble for bringing a penknife to school. Kids were unsure whether Nathan planned to use it as a weapon but thought of him as a nonviolent person. Once, when a bully videotaped Nathan in class with his cell phone camera, Nathan just took the phone away, waited for the teacher to arrive, and reported the incident.

Brandon Downer sat at his desk as other classmates filled the seats around him. The teacher had also arrived and was organizing the day's lesson plan. Downer swept the classroom with his eyes once more, but Nathan Carman was nowhere to be found. In fact, he would never return to class at Middletown High School again.

CHAPTER FIVE

John Chakalos loved Nathan Carman. As the eldest of his nine grandchildren, Nathan held a special place in his grandfather's heart as well as being groomed by the eighty-five-year-old multimillionaire real estate developer to play a prominent future role in the family business. Because Nathan was Chakalos's firstborn grandchild, the Greek American businessman overlooked the awkwardness and difficulties that came with Nathan's social disorder and treated him as his heir apparent. "Without family, you've got nothing; family is everything," Chakalos often told his four daughters, Linda Carman, Elaine Chakalos, Charlene Gallagher, and Valerie Santilli. As young girls, they had watched their father scrape, sweat, and toil to build a successful real estate enterprise that specialized in assisted living facilities. Chakalos Investments Inc. had grown out of the family's modest three-bedroom home in Windsor, Connecticut, with the support and assistance of the entrepreneur's devoted wife, Rita.

The couple met while attending Woodrow Wilson High School in Middletown, Connecticut, in the 1940s. Raised in a Polish American household by staunchly Roman Catholic parents, the former Rita Baranowksi was drawn to Chakalos, the son of Greek immigrants, for his rugged good looks, his quick wit, and his tenacity. Born in Keene, New Hampshire, Chakalos was one of six children and the only boy in the family. He had a twin sister named Vasiliki, whom the family called Kiki. Growing up, Chakalos struggled in school because of a learning disability. But he had the dogged persistence of a pit bull and fought to maintain passing grades.

At the outbreak of America's involvement in World War II, Chakalos put his education on hold and enlisted as a private in the U.S. Army. As a member of the Eleventh Airborne Division, he was sent to jump school at Fort Polk, Louisiana, in early 1944 before deploying to New Guinea in the southwestern Pacific for final preparations for a daring Allied assault on the Philippines in an effort to retake the island chain from the Japanese following General Douglas MacArthur's embarrassing retreat from the island of Corregidor in March 1942. In November 1944, Chakalos, then just eighteen years old, launched himself out of an airplane with his fellow paratroopers and landed in the jungle in Leyte, Philippines, where he helped to destroy two Japanese divisions near the city of Jaro. Two months later, Chakalos fought under U.S. Army general Edwin D. Patrick's Sixth Infantry Division in the Battle of Luzon, where eight thousand American soldiers were killed during two months of blood-drenched, terrifying combat before eventually liberating the capital city of Manila.

When Chakalos returned home from the war, he met and fell in love with Rita. After both had graduated from Woodrow Wilson High School, Chakalos attended the Bradford Durfee College of Technology in Massachusetts under the GI Bill, while Rita studied to become a nurse at the Waterbury Hospital School of Nursing in Connecticut. Following college, they got married and settled down in the town of Windsor, where they raised their four daughters.

The girls all had unique personalities when they were young. Elaine Chakalos, the eldest daughter, was studious like her parents and followed her mother's path into nursing. Elaine attended a small Catholic school, Our Lady of the Angels Academy in Enfield, Connecticut, where she served as class treasurer and was voted Most Quiet by her classmates. She then went on to study at Quinnipiac University and received her nursing degree in 1984. Younger sister Charlene, with her feathered blond hair, was more carefree. In her Windsor High School yearbook, *Tunxis*, the 1981 graduate pledged her love for her mom and dad while also promising to "party on forever" with her party crew. Sister Valerie followed Charlene's footsteps at Windsor High School where she graduated in 1988. Unlike Charlene, Valerie was as professionally driven as their father was. In her high school yearbook photo, the teenager appeared no-nonsense, as if she were posing for an executive profile at a Fortune 500 company. Wearing smart earrings and a necklace under a dark blazer and light sweater, Valerie looked like she was ready to take on the world, and just like her big sister Charlene, she too thanked her mom and dad for their support through the years.

And then there was Linda, John and Rita's second daughter.

Linda Chakalos, the problem child.

Even when she was young, Linda butted heads with her father over just about everything. She could not understand why, when her father was earning millions of dollars developing convalescent homes across New England, the family was still living in a seventies-style mustard-colored ranch home in a blue-collar neighborhood in Windsor. If her father had all this money, why wasn't he spending it on his family? All but one of John Chakalos's four children went to a local public school. The Chakalos home was a far cry from the opulence that Linda had seen on popular '70s and '80s television shows like *Dallas*, *Dynasty*, and *The Lifestyles of the Rich and Famous*.

While her sisters remained relatively close to home after graduating from high school and college, Linda Chakalos had wanderlust. She tried to win her father's affection by serving as an airman first class in the Connecticut Air National Guard for fourteen months. Although John Chakalos was proud to have one of his children serving in the military as he had done, he and Linda still argued regularly. After receiving an honorable discharge in 1985, Linda moved out to California, where she eventually met Clark Carman. The two bonded over their mutual love for the outdoors, whether it was hiking in the California mountains, fishing in fast-flowing streams, or enjoying the rumbling surf of the ocean. "We were both members of a ski club in Los Angeles, California. We would bus up to Mammoth [Mountain] and ski on weekends," Clark recalled. "The club had activities in the summers too, like building sand castles and playing softball. So we got together at one of the outings. I didn't know her that well at the time. We went to a water park, and we got talking, and things went well. She had gone with someone else, and I offered to take her home, and things budded from there."

The couple dated for a year and would take off together in Linda's Ford Ranger to state parks and sleep in the back of the vehicle. Linda and Clark got married and wanted a baby of their own, but Linda had trouble getting pregnant. They saw a team of fertility doctors, and she underwent a number of different treatments before conceiving a child.

Linda had been estranged from her father for several years but saw the impending birth of her first child as an olive branch to extend to her family back home. She telephoned her parents with the news, and they were elated. However, her father did express concern about how the couple would care for the baby. John Chakalos worried that his daughter could barely take care of herself and that her new husband did not have many job prospects in California. Clark had worked as a financial analyst in the aerospace industry but had recently fallen victim to a corporate layoff.

Now that there was a baby to be considered, and not just any infant but his first grandchild, Chakalos thought the best way to take care of the child would be to keep him close by.

"I'll buy you a Dunkin' Donuts franchise if you come back to Connecticut," he told his daughter over the phone.

Linda and Clark returned to Windsor with the expectation and hope of owning one of the most profitable coffee and doughnut franchises in New England. There wasn't a Dunkin' on every street corner in Connecticut, but it surely appeared that way. While other fast-food franchises like Krispy Kreme and Pizza Hut blew into towns and often struggled to survive, Dunkin' was considered the surest bet possible because customers were hooked on its delicious coffee. John Chakalos believed that he would be providing a fail-safe business for his daughter and son-in-law to run. But once the couple arrived in Connecticut, Chakalos had some misgivings.

Linda was still bullheaded, irascible, and unpredictable, and her new husband projected zero confidence in his ability to run a business.

Chakalos was both a father and a business owner. While the parent in him wanted to fulfill the promise he had made to his daughter, his business-man side thought it would be a disaster. He reneged on his offer to buy the Dunkin' Donuts franchise for Linda and her husband, which created a deeper chasm in their relationship.

"When we got to Connecticut, there was nothing," Clark remembered. "There was no Dunkin' Donuts franchise. John never explained to us why he didn't fulfill his promise. He just said, 'No.'"

Linda's resentment toward her father grew while Clark built up animosity against Linda for allegedly duping him into leaving his native California and moving nearly three thousand miles east to Connecticut, where no job awaited him. The only person who was satisfied with the arrangement was John Chakalos. The developer was at the hospital when Nathan James Carman was born on January 21, 1994. His new prized possession, his first grandchild, was now close by, and the elated grandfather vowed that he would never let the boy out of his sight again.

To ensure that the infant was provided with everything he needed, Chakalos purchased a house for Clark and Linda in nearby Middletown and handed out weekly allowances to the couple. During one visit to their home, Chakalos urged them to put up a fence to ensure that Nathan could not wander off. "You put it up, and I'll pay for it," he promised. Linda and Clark had the fence installed but were never reimbursed by Chakalos. Like the Dunkin' Donuts franchise, this promise also went unfulfilled.

Linda spent her allowance frivolously and often blew much of it at the Foxwoods Casino, which was only about a fifty-minute car ride from their home. But it was not his wife's unpredictable behavior that drove Clark away; instead, it was her father's domineering stranglehold on the family that led him to leave. John Chakalos paid for everything and therefore felt that he could control all the couple's decisions, especially when it came to their son.

Clark and Linda Carman divorced in 1996, when Nathan was only two years old. Clark could not stand up to the boy's stern grandfather, so he just disappeared. He fled back to California, forcing Linda to raise the toddler virtually on her own.

Still, every decision that she made for Nathan was second-guessed or overruled by Chakalos, who, as Connecticut's modern-day version of King Lear, often doled out money to his daughters in exchange for their love and loyalty. Linda happily took the payouts, but she also wanted to raise her son her way.

Nathan had always been different. When he was a toddler, Linda and Clark recognized that he was not developing at the same rate as other children. "When he was very young, he was very smart but not socially adept with children his own age," Clark remembered. "He could converse with adults with no problems whatsoever, but he had no desire to play with other kids."

Yet Nathan could become totally obsessed with a toy or a cartoon. When he learned to talk, his speech pattern sounded robotic, and he maintained a blank facial expression regardless of how he was feeling at the time. "His demeanor gave the impression that he had no empathy or emotions, but he really felt deeply about all kinds of things," his father explained.

John Chakalos, a wealthy real estate developer, doted on his grandson Nathan Carman since the day he was born. (courtesy of FindAGrave.com)

Linda shared her own concerns about their son with her ex-husband over long-distance telephone calls to California. They agreed to have their child tested for autism when he was five years old. A neurologist told them that Nathan's behavior was consistent with autism spectrum disorder. "We studied up on the disorder and then placed our son in after-school programs and therapy," Clark said. "It's not like we just left him alone. We tried to help him through all that."

When Linda first raised the idea that her son may have a disability to her father, he scoffed at it. Chakalos grew up during the Great Depression and had fought his way through World War II. He believed that any mental or physical obstacle could be overcome with determination and the right training. In his mind, Nathan's challenge was no different, and he refused to handle his first grandchild with kid gloves. Chakalos had lofty dreams for the boy. His wish was that Nathan would one day take over the family business, which was now estimated to be worth north of forty million dollars, and he was laser focused on making that happen.

CHAPTER SIX

Clark Carman failed to paint a full picture when he told columnist Randy Beach that his son had missed several classes during his junior year in high school in 2011 after his beloved horse Cruise died. Nathan did not take time off from school to mourn Cruise. Instead, he had been admitted to a psychiatric hospital for treatment.

During that year, Nathan stopped talking to his mother. They communicated only through passed notes. After Nathan's verbal assault of two school administrators, whom he called "Satan" and an "agent of the devil," Linda poured out her frustration over her troubled son's "psychotic episode" at school in an online message board. She had entered the digital forum to get advice about how to cope with her son, who had stopped taking his daily antianxiety medications. **Yes, he is a complicated mess**, she wrote. Linda went on to describe how Nathan was suffering from "paranoid delusions" and what she called "religious idiocy."

In April 2011, Linda drove her son from Middletown to Hartford and checked him into Mount Sinai Rehabilitation Hospital, a sixty-bed inpatient facility that specializes in treating neurological injuries. Nathan was given his own room close to the hospital's Seaver Autism Center for Research and Treatment. His anger toward his mother grew after he was confined to the psychiatric hospital. The teenager believed that Linda was trying to control every aspect of his life and rob him of his independence. His father agreed.

"She always doted on him, took care of him," Clark later recalled. "But he was resistant to it."

Nathan refused to let his mother visit him in the hospital, and he never left his room. While Linda hoped for regimented treatment for her son, Nathan would not participate in most therapy sessions. Among the questions that Linda was hoping to find answers to was why Nathan had recently exploded into a fit of rage and thrown a tray of cookies against the wall after she burned them and why he had given trick-or-treaters ziplock bags filled with fish guts on Halloween, an incident that had triggered a visit from a police officer. Nathan refused to discuss any of his current or previous behaviors with professional therapists.

The boy's only regular visitors were his grandparents, John and Rita Chakalos. His grandmother brought him candy while his grandfather delivered daily editions of the *Wall Street Journal* and supplied him with a radio so that he could listen to his favorite conservative talk shows. Once again, Linda was on the outside looking in at her son's treatment, or lack thereof.

With no one to turn to, Linda opened her laptop and returned to the online message board and began typing furiously. **His grandfather has insisted for 17 years that my son belongs to HIM and all his problems are the result of me, his mother,** she wrote. **This man (his grandfather) is allowed to sit with him in his room, behind closed doors, unmonitored for 5 hours at a time.**

Word got back to John Chakalos that his daughter was sharing her frustrations with him with an anonymous, online community. He called a family meeting at Mount Sinai. Both Linda and her father knew that the meeting would be intense. Their arguing was part of the family's rhythm. They had both sharpened their verbal knives and cut into each other around the dinner table at Greek Easter and other Chakalos family gatherings.

Linda's sisters did their best to ignore the noise, as it was just part of the tumultuous relationship between the father and daughter. After shouting at each other, they would retreat to their neutral corners before eventually reconciling. Passions ran deep in the Chakalos household.

But when Linda arrived at Mount Sinai on that fateful morning in April 2011, her demeanor was different. She was ready for a fight—a physical one.

At home, Linda flipped through the pages of her photo albums and the pictures stored on her phone and wondered when she had lost her connection with her only son. There were photos of the two enjoying each other's company during a trip to Atlantis in the Bahamas, where they had the opportunity to swim with dolphins. Other pictures showed the mother and son showing off their prized catches during one of their countless fishing trips. Linda hated to fish but loved spending time with Nathan. In one photo, the normally stoic Nathan appeared to be smiling. Most of their photos were taken while both were dressed in their fishing gear and on the water. Linda's wanderlust had never waned, and she continued to travel extensively as an adult, most times with Nathan. They traveled to Greece and visited the ancient seaside town of Eretria, where Linda's grandmother Kalliope Kyriazis was born and lived before immigrating to the United States in 1918. Linda and Nathan took an RV trip across Alaska, where they fished in pristine lakes and rivers, spotted grizzly bears in the rugged wilderness, and enjoyed hot meals by a flickering campfire. Linda feared that she would never experience such closeness with her son again. According to her, the wedge between them had nothing to do with Nathan's autism spectrum disorder. Instead, she blamed her father, who she firmly believed had wanted to claim her son for his own.

Linda was in full battle mode when she met John Chakalos at Mount Sinai Rehabilitation Hospital. Clark Carman had traveled back to Connecticut while Nathan was hospitalized and joined his ex-wife for the meeting in an effort to keep the peace. Linda and her father engaged without pleasantries. Instead, they went right at each other, shouting and pointing fingers inside a conference room. Although Chakalos was paying for his grandson's expensive psychiatric treatment, he had disagreed vehemently with his daughter's decision to commit the boy. Linda refused to listen to her father's reasoning and told him to butt out when it came to the upbringing of her child.

"Nathan was supposed to be there to get help," Clark explained. "But his grandfather was there every day. He brought him newspapers. He brought him pizza. He brought Nathan anything he wanted. Linda wasn't happy with that, because our son wasn't really getting the help he needed because John was always there."

Chakalos stood his ground and loudly reminded Linda that he was paying for Nathan's clothes, his food, all her utility bills and mortgage payments, as well as the lavish trips that she took all over the world with her son. Chakalos felt that Linda was doing a terrible job as a mother and then asked Nathan's father, Clark, to move back to Connecticut permanently to help raise the teenager.

"I'll give you a job," he told Clark, who had difficulty finding steady work.

Chakalos's words served as a trigger for Linda, who remembered the similar unkept promise he had made to Clark involving a Dunkin' Donuts franchise. She erupted with profanities toward Chakalos, who immediately threatened to completely cut her off financially.

"I've only been giving you money because I love my grandson!" he told Linda.

Linda Carman had difficult relationships with her son, Nathan, and her father, John Chakalos. (Twitter photo)

As their conversation grew more heated, Clark braced himself for the worst. He had witnessed nasty arguments between his ex-wife and her father in the past. "They were of the same ilk. When Linda worked in her father's office, they yelled and screamed at each other constantly. It wasn't an atypical situation."

Clark watched as Chakalos leaped up from the conference room table and started pulling his daughter's hair. Linda closed her fist and threw punches at her father in return. She scratched and kicked him as he tried to escape. As Chakalos tried to force his way out of the conference room, Linda reached down and grabbed her father's testicles and squeezed as hard as she could.

"I finally was able to get between them and stop it," Clark said. While trying to break up the fight, Clark was hit with a wild punch to the mouth from his ex-wife.

The fracas got the attention of hospital security guards, and the local police were called.

Officers slapped a pair of handcuffs on Linda's wrists and arrested her for assault on an elderly person. "She was made out to be the bad guy, and she had her part in it, but it wasn't her fault that this had occurred," Clark contended.

While she was getting booked on the charge, Linda continued to rail against Chakalos.

"My father is worth $300 million, and I want my share," she screamed at police officers while inflating her father's wealth. "He is not going to cut me off. I need the money!"

But Linda's fight with her father barely raised an eyebrow within the family, according to Clark. "That was the Chakalos family dynamic," he insisted. "The sisters all argued with each other, and they battled their father constantly. When we would all gather for the holidays, it would just be a matter of time before the yelling would start. They were all quite volatile and outspoken." Clark also described heated debates between Chakalos and his youngest daughter, Valerie, over the family business as well as insults tossed Chakalos's way from his eldest daughter, Elaine. "She was always a bit quiet, but she knew how to dig under her father's skin," Clark said.

But the most recent episode between Chakalos and Linda was violent. He had suffered minor injuries, and she was facing jail time. Added to Chakalos's physical wounds was the sheer embarrassment he felt over such a sad spectacle. Linda's arrest was public information, and people in the community talked. Chakalos, the prominent businessman, was now seen by many as someone who could not control his family, especially his wild daughter, Linda. In an effort to regain some privacy and shield his daughter from prosecution, Chakalos dropped the assault charge against her. In doing so, he also protected himself against any allegations she might make against him at trial.

But Chakalos was not about to let bygones be bygones. He would exact his revenge by taking from her what she cherished most in the world—her son.

CHAPTER SEVEN

Nathan was released from Mount Sinai Rehabilitation Hospital after a couple of weeks of observation. Despite Linda's assertion that her son was delusional, doctors there found no evidence that Nathan was schizophrenic or psychotic. The teenager returned to Middletown and finished his junior year of high school. But Linda saw little improvement in her son's behavior as he retreated to her RV and rarely came out. He ate all his meals in the motor home parked in Linda's driveway and filled it with half-eaten cartons of food, stacks of dirty plates, and piles of clothes that he refused to wash. Nathan urinated in empty water bottles and smashed the inside of the RV with a baseball bat. The motor home looked like it had been hit by a tornado, and the interior reminded Linda of one of those hoarding shows on television.

After repeated outbursts, she called a local social services hotline, pleading for help. A police officer was sent to the RV to conduct a wellness check on Nathan. Linda told the cop that her son was struggling with autism spectrum disorder and that his moods were unpredictable. The officer knocked on the door of the RV and waited several seconds for Nathan to answer. The teen opened the door slowly and was startled to see the uniformed police officer in front of him. The officer asked if Nathan was okay, and he replied that he was doing fine. Since there was no crime committed and no search warrant issued, the officer thanked Nathan for his time, got back into his squad car, and exited the driveway. Nathan was outraged, not at the police officer but at his mother for once again trying to control his life and dictate his future. Two days later, he jumped on his bicycle and disappeared.

When he was discovered by police in Virginia and returned to his parents days later, Nathan retreated to the safety and security of the RV, the same mobile home that he and Linda had traveled in on their cross-country trek to Alaska and back. He rarely spoke to his father and did not speak at all to his mother. But he did write her a two-page letter, blaming her and others around him for his decision to run away from home. The only person to escape Nathan's scorn was his maternal grandfather, John Chakalos.

As Nathan's legal guardian, Linda would make one more desperate attempt to manage his mood swings when she decided to hand him over to counselors at a behavioral boot camp in Idaho. Both Linda and Clark signed over guardianship of their son to camp officials, and soon after, counselors showed up in Middletown one evening and took him away. The boot camp in Idaho promised a healthy and temporary time apart for teens and a respite for their exhausted parents. After running away from home, Nathan now felt like he was being kidnapped.

He returned to Middletown, Connecticut, two months later, and both Linda and Clark noticed improvements in their son's demeanor, despite the concern from many experts who believed that rigid behavioral boot camps were detrimental for teenagers on the autism spectrum. As an honor roll student, Nathan had accumulated enough high school credits to begin taking classes at Central Connecticut State University in New Britain, Connecticut, just a two-dollar bus ride from Middletown.

After turning eighteen, Nathan moved away from Linda's property for good. He abandoned the RV, packed his bags, and stayed with a cousin. Linda was devastated, but his grandfather welcomed the move as it would create a deeper separation between mother and son. John Chakalos bought Nathan a 2009 Nissan Titan pickup truck, gave him money to rent his own two-bedroom apartment in the nearby town of Bloomfield, and handed him a credit card with a $5,000 spending limit. Chakalos also began showing him the ropes of the family business. As part of his professional development, Nathan created his own LinkedIn page, but he did not post anything.

During this time, Linda tried desperately to reconnect with her son. She couldn't stomach the idea of him bonding with someone else, especially his grandfather. Nathan visited Chakalos at least once a week at his home in Windsor. Chakalos proudly introduced him to his business associates, and Nathan felt valued and supported for the first time in his life. No longer under the protective yoke of his mother, who would not even introduce her son to many of her friends out of fear that he would act out, Nathan began to think about his life beyond his disability and gained confidence that he could one day run the family's business empire.

Chakalos had four daughters and eight other grandchildren, and many questioned why he was elevating Nathan to the lofty position as his eventual successor. While his adult daughters, all but Linda, may have been capable of running the family business, Chakalos was old-fashioned and treated his Greek family as an archaic patriarchy where women did not hold the same value as men. He also placed a special emphasis on Nathan's status as his first male grandchild. To his credit, though, Chakalos willingly overlooked the challenges of Nathan's autism spectrum disorder and the stigma that came with it. When donating a pair of new fire engines to the local fire department, the developer brought Nathan to the ceremony and insisted that both trucks bear a plaque naming the teenager as the official donor.

In a relatively short time, Nathan had gone from an awkward, galoshes-and-khakis-wearing social outcast to a clean-cut, collegiate young businessman in training. A stickler for detail, Nathan became his grand-father's eyes and especially his ears when it came to the family business.

"John couldn't really hear anything anymore," claimed Clark. "He was very hard of hearing. He had hearing aids, but those didn't work, so Nathan listened intently on behalf of his grandfather at all of his business meetings and made recommendations on prospective deals."

The derogation that had accompanied the public's overall lack of under-standing of autism spectrum disorder had been momentarily lifted for Nathan. But his sense of self was shattered, as were the lives of so many people in his home state of Connecticut, when an armed gunman entered the Sandy Hook Elementary School in the town of Newtown on December 14, 2012, and opened fire on innocent children and adults in one of the most heinous mass shootings in American history. In all, twenty-six people were killed, including twenty children between the ages of six and seven years old. The gunman, who took his own life after committing the carnage, was twenty-year-old Adam Lanza. As news quickly spread of the massacre, it was noted by the media that Lanza had been diagnosed with sensory integration disorder and later with autism spectrum disorder, or Asperger's syndrome, as it was commonly referred to then. "It would be unfair to say that every child with Asperger's will become a mass murderer," renowned autism advocate Nancy Alspaugh-Jackson told a reporter from the *New York Daily News* at the time. "But combining Asperger's with a troubled family situation…and no care or treatment, is a recipe for disaster."

The backlash against people with autism spectrum disorder spread across the country. "The reason why this man shot little kids is because he has autism," one Utah middle school student told his teacher.

Calls to Autism Speaks, a national research and advocacy group, rose 130 percent in the days following the Sandy Hook tragedy as parents of autistic children feared their kids could be targeted for retribution. "It seems that [the public is] wanting to put the blame squarely on the fact that the shooter may have had autism," said Peter Bell, an executive with Autism Speaks. "This rush to put a label on the situation has caused significant harm already."

Lanza's mother, Nancy Lanza, had been murdered by her son before he arrived at the Sandy Hook Elementary School armed with a Bushmaster AR-15, a Glock 10 mm, and a 9 mm Sig Sauer handgun. On the morning of December 14, 2012, before making that fateful trip to Sandy Hook Elementary, the school that he had attended as a child, Adam Lanza shot his mother four times in the head while she was in bed.

While some people laid blame for Lanza's murderous act on his easy access to guns and his obsession with violent video games, others unfairly linked the killings to Adam Lanza's struggles with autism spectrum disorder. This lack of understanding about people on the autism spectrum wound its way from Newtown forty miles north to Middletown, Connecticut, where some of Nathan Carman's former classmates openly wondered whether he also had the makings of a school shooter. One of Linda's boyfriends was concerned that she would meet a similar fate as Nancy Lanza. "Soon enough, he's gonna slit your throat while you're sleeping," he warned.

Linda waved off the boyfriend's morbid prophecy. Her son did not scare her. Her only fear was that she was losing Nathan's love and loyalty to her father.

Linda rebelled against the growing bond between her father and her son by acting like the troubled teenager she had once been. She took off on a ten-day gambling trip to Mississippi and bounced back and forth between Middletown and the Mohegan Sun Casino in Uncasville, Connecticut. Since she had no job of her own, Linda worked quickly to spend the monthly allowances from her father and even depleted a trust fund that Chakalos had set up for Nathan. Feeling fed up with Linda's irresponsible, spendthrift ways, her father created a new trust fund for Nathan and appointed her younger sister Valerie Santilli as the executor. This was a slap in the face for

Linda. But instead of attacking her father, physically or verbally, she took out her frustrations on her son. On September 26, 2013, Linda secretly rewrote her will, stating, "Nathan Carman is my only child. I have intentionally omitted Nathan and all of his descendants as beneficiaries under my revocable trust."

After cutting Nathan out of her will, Linda pledged her $5.7 million share of her father's estimated $43 million inheritance to her sisters, Elaine, Charlene, and Valerie, and left her horse, Sophie Belle, to a close friend. Linda's millions were tied up in what was known as a dynasty trust that was controlled by Valerie's husband, Lawrence Santilli, the millionaire CEO of Athena Health Care Systems, which operated close to fifty assisted living centers in Connecticut.

Linda gave no reason as to why she was omitting her son from her will. She did not share information with any of her family members, including Nathan, and she hoped that he would not find out, as it would create an even greater divide with her son. It was a secret that Linda had promised herself she would take to her grave.

Chapter Eight

As Linda Carman was revising her will, both her son and her father were attending the groundbreaking of a new assisted living facility named in her honor. John Chakalos brought Nathan to a ceremony in Leeds, Massachusetts, where the developer formally announced the construction of the Linda Manor Extended Care Facility, a $16 million, 122-bed nursing home that was built for people living with dementia and Alzheimer's disease. Standing with a shovel in hand next to the town's mayor, Chakalos spoke to a small crowd of dignitaries about his goal to offer seniors the choice of independent living units and around-the-clock nursing care.

"These are the kind of services for people that want options," Chakalos said proudly while Nathan clapped enthusiastically with fellow attendees.

Among Chakalos's large portfolio of assisted living facilities were two others named for his daughters; Elaine Manor in Hadley, Massachusetts, and Charlene Manor in nearby Greenfield, Massachusetts, along the picturesque Johnny Appleseed Trail. Chakalos had also built Valerie Manor in Torrington, Connecticut, which was operated by Athena Health Care Systems, the company run by his daughter's husband, Lawrence Santilli. Adding to the family legacy, Chakalos had recently won approval from the town of Northampton, Massachusetts, to build a ninety-bed facility called the Zoe Life Retirement Community, named for one of his granddaughters, Zoe Santilli. The project's expected price tag was between $10 million and $15 million. Chakalos had never been busier, and friends and colleagues were awed by the eighty-seven-year-old's energy and enthusiasm for growing his business.

But due to his advanced age, the millionaire developer was on borrowed time. Chakalos would soon have to name a successor. Daughter Valerie Santilli was the obvious choice. She had inherited her father's determination and drive, and she was smart and more business-savvy than her three sisters. Despite taking all her positive attributes into account, her father still dreamed of passing the business to his closest male relative and his firstborn grandson, Nathan Carman. He saw in Nathan what others in the family had routinely overlooked. While Linda and her sisters focused on the teenager's social awkwardness and his numerous vulnerabilities, Chakalos continued to see through Nathan's disorder and boasted about his grandson's high intelligence and his meticulous attention to detail. The grandfather and grandson shared a singular mindset. "John [Chakalos] was very black-and-white," Clark Carman recalled.

To Chakalos, it was a clear case of nature versus nurture. He strongly believed that his grandson's development had been stunted by his overbearing mother. Chakalos was determined to empower Nathan and instill in him the confidence that he would need not only to run the family business but to run his large Greek family after the old man's death.

The idea of mortality wore heavily on the mind of John Chakalos during the final months of 2013. He visited a cemetery monument store in Windsor to order as many as thirty burial plots in Hartford for himself and his family. Chakalos's wife, Rita, was suffering from an advanced stage of breast cancer and was now in hospice care. She was eighty-four years old and had dedicated her life to her family and to her community. The family matriarch doted on her daughters and grandchildren and even their pets, which she referred to as her "granddogs." Rita, a devout Catholic, had served for many years as a eucharistic minister at her local parish, St. Gabriel Church in Windsor. She was a member of the Catholic Daughters of the Americas, one of the oldest and largest volunteer organizations of Catholic women in the Western Hemisphere, where she helped victims of domestic abuse, offered spiritual guidance to prisoners, and administered academic scholarships to local students. Rita Chakalos also organized a large holiday food drive in the couple's adopted hometown of West Chesterfield, New Hampshire. While they maintained a modest lifestyle at their ranch-style home on a dead-end street in Windsor, the couple spent lavishly on themselves in New Hampshire, where they had built a 15,707-square-foot mansion in the rural town of West Chesterfield in 1991 and moved in in 1994. John and Rita Chakalos even gave the estate an aristocratic nickname: the Farm at Pond Brook.

One close family member believed the developer had built the opulent oasis "as a monument to himself." But he also said that Rita was somewhat embarrassed by it and did not visit there often. "They were simple people and he built that place because he made money."

Having grown up poor in nearby Keene, New Hampshire, Chakalos had always dreamed that he would one day return as a conquering hero. "Someday, I'm gonna build me a big mansion up on a hill," he told his family. He still had strong ties to the community there and shared many fond memories with childhood friends. While he lived and worked in Windsor, the developer always said that his roots were planted firmly in the ground in New Hampshire.

Sitting on eighty-eight acres of land, Chakalos's three-story Georgian brick colonial mansion came with six spacious bedrooms, a grand foyer with a double staircase accentuated by a massive crystal chandelier, an elevator, a gourmet kitchen, several murals hand-painted by a local artist, an indoor swimming pool and spa, a billiard room with a soda fountain, a tennis and basketball court, a putting green, miles of ATV trails, and a pond with a gazebo.

Originally, it had been part of a sixteen-hundred-acre property owned by a local dairy farmer named Henry Putnam. John Chakalos toured the property several times before he decided to buy a parcel of land and build on it. He hired Putnam's granddaughter, Joy Washburn, who lived next to the property, to help oversee the construction of the mansion and then take care of the estate.

"I became John's right-hand man and woman," Washburn said about their work relationship. "People both loved and hated John, and he had a way about him that could make you dislike him. John called me 'stupidly honest' because I always told the truth, and that's why we got along just fine. I took care of the place, checked on it weekly, and was on call twenty-four seven."

Washburn said that Chakalos was a very impatient man and would call her up to fifteen times each day to check on the progress of his builders and subcontractors.

"You told me to give you a weekly report, but now you've got it down to the minute and the seconds," Washburn said jokingly to him.

In West Chesterfield, John Chakalos could live like the real estate titan that he was, and he wanted to give his number one grandson a taste of his affluent lifestyle. In 2012, Nathan was invited to live at the Farm at Pond Brook, where he could spend more time with his grandfather and time alone while roaming the plush, manicured acreage and surrounding woods, hills, and mountains. Nathan was excited by the idea and had even switched the license plates on his truck from Connecticut to New Hampshire. He also obtained a New Hampshire driver's license and listed his address as 140 Pond Brook Road, his grandparents' mansion in West Chesterfield.

One Thanksgiving, Chakalos called his caretaker at home because Nathan had turned the water on in the shower and then forgot about it and fell asleep. There was water coming through the ceiling, so Washburn rushed over to the estate and organized the cleanup of the mess. When she arrived, Nathan was yelling at members of his family who had accused him of ruining their Thanksgiving dinner with the water leak.

"Fine, I know you all hate me," he shouted. "I'm going back to Connecticut. Fuck you all!"

Nathan ran out of the home while Washburn got a mop and bucket and began soaking up the excess water.

"It wasn't just Nathan. They were all very irresponsible people," Washburn said of the family.

She was called to the mansion on several occasions, including a time when Linda Carman had thrown a birthday party at the estate for Nathan. Washburn inspected the home after Linda left and saw a half-eaten birthday cake left out on the granite countertop and empty wine bottles and beer bottles strewn across the billiards room.

"There were maggots crawling in the sink, and she had left out macaroni salad and potato salad," Washburn recalled.

The caretaker called Rita Chakalos and told her about all the rotting food and the empty and half-drunk bottles of booze that Linda had left behind.

"That was supposed to be a kids' party for Nathan," Rita pointed out. "There shouldn't have been any drinking there. Don't touch a thing. Just leave it there." The family matriarch ordered Washburn to photograph the mess with a disposable camera and send the images to her.

When John Chakalos saw the pictures, he ordered Linda to drive up to West Chesterfield and clean up the leftover food and bottles, but Linda refused. Washburn was tasked with the dirty job instead.

"Put down your time and what it took to clean the place up," Rita told her.

The Chakaloses ordered Linda to pay Washburn out of her monthly allowance from the family business. They then clamped down on any unsupervised visits to the farm by their daughters and their grandchildren. According to Washburn, Linda still snuck into the home and stayed there with her friends while coming back from ski trips without her parents' permission. The grandchildren did the same, leaving empty red Solo cups and empty beer bottles for Washburn to clean up after their underage drinking parties. Washburn was also ordered by John Chakalos to supervise the grandkids while they were riding ATVs on the property.

"John told me the kids could ride the vehicles in the fields around the property and on the long driveway but not to go in the woods with them, especially during hunting season, for their safety."

But the grandchildren, including Nathan, paid no attention to the caretaker.

"They almost ran me over when they took off," Washburn recalled. She raised the issue to Chakalos's daughters and was told simply, "Boys will be boys."

"Nathan drove those ATVs like crazy," Washburn added. "He knew where all the humps and bumps were, and he'd have the wheels off the ground, flying through the air."

The caretaker said that Nathan had once bent the suspension on a vehicle, and his grandfather had to get it fixed. "It was one of the reasons that John didn't want Nathan doing that kind of stuff, because he was afraid he'd get hurt," she recalled.

Acting like spoiled members of the Kennedy family, the kids flaunted Chakalos's wealth and took advantage of their privilege. In late 2012, the grandfather called a family meeting at the estate. It was time for him to put his foot down.

"That damn does it," Washburn heard Chakalos tell them all. "No more wild rides and no more underage drinking parties in my home!"

The caretaker also claimed to have witnessed her boss argue with his daughters over money.

"They wanted to take cash out of Charlene Manor [a Chakalos-owned assisted living facility] to buy Christmas presents, and John told them no," Washburn said.

"If anybody gets money out of that account, it will be your mother and I, but the rest of it stays there," he shouted over the phone. "You'd better figure out another way to do your Christmas shopping, every one of you. What the hell's the matter with you? You should all be working, making money of your own, and putting the Charlene Manor money aside for your retirement. The answer is no, it's not happening, and forget it!"

Chakalos slammed the phone down and looked up at his wife, Rita. His blood was boiling.

"I don't know where we went wrong," he told her while Washburn was in the room. "I have never seen such a bunch of backstabbing, money-hungry, greedy bitches in my life."

Rita's eyes bugged out, and her mouth went wide. "John, John, you shouldn't be saying these things about the girls, especially in front of Joy."

"Well, it's a fucking fact. I just don't understand them. They've got everything. It's not happening this year." He looked over at the caretaker. "Can you believe that shit?"

"It's not my business," Washburn replied. "But that's what happens. Money goes to people's heads."

"They're all gonna get a lesson now," Chakalos promised. "They're all gonna start getting cut, because I'm fed up with it. It's time that I started using some of that money to do what I want to do."

John and Rita Chakalos normally drove up from Connecticut on Wednesdays and would stay at the mansion through the weekend before returning to Windsor.

Not only did they share their estate with Nathan and other family members, they also allowed members of the community onto the vast property during the holiday season.

For the past ten years, John and Rita had acted as Mr. and Mrs. Santa Claus for neighbors and strangers alike by illuminating their estate with six million Christmas lights. At first, the couple asked Washburn to hang a few Christmas ornaments and invited kindergarten students from nearby Chesterfield School to enjoy their display, but soon after, they allowed people from far and wide to travel down their long, winding driveway and see all the sparkling lights and large holiday decorations over a span of ten days each December. John Chakalos oversaw the project, taking photos of holiday displays he liked and then employing a local welder to build him the same thing for his property. At one point, Chakalos had tapped all the available electricity provided from the town and had to build his own power plant on the property, along with several generators.

John and Rita used their holiday display as a mechanism to raise money for Joan's Food Pantry, which operated out of the Asbury United Methodist Church in Chesterfield. Volunteers from the church stood at the front gate of the Chakalos estate to receive donations and nonperishable food items from the estimated nine thousand visitors each year.

"The display was gorgeous. You'd come around the corner, and the property would just glow. John Chakalos knew what was going on in the community and knew what the town needed," said Cornelia Jenness, a food pantry volunteer. "The pantry has just been a godsend, and we now serve seventy local families. John and Rita both played vital roles in our growth."

But despite the goodwill shown to the town, the holiday display created even more turmoil within the family. At least one of his daughters complained that Chakalos was spending too much money on "Christmas shit." According to caretaker Joy Washburn, that same daughter argued with Chakalos over putting up blue-and-white sparkling lights on the arches over the driveway because they were the colors of Hanukkah. "We're not Jews," the daughter argued.

"Look, as a Greek Orthodox Christian, I cover all religions here," Chakalos replied. "People from all over drive through here and give something to the pantry, so like it or not, I'm covering all religions here."

During the last Christmas in 2012 when the entire family gathered at the farm in West Chesterfield, Washburn said she witnessed an epic fight between Chakalos and his daughters over two missing bottles of expensive wine. Chakalos interrogated several family members and pointed his fingers at his daughters and grandchildren. Someone then questioned whether the caretaker stole the wine, and the attention suddenly shifted to Washburn. At that moment, the caretaker had reached her breaking point and unloaded on the family.

"In all the years that I've worked for you, you dare question me and ask me if I took it?" Washburn asked them all. "I am appalled that you would think that I would do such a thing." She then recited a laundry list of her own complaints and detailed the inappropriate behavior of certain family members that she had witnessed over the course of her years working at the farm.

When the dust finally settled, the person who had taken the expensive bottles of wine never came forward. But Washburn's outburst and her airing of Chakalos family secrets was never forgotten.

"One family member threatened me and said that she had influential friends and that I may go missing and never be heard from again," Washburn claimed.

In 2013, Rita Chakalos was diagnosed with breast cancer and fought the disease bravely for several months before entering hospice care in November. At that time, Washburn claimed that John Chakalos approached her at the farm with an unusual proposition.

"His wife was dying, and he asked me to marry him," Washburn said.

"He called it a marriage of convenience and said it was the only way he could change the family trusts, by adding me as his wife."

Washburn said she was appalled by the idea, as Rita Chakalos was lying on her deathbed at the time. "Don't you dare ask me that question until Rita has passed," Washburn told him. "I respect your wife as well. I love her and care about her. After she's gone, I'll think about it because I know it won't be an easy life living with you."

Washburn claimed that Chakalos also offered her $10,000 per month to marry him. He then looked her over from head to toe.

"The only thing is that you're a little chunkier than most women I've been with," he told her.

"You won't have to shake the sheets to find me then," Washburn replied with a laugh.

The caretaker said that Nathan was standing out on the terrace and had overheard their conversation.

Joy Washburn did not discuss the matter with her boss again.

Rita Chakalos succumbed to breast cancer and died a week before Thanksgiving in 2013, surrounded by her family and her hospice care nurse.

Washburn attended the funeral and claimed to have received another bizarre proposal at the reception following the service.

"An associate of the family came up to me and told me that no one could stand John [Chakalos] anymore," she recalled. "The person asked me to take John out hunting in New Hampshire and kill him and make it look like an accident. I don't think this person was joking."

John Chakalos appeared shaken by the loss of his wife of fifty-nine years and told friends that he did not want to live anymore without her. His daughters stayed with him for the first few days over a concern that he was growing depressed. They also urged him to sell the massive home in New Hampshire, but Chakalos was vehemently opposed to the idea. He had given his heart to the community, and they had returned his affection.

Folks in the Chesterfield, New Hampshire, area rallied around the grieving widower and paid tribute to the memory of his late wife by decorating a tree in front of the Chakalos estate in Rita's honor.

"It's for our angel who, for all those years, helped feed so many people in our community," said food pantry volunteer Val Starbuck.

Joy Washburn had considered putting up pink lights that holiday season to symbolize breast cancer but decided against it because she was worried that the family did not want to be reminded of Rita's death so soon.

But Chakalos was not spending much time grieving at the Farm at Pond Brook. He had a dark secret of his own. To the outside world, he was a dedicated and loving husband. But in reality, the elderly widower had been engaged in an illicit affair with a woman less than half his age.

While family members were trying to cope with the loss of Rita Chakalos, her widower husband was enjoying a long weekend with his young blond mistress at the Mohegan Sun Casino. John Chakalos was especially excited to see her after she had recently undergone $3,500 worth of breast enhancement surgery, a procedure that he had paid for. At his advanced age, Chakalos may still have had stamina in the boardroom, but he could no longer perform in the bedroom. Still, the thought of being alone with a beautiful twenty-five-year-old woman excited him and made him feel young again.

He had met her in the spring of 2013 while she worked for a property management firm in New Hampshire. Chakalos owned a large apartment complex in Keene, New Hampshire, and the pair struck up a conversation that led to a relationship during his many visits to her office. While Rita was battling breast cancer, her outwardly devoted husband spent much of his time trying to seduce his new girlfriend. He began taking her to lunch and offering her gifts of cash of $100 at first. Chakalos also promised to pay for her college tuition. The woman was living with a boyfriend in New Hampshire but had moved to Connecticut in September 2013 to be closer to Chakalos. He increased the cash offerings to her from $100 to $800 when she agreed to perform sexual favors. During their getaway to Mohegan Sun in mid-December, just a few short weeks after his wife's death, Chakalos brought a bag of sex toys up to their hotel room. He asked her to use them on herself while he watched. The blond took one look at the size of the dildo he had pulled out of the bag and shook her head no. "[It's] way too big," she told him.

Chakalos kept his illicit affair a secret from his family members. Otherwise, they might have confronted the patriarch about his lewd, disrespectful behavior, especially while his wife was withering away. After Rita's funeral service at St. Gabriel Church in Windsor, followed by her burial at Cedar Hill Cemetery in nearby Hartford, Chakalos did not see much of his family. He planned to avoid them over Christmas as well while spending the holidays in New York City with his mistress. That year, the Rockefeller Center Christmas tree, a seventy-six-foot-tall Norway spruce, had been chopped down in Shelton, Connecticut, about an hour's drive away from Chakalos's Windsor home. Upon returning from his holiday getaway, the millionaire businessman planned to move out of the mustard-colored middle-class home where he and Rita had raised their four daughters and into a luxury apartment in Hartford's trendy Blue Back Square, where he and his new girlfriend could enjoy the city's best shops and restaurants. John Chakalos felt young again.

CHAPTER NINE

In the early evening on Thursday, December 19, 2013, Nathan Carman joined his grandfather for dinner at a Greek restaurant on the Berlin Turnpike in the town of Newington, Connecticut, just fourteen miles from Chakalos's Windsor home. Chakalos rarely ate meals at home and enjoyed the restaurant's authentic menu of Greek dishes that included lamb *youvetsi* and chicken *spanaki* à la crème. He looked forward to these dinners alone with his grandson, where they could discuss business matters and the news of the day. Chakalos wanted to make sure that Nathan was keeping up with his reading of the *Wall Street Journal.* The big news on this day focused on Hillary Clinton's televised interview with Barbara Walters about whether she would run for the presidency in 2016. The grandfather and grandson were both staunch Republicans and shuddered at the thought, although a strong challenger from the GOP had yet to emerge.

They finished their meals, and Chakalos asked for the check. He left the restaurant and climbed onto the passenger seat of Nathan's Nissan Titan pickup truck. It had snowed recently, but the sky was clear, and the temperature hovered around thirty-eight degrees with little wind. Since 2011, Chakalos had relied on others to drive him around after losing his license because of his failing eyesight, paying one of his nephews nearly $6,000 a month to help him run errands around town during business hours. The eighty-seven-year-old man had also been hospitalized after crashing his car in New Hampshire. On this night, Nathan had offered to take his grandfather to dinner and back home again.

During the drive, they listened to a conservative talk radio station and discussed their mutual disdain for Hillary Clinton. They reached the family home on Overlook Drive at 8:30 p.m. Nathan then escorted his grandfather inside, where they spent a few minutes talking before being interrupted by a phone call. It was Chakalos's girlfriend on the line, and she was in a playful mood. Earlier that day, the widower had visited the Luv Boutique, a sex shop in Hartford that specialized in toys and fantasy wear. While browsing the store's vast collection of dildos and vibrators, he tried calling his girlfriend on the phone, but she did not pick up. Later, Chakalos was seen on a bank surveillance camera withdrawing cash from an ATM. He had an unidentified blond with him.

The girlfriend called Chakalos at 8:36 p.m., purring on the phone, wanting to engage him in phone sex. The elderly man could not resist such a tantalizing conversation with the young blond, so he quickly cut his visit with Nathan short and escorted him to the front door while he still had his cell phone to his ear.

"Nathan's just leaving," Chakalos whispered into his cell phone. "Give me a minute. I want to say goodbye to my grandson."

Chakalos hugged Nathan and then closed the front door and continued the erotic discussion. After about twenty minutes of phone sex, they finished their call by finalizing their holiday getaway plans to New York City. "I didn't like what happened at Mohegan Sun," he told her, likely in reference to her refusal to perform with the large sex toy he had purchased for her. He planned to bring the new batch of toys, which he had purchased that day with a credit card at Luv Boutique, with them to New York.

After hanging up with his mistress, Chakalos took two more phone calls between 9:00 and 10:30 p.m. One call was from his daughter Linda, the other from his caretaker, Joy Washburn, who reported trouble with the Christmas lights display at the Farm in West Chesterfield.

"We were working up there. It was the second night of the Christmas display, and part of the lights went out," Washburn remembered. "We were up there working, unplugging and pulling thousands of light bulbs. I told John that we were fixing the problem."

Chakalos went to bed after the phone call with his caretaker, as he had plans to go to his granddaughter's recital the following day before heading up to his New Hampshire estate.

Early the next morning at approximately 2:00 a.m., a neighbor living next door to Chakalos was startled awake by a loud bang. An hour later, the same neighbor said she heard the squeal of tires from a car as it left the street. The commotion was unusual for such a quiet neighborhood. Still, the neighbor did not call the police and instead tried to go back to sleep.

When daylight broke, Elaine Chakalos left her two dogs, Stetson and Riley, and drove from her home in West Hartford to visit her father for breakfast. A registered nurse, Elaine wanted to make sure that her dad was taking his heart medications, which he kept on the right-hand side of the kitchen sink. She arrived at the home at 52 Overlook Drive at approximately 8:15 a.m. and parked next to her father's car. Elaine then let herself into the house and called out his name. She was met with silence. John Chakalos had been an early riser since his army days in the 1940s and would normally be working furiously at his desk by this time of the day. Elaine peeked her head into his office and saw that her father's desk was undisturbed. There was no paper shuffling and no smell of freshly brewed coffee wafting through the small house.

Elaine crept toward her father's bedroom. For a moment, she feared that he had died in his sleep or maybe was struck unconscious after falling out of his bed. She opened the bedroom door slowly. The space was dark, with only a small beam of light coming in from the bedroom window. Elaine saw her father lying still on the king-size bed. The sheets and comforter were covered with fresh blood. Elaine let out a terrified scream. She ran outside and, with trembling fingers, dialed 911 on her cell phone. The time was 8:23 a.m.

Within minutes, the neighborhood was overrun by officers from the Windsor Police Department and detectives from the Connecticut State Police Central District Major Crimes Squad. Crime scene investigators crossed the snow-covered front lawn, entered the home, and found that most of the house had been left undisturbed, including stacks of cash that Chakalos always had on hand in case of an emergency. The master bedroom, however, was a gory mess. The millionaire businessman was unrecognizable, as half of his head appeared to have been blown off. Detectives surmised that Chakalos's killer had stood at the foot of the bed and unloaded a series of rifle blasts into the elderly man's body while he was asleep. The first shot hit the millionaire developer in his stomach and traveled up through his chest toward his head. The killer then fired two more shots into Chakalos's skull to make sure that he was dead.

Neighbors stood out in the cold morning air, craning their necks for a closer look at the flurry of police activity outside the home. Soon, an ambulance was called. and a stretcher was wheeled into the house, followed by a dour-looking medical examiner. Investigators continued to go about their grisly work without acknowledging the crowd of onlookers huddled together on the dead-end street. They would all be questioned later by police.

The killer had been methodical and had taken the murder weapon and the rifle's shell casings when they made their escape. The window in the back door was broken, and as investigators later discovered, the bag of sex toys bought by Chakalos the day before was gone.

Joy Washburn was first alerted to the situation by a subcontractor who lived close to John Chakalos in Windsor. He drove through the neighborhood and placed a frantic call to the caretaker.

"Joy, I just went by John's, and there's tape up and cops and ambulances. I don't know what's wrong, but something must've happened to John."

"I just talked to him last night and told him that we're doing repairs on the Christmas display," Washburn replied. "He's supposed to come up today. Shit."

The caretaker said she tried calling Linda Carman and Elaine Chakalos but got no answer. She then reached Valerie Santilli at home.

"Valerie, what's happening? There's an ambulance and police at your father's house."

Washburn claimed that Valerie told her that Chakalos was "very sick" and that he was on his way to the hospital for treatment. Washburn surmised that it had something to do with her boss's low blood sugar and that he may have slipped into a diabetic coma.

"Please keep me posted about your dad and how he's doing," the caretaker said. "Let me know what hospital he's in so that I can come down and visit when he's a little better."

Washburn went back to work repairing the Christmas lights before being called home to retrieve two cows that had escaped from her property. She had finally corralled the animals and fixed the fence on her property a couple hours later when her cell phone rang again. The call was from a police officer from Connecticut, offering his condolences to her for the loss of her boss.

Washburn was confused. "Huh? Rita died last month. I was there at the funeral."

"No, I'm talking about John," the officer said.

"I just talked to him last night. But Valerie told me that he was extremely sick and that he was on his way to the hospital."

The officer corrected her. "No, not at all. But he was found dead by his daughter."

"What? Oh my God!"

Washburn hung up the phone and stood still by the fence of her property.

Why would Valerie say such a thing to me? she asked herself. *Maybe she's in shock and doesn't want to believe what has happened to her father.*

The caretaker felt numb. She immediately recalled the strange conversation she had had just a few weeks before with a family associate who asked her to murder Chakalos and make it look like an accident. She had nervously laughed off the cryptic conversation then, but she wasn't laughing anymore. Joy Washburn was terrified.

CHAPTER TEN

Nathan said he dropped his grandfather off at home and then drove his pickup truck to his two-bedroom apartment in nearby Bloomfield and left there a few hours later for a late-night ice cream run to a Stop & Shop supermarket, where a security camera captured him entering and leaving the store. He then returned home and ate his frozen dessert while playing online chess. A surveillance camera at the housing complex showed him leaving the apartment at 2:57 a.m., about an hour after Chakalos's neighbor heard a loud bang coming from his home. Nathan had planned to meet Linda for an early morning fishing trip in Rhode Island. The two were supposed to rendezvous in Glastonbury, Connecticut, at 3:00 a.m. and then pile into one vehicle for the ride north to Rhode Island. Linda waited in her car for thirty minutes before deciding to turn around and return home to Middletown. Nathan arrived in Glastonbury at 4:00 a.m. and saw no sign of his mother. He used a credit card to buy gas for his truck and then called Linda on his cell phone to let her know that he had finally reached their meeting spot. Asked why he was late, Nathan told her that he lost track of time while playing chess. Not wanting to miss an opportunity to spend time with her son, Linda hopped back into her car and drove to Glastonbury. From there, they traveled to Rhode Island and spent the morning fishing.

While Linda enjoyed time with her son, seemingly blissfully unaware of her father's murder, her sisters Valerie and Elaine were questioned by the police. When asked about a possible motive for the slaying, Valerie told investigators that it could have had something to do with Chakalos's business and the tens of millions of dollars he had left behind that would now go to the sisters. "One of the daughters [Valerie] lived in West Hartford, and they were fearful that they could be next and that this was a targeted murder over the money," said Don Melanson, later the chief of police in Windsor, Connecticut, who was working as a police officer in West Hartford at the time. "She actually hired West Hartford police to provide security at their home for a short period of time following the murder."

According to Melanson, the sisters were fearful of Valerie Santilli's first husband, who had been arrested a decade before for threatening and harassing her over the phone. Valerie had filed for divorce from him after alleging that he had beaten her and had verbally abused her during their marriage, which had lasted for only two years.

During their marriage, Chakalos had set the couple up to run a restaurant. Soon after opening the place, Valerie accused her husband of cheating on her with several waitresses. When word reached Chakalos, he told Joy Washburn, "That guy deserves a pair of cement shoes!"

"At the time, Linda offered Valerie a place to stay so she could leave the guy," Clark Carman recalled. Instead, Valerie moved back home with her parents, but her former husband continued to intimidate her. "I won't quit until you give me one more chance," he threatened.

Valerie filed a restraining order against him, which he violated repeatedly.

"I just want him to leave me alone," she told the court. "I don't know if he will honor a protective order."

In November 2002, the ex-husband traveled from his home in Fort Lauderdale and surrendered to authorities in Connecticut, where he was arraigned on two counts of threatening and second-degree harassment.

Valerie worked to put the ugly episode in her rearview mirror and, eleven years later, was remarried with kids of her own. But she was still worried that he would return someday and do harm to her or a member of her family.

Detectives from the Windsor Police Department worked to establish a timeline of John Chakalos's last day through interviews with his daughters and other family members and by analyzing his credit card receipts and phone records. After visiting the sex shop on December 19, Chakalos spent time at the St. George Greek Orthodox Cathedral in Hartford. Later, he had dinner with Nathan and then had phone sex with his mistress. At 9:03 p.m., Chakalos received a call from Linda Carman. He took one more phone call from Joy Washburn at 9:54 p.m. before going to bed.

Interviewing the residents living on Chakalos's street, police discovered that a neighbor had heard someone running in the area at around midnight.

A person living directly next door to the murder scene told investigators that they had heard noises a couple of hours later at 2:00 a.m. "I was home and in my mom's bedroom, which was located in the northeast corner of our house," the witness said. "I heard a loud bang coming from the direction of my neighbor's house at 52 Overlook Drive. My dog began barking at about the same time, which I thought was unusual for the hour. At 3 a.m., I was lying in my mom's bed and heard traffic out in front of our house. I heard multiple cars drive by. I heard one of the cars either brake or turn around and it made a squealing noise."

While questioning family members and neighbors, Windsor police managed to keep the media at bay for the first couple of days, which was surprising given the gravity of the crime and the victim's well-known ties to the community. The first mention of John Chakalos's murder in the press came on Sunday, December 22, 2013, in a brief write-up in the *Hartford Courant*. The story was relegated to a back section of the newspaper and had reprinted information from a news release that was distributed to reporters by the Windsor police. The story noted that Chakalos "was killed by a bullet to the head" and that investigators from the Windsor Police Department along with detectives from the state police Central District Major Crime Squad were treating his death as a homicide and not a suicide. The *Courant* story also supplied a hotline number urging anyone with information to call police.

Word of John Chakalos's murder quickly spread to Massachusetts, where he had several business ventures, and to New Hampshire, where he maintained his lavish home. Reporters working for community newspapers in both states dropped what they were doing and jumped on the story.

Dan Crowley, a reporter from the *Daily Hampshire Gazette,* called Windsor police and got the department's communications officer on the phone. "We have many investigators working on it, going over every aspect of Mr. Chakalos's life at this point," Windsor Police Captain Tom LePore told Crowley. "We're not going to leave any or many stones unturned or any possible motives. There's a lot of stuff to go over, as you can imagine."

The reporter noted that the Connecticut state's attorney's office was now on the case.

Crowley also interviewed local business associates and friends who were devastated by the news and remembered Chakalos fondly. "He was a dynamic, hardworking, larger-than-life figure who was at it every day," said Patrick M. Goggins, a Northampton, Massachusetts, real estate developer who had partnered with Chakalos on a forty-two-unit luxury town house condominium development project. "He had a strong work ethic and approached everything he did with an energy and enthusiasm that would belie his eighty-seven years. He left an impact on the area and was known for a lot of good projects."

Chakalos's caretaker also shared her dismay and disbelief with reporters.

"I have bawled all day long. I'm just so stunned by everything at this point," Joy Washburn told a reporter from the *Keene Sentinel.*

Despite the violent tragedy, Washburn had no plans to shut down the holiday lights display that had been attracting thousands of residents over the past week and was scheduled to run through Sunday, December 22. "[The Chakaloses] are very generous people and have done a lot for the people here in town," she added. "I know that it would be their wish for the light show to go on."

The Chakalos family gathered together over the holidays at Valerie Santilli's home, where Nathan tried to comfort Valerie's daughter by teaching her how to play the piano. Memorial services for the slain patriarch would be held over a two-day period in late December. A wake was held at a local funeral home in Windsor, followed the next day by a Greek Orthodox mass at St. George Cathedral and a graveside service at Cedar Hill Cemetery in Hartford where family members had gathered the month before to say goodbye to Rita. But at least her death had been expected and planned for. John Chakalos had been shot and killed in cold blood, and his murderer was still on the loose.

Uniformed police officers and plainclothes detectives placed themselves strategically outside the church to monitor comings and goings in case the killer wanted to see his handiwork or shoot other members of the Chakalos family. Mourners entered St. George Cathedral and signed their names in a guest book, while others paid tribute online, writing their condolences to the family in a digital funeral program. The website showed a photo of Chakalos half smiling and included a poem from the writer Alex MacLean and a quote incorrectly attributed to another shooting victim—President Abraham Lincoln: "In the end, it's not the years in your life that count, it's the life in your years."

The common narrative among friends who left testimonials in the dead man's memory was that he was larger than life, had a wicked sense of humor, and was always quick to help those in need. As one mourner proclaimed, "John was truly a superman, a hero who the whole world will miss."

Linda Carman had immediately called her ex-husband when she learned of her father's murder, and he grabbed a flight from Los Angeles to Connecticut. Clark Carman attended the funeral with Linda and Nathan. While the other grandchildren openly wept, Nathan showed no emotion, which his father blamed on his disorder. "His demeanor was very cool and off-set," Clark recalled. "But he was sad, and I could tell. He was absolutely crushed."

Inside the church, no one discussed the murder, although it was surely front and center on their minds. Chakalos's obituary, which was printed in local newspapers, stated that he "had passed away unexpectedly at his home in Windsor." It was a peaceful description of a violent death, as if he had gone to sleep one night and never awoke. That may have been partly true, minus the terrifying image of his killer standing with a loaded rifle at the foot of his bed.

A military honor guard presented the family with an American flag signifying Chakalos's bravery during WWII. No one mentioned the terrible irony that he had fought and survived for months against Japanese mortar rounds, gunfire, and bayonets in the Pacific theater only to get blown away in the comfort of his own home while in the twilight of his life.

Clark Carman racked his brain, trying to figure out who had murdered his ex-father-in-law. He thought back to how Chakalos had reneged on his promise to set him and Linda up with their own Dunkin' Donuts franchise. *I wonder if he conducted his business in a similar fashion, lying to people, and what kind of enemies he made in doing some of his deals?* he asked himself.

Joy Washburn attended the funeral and, adhering to the Greek Orthodox religion, was asked to view Chakalos's body.

"It was a closed casket funeral, but when they opened the casket, I could see there was nothing left of his head," she recalled. "It's an image that continues to disturb me to this day."

Once again, her mind raced back to the previous month when someone had approached her about killing John in the woods and making it look like a hunting accident. Washburn did not share the story with anyone at the funeral, but she would tell authorities about it later.

At the funeral reception, Washburn claimed that Valerie approached her quietly with a stunning accusation.

"Nathan killed my father," Valerie allegedly said.

"Well, why is he here and not in jail?" Washburn asked.

"He'll never be prosecuted for it. If anything, they'll place him in a mental institution."

Valerie then walked away.

CHAPTER ELEVEN

Sergeant Bill Freeman led a team of investigators that was assigned to the case by the Windsor Police Department. He met with his detectives every day from December 23 to January 8. The team interviewed several of Chakalos's business associates, including Bill Rabbitt, a certified financial planner. Rabbitt had been working as Chakalos's financial advisor for the past five years, and they had attended numerous business meetings together. During his interview with police on January 7, 2014, Rabbitt described the nature of all Chakalos's business ventures as well as his estate plans for passing his $43 million fortune to his daughters and establishing college funds for his nine grandchildren, including Nathan Carman. He also offered his insight into the family dynamics and described how Chakalos kept certain details about his business dealings to himself.

"I would tell you, out of all of his advisors, nobody really knew everything, so we had to rely on each other," Rabbitt told investigators.

Chakalos was good at keeping secrets, as Sergeant Freeman and others would discover when telephone records from the day before the murder led them to the elderly man's new girlfriend, whom investigators later dubbed Mistress Y. When pressed by detectives, the young woman offered all the sordid details about their affair. While Chakalos may have believed that he had stumbled into a May–December romance, his mistress treated it as a transactional relationship where she offered companionship and performed sex acts for him in exchange for cash. While dating Chakalos, the woman also had a steady boyfriend who allegedly sold drugs.

Although Chakalos had shielded his family from any knowledge of his affair with the young woman, his infidelity had long been a topic of discussion within the large Greek household.

"John had cheated on his wife at least once before, and Rita found out about it," Clark Carman claimed. "It was quite volatile for a while. Rita took a lot of abuse from John, both physically and mentally. Linda tried to get her to leave him before her death, but she wouldn't go. She was fearful of being out on her own."

Clark was visiting the family home when his ex-wife confronted her father about one of his extramarital affairs. "The two got into it," he vividly recalled. "They fought each other. John was a large man, five ten and stocky. He was an imposing figure, even at his advanced age, and especially when he got mad. His face would turn beet red, and he'd start snarling." But Linda refused to back down, and punches were thrown once again. This time, Clark managed to break up the scuffle before anyone got hurt; therefore, there was no need to call the police.

———

One of Sergeant Freeman's investigators, Detective Russell Wininger, was an eighteen-year veteran of the Windsor Police Department, and he was assigned with the task of tracking down the phone records of eleven people who had all emerged as potential suspects in the murder.

One of them was Linda Carman, who had spoken with her father on the phone just hours before he was killed. The team gathered information about her antagonistic and violent relationship with her father. Investigators pulled the 2011 police report that detailed how she had punched, scratched, and grabbed Chakalos's testicles during their confrontation over Nathan's care, along with her comments to police sharing her belief that her father was worth $300 million and that she wanted her share. Her father had cut her off financially on many occasions, although she was still in line to inherit millions upon his death. The fact that she had gone fishing during the early morning hours after her father's murder was not lost on investigators. Was Linda trying to establish an alibi? She hired an attorney within days of the killing, as did her three sisters.

"The whole family had lawyers," recalled Windsor police chief Don Melanson. "They mobilized [their attorneys], which complicated the investigation. Any time you can't speak directly with someone and now you're scheduling a meeting through an attorney, it slows things down."

But it appeared that investigators were not casting a wide net in their search for the killer and failed to interview people who were close to Chakalos and close to the family.

"I was never interviewed by any legal authority after John's death," Clark Carman claimed. "I was never contacted by anyone from Windsor police, which was totally odd to me why that would occur."

Valerie Santilli did discuss with investigators her suspicion that her nephew Nathan Carman was capable of murdering his grandfather. She spoke of an incident involving Nathan where he allegedly held another boy at knifepoint. Detectives were curious about why he had arrived late for the early morning fishing trip with his mother on the morning of the murder. Nathan told them he had lost track of time while playing chess on his computer and then got lost and ended up on the wrong highway. He then circled around and stopped at a convenience store to buy a soda before finally arriving at the pre-planned meeting spot and calling his mother. Nathan said that he routinely showed up late for activities with Linda. He also described a growing jealousy in the family over his close relationship with his grandfather. He claimed that both Valerie Santilli and Elaine

Chakalos were angry over their father's plans to buy a new Ford F-150 Platinum truck for Nathan at the cost of $50,000, while Chakalos had recently purchased a less expensive used car for Elaine's daughter Hailey.

All four sisters were asked to take a polygraph test. Each daughter accepted the request, and all of them passed. Investigators also asked Nathan to submit to a lie-detector test, as he was the last person to see his grandfather alive. But the teenager refused to cooperate. In a written response to investigators, Nathan stated that he was refusing "because the accuracy and reliability of polygraph results are questionable and the principle of attempting to prove my innocence, a seeming waiver of one of the most fundamental human rights, the right to be presumed innocent until proven guilty, is abhorrent to me."

Nathan told investigators that he had no motive to kill John Chakalos, who treated him not as a grandchild but as a son. The elderly man had spent more than $100,000 on Nathan over the past year in cash payments and had made sure that all his bills were paid. He had promised to pay for Nathan's tuition and living expenses if he enrolled at Keene State College and gave him unrestricted use of the family mansion in West Chesterfield. According to Nathan, Chakalos also wanted him to become heavily involved in the building of an assisted living project on Cape Cod.

"He was grooming Nathan to take much more responsibility in his businesses, and I think that affected how his aunts treated him," Clark Carman said. "Nathan was the firstborn grandchild in a Greek family, and his grandfather doted on him even before he was born."

"My relationship with my grandfather represented the best opportunity for personal and professional growth which I had ever had," Nathan said. "And it held the promise of future opportunities to receive financial support if I should ask or the need arise, as well as opportunities to develop relationships with high-level business leaders and other distinguished individuals."

According to financial records and a police interview with John

Chakalos's financial advisor, the patriarch had also set up two bank accounts naming Nathan as a beneficiary upon his grandfather's death. One account held $150,000, which was created to pay for Nathan's college education. The other account contained $400,000 and listed both Nathan and Linda Carman as beneficiaries.

While members of the Windsor police investigative team worked to establish a motive for the murder and tried to determine who had the most to gain from John Chakalos's death, detectives from the Connecticut State Police Central District Major Crimes Squad were analyzing pieces of six bullets that had been recovered from the crime scene. A month after the slaying, forensic experts reported that two projectiles came from a ".30 caliber boattail jacketed bullet," and another was a hollow-point bullet, which were lethally designed to expand on impact. "If any .30 caliber class firearms are developed in this case, they should be submitted to the laboratory for further examination," the forensic expert recommended in the report. "A Sig Sauer rifle fires either .308 caliber bullets or a 7.63 mm cartridge."

While examiners could not say definitively what type of firearm was used to kill John Chakalos, detectives were now narrowing their investigative focus to anyone close to him who owned a Sig Sauer rifle, the likely murder weapon.

CHAPTER TWELVE

Within a week of John Chakalos's murder, Windsor police detective Russell Wininger had successfully obtained telephone records for eleven potential suspects, including Nathan Carman, but for some reason, he kept the phone records to himself. During weekly meetings with Sergeant Bill Freeman and other members of the investigative team, Wininger was asked about his progress. He lied to the group and claimed that he was still working to gather the evidence. Without Freeman's knowledge, Wininger had taken the records to a friend at the Hartford Police Department and asked him to perform a mapping process that would show a cell phone's exact location at the time of a call. The Hartford police officer did not feel any urgency to handle Wininger's request and took off for vacation in early January. Wininger himself then left on vacation on January 8, 2014.

While he was out of the office, another detective was asked to follow up with the phone companies about the records. The investigator was startled to learn that the records had already been sent back to the Windsor Police Department, some as early as December 23, three days after the murder. Had Wininger simply forgotten to share this information with his colleagues? Detectives searched his work computer and discovered emails that included the phone records. Wininger had even taken the time to transfer the records into his own computer files. "Detective Wininger's withholding of the records not only deprived the team for over two weeks of important information provided in the records in addition to the mapping, it also delayed the mapping process [during] a similar two-week period," said Kevin Searles, who was the chief of Windsor police at the time. Chief Searles was also concerned that the delay could have resulted in the erasing of critical surveillance video of potential suspects. Windsor's town manager blasted Russell Wininger in a letter to the department, stating that his actions "had a significant negative impact upon an ongoing homicide investigation."

Detective Wininger himself offered no reason as to why he would lie about obtaining the phone records. In a statement that he later released to the *Hartford Courant*, Wininger said, "I would never, nor have I intended to do something that would hamper any investigation. I would hope that my reputation as a Police Officer in the Town of Windsor for the past 19 years would speak for itself."

Russell Wininger would later be demoted, and he was suspended for ten days without pay for making false statements and for withholding evidence. Detectives now feared that their investigation into the biggest murder case in the town's history was coming off the rails. They needed to catch a break in the case soon.

At around this same time, investigators discovered that large sums of money had been taken out of John Chakalos's various bank accounts before his murder. Poring over banking records that dated back several years, detectives learned that the millionaire's bookkeeper had embezzled $416,000 from him. The thefts began in 2009 and continued through 2013. On May 6, 2014, police arrested the bookkeeper, fifty-five-year-old William D. Satti, at his home in Pawtucket, Rhode Island. Satti waived extradition and was brought across state lines to Connecticut to face charges. The bookkeeper was then arraigned on larceny charges and held by the Connecticut Department of Correction on a $500,000 bond.

Despite the fact that Satti may have had motive to murder his boss in an effort to conceal his plundering of Chakalos's bank accounts, Windsor police captain Tom LePore, the spokesperson for the department, quickly added that the bookkeeper's arrest was "unrelated to the death" but that he had no information to release regarding the investigation. Satti later admitted that he had stolen large amounts of money from his boss but not $416,000 as investigators had claimed. The bookkeeper spent some of the money on expensive cars and said that he viewed it as a personal loan from the millionaire developer, only without John Chakalos's knowledge. "I'm sorry," Satti told a judge in 2015. "I did mean to put the money back in the account."

While Windsor police were determined to treat Satti's embezzlement and Chakalos's murder as unrelated events, the bookkeeper's own lawyer did not seem so sure. Attorney Charles D. Hines of Enfield, Connecticut, was surrounded by news reporters on the day that his client was sentenced to three and a half years in prison for robbing from his wealthy employer. When asked where all the stolen money had gone, Hines pondered the question and answered that it was "part of the greater mystery of what happened to Mr. Chakalos."

In June 2014, family members marked the half-year anniversary of John Chakalos's murder with a Greek memorial service, called a *mnimosino*, at St. George Greek Orthodox Cathedral in Hartford. Both Nathan and Linda attended the Sunday service along with Valerie, Elaine, and several of Chakalos's grandchildren. The sisters expressed their mutual frustration over the lack of progress being made by investigators but did not share with each other what they had discussed with the police. The arrest of William Satti had been a curious development, but investigators said that they could not tie the bookkeeper to the likely murder weapon.

However, members of the investigative team had recently discovered that Nathan had used his New Hampshire driver's license to buy a $2,000 Sig Sauer 716 rifle at Shooters Outpost, a large, family-run gun shop in the town of Hooksett, on Tuesday, November 11, 2013, just five weeks before his grandfather's murder. Kellie Senecal, a special agent for the Bureau of Alcohol, Tobacco, Firearms, and Explosives, had been visiting New England gun shops and asking staff members if anyone had purchased such a weapon around the time of the deadly crime. When gun seller Jed Warner saw her walk in, he knew exactly why she was there. In late fall the previous year, a disheveled young man in dirty clothes had walked into Shooters Outpost with a specific request for a Sig Sauer. To Warner, the shaggy-haired customer did not look like a typical sportsman, especially one who could afford such an expensive weapon.

"A Sig Sauer is one of the premier firearms on the market, and if you looked at that kid on the street, you wouldn't think he could afford that kind of rifle. He didn't really fit the bill," Jed Warner recalled.

Initially, the man, later identified as Nathan Carman, was working with another employee at the store. Warner observed their interaction and jumped into the conversation. "My job was to sell firearms and be helpful to our customers, but I also like to ask questions as kind of a preliminary background check."

Warner's bosses at the gun store gave him plenty of leeway when it came to deciding whether to sell a weapon to a customer. "Even if the customer passed a background check, if my 'Spidey-senses' went up, if I had a gut feeling about someone, I could refuse to sell them a firearm," he recalled. "I'm releasing these weapons out into the world and potentially around my friends and family. I was always super cautious about who I sold them to."

Despite Nathan's unkempt appearance, he did not project a weird or potentially dangerous demeanor while shopping at the gun store. "He also handled the rifle pretty well. It looked like he knew what he was doing."

When asked by Warner what he planned to use the weapon for, Nathan replied, "Target shooting."

Since he would only be using the gun to shoot clay pigeons, Warner tried to steer Nathan away from the pricey weapon toward a more economical brand.

"No, I have done my research, and this is what I want," Nathan told Warner matter-of-factly.

Knowing that the customer had made up his mind, the gun seller then talked about ammunition. Warner informed Nathan that the Sig Sauer was capable of firing two different kinds of bullets: a 7.62 NATO military-caliber bullet as well as a less expensive .308 commercial-grade bullet. Warner explained that Nathan could use the ammunition interchangeably with the Sig Sauer.

When filling out the paperwork to buy the rifle along with several cartons of ammunition, Nathan showed his New Hampshire driver's license to Warner. The gun seller flipped it over and noticed that there was also an address for a post office box in Connecticut printed on the back of the identification card.

"Dude, you're from Connecticut," Warner told him. "I can't sell you this rifle, Connecticut says no."

"I live in New Hampshire, and I have property here," Nathan told him.

"I need something that proves that you are a resident of New Hampshire, that you have a domicile here, or else I can't let this gun leave the store. Is your car registered in New Hampshire?"

Nathan nodded his head yes and returned to his truck to retrieve the vehicle's registration. He presented it to Warner, and they continued to fill out the paperwork. Warner called over a fellow employee, who was a retired ATF agent, to review the documents.

"We now know you have ties to Connecticut, family or whatever, but this firearm cannot cross state lines," Warner warned Nathan. "This weapon must stay in New Hampshire."

"Yes, I understand. I know that," Nathan replied.

The teenager left the store with the Sig Sauer, and Warner continued on with his day. When he later learned that a millionaire with a house in West Chesterfield had been killed by a rifle in Connecticut, his Spidey-senses tingled. *Did I sell the weapon that was used in the murder?* he asked himself.

Warner's worst fears were realized when ATF agent Kellie Senecal entered Shooters Outpost. Senecal showed her badge to another employee, who waved Warner over to a back room and away from other customers. Together, they showed Senecal a file of recent Sig Sauer rifle sales. Nathan Carman's paperwork was at the top of a small stack of customer receipts. Special Agent Senecal asked Warner what he remembered about Nathan, and the gun seller recounted their exchange from November 11, 2013. Senecal handed Warner her business card and left with the paperwork.

Ironically, John Chakalos paid for the weapon and for Nathan to get trained on the Sig Sauer, and they presented the rifle to Joy Washburn at the Farm in West Chesterfield.

"Show Joy what you just got," Chakalos told him.

Nathan was reluctant to fetch the weapon.

Chakalos pressed. "C'mon, Nathan, you know she hunts. She'd love to see it."

"Fine."

Nathan pulled the Sig Sauer out of the back of his truck and opened the box.

"Nice," Joy said.

"Nice all right," Chakalos replied. "I tried to get him to buy something cheaper, but he had to have that Sig Sauer."

Chakalos took the rifle out of its box and handed it to the caretaker.

Washburn was impressed. "Wow, this has got a nice feel to it." She stepped sideways and put the rifle to her shoulder. "This is nice," Washburn repeated. "Nathan, you ought to be proud of yourself. It's got a good feel to it, and it locks right into your shoulder. It's comfortable, even for me."

Nathan grew frustrated as he watched Washburn aim the empty weapon.

"Okay, you've had your hands on it long enough," he told her. "Put it back in the box now, and wipe your fingerprints off it too!"

"Don't be like that," Chakalos scolded his grandson.

Nathan grabbed a rag, wiped down the rifle, placed it gently back in its box, and returned it to the back seat of his truck, where he threw a blanket over it.

"I bet Joy could teach you how to shoot that rifle," Chakalos suggested to Nathan. "She's been hunting her whole life and knows her way around guns."

"No," Nathan replied coldly.

Washburn said that Nathan and Chakalos took the Sig Sauer down to Connecticut illegally, and she never saw the weapon again.

With proof of Nathan's purchase of a Sig Sauer shortly before his grandfather's murder, investigators obtained a search warrant for his residence at the Knoll Crest Apartments on George Street in Middletown, where he was now living, and for his pickup truck. It was a search and seizure warrant for firearms against a "person posing [a] risk to self or others." The warrant listed a number of reasons for the search, including that he had discarded "both the hard drive of his computer as well as the GPS unit used on the morning of December 20, 2013" and that he'd purchased a high-caliber rifle, identical to the weapon used to murder John Chakalos.

With the search warrant in hand, investigators entered Nathan's apartment on July 18 and found a Remington tactical shotgun and rifle scope along with a pellet gun and several boxes of ammunition. Investigators also discovered several notes written by Nathan with intricate details about sniper rifles with a stabilizing platform and camera that collected facial recognition data and self-propelled improvised explosive devices. While interviews were being conducted with residents at the George Street apartment complex, one neighbor dubbed Nathan "Murder Boy." "He's a time bomb waiting to go off," the neighbor said.

Yet despite an exhaustive search of the apartment, investigators found no sign of the Sig Sauer 716 rifle.

Detectives from the Windsor Police Department took possession of Nathan's shotgun and ammunition. Nathan told police that he had experience shooting guns at shooting ranges. He also led them back to his grandfather's home on Overlook Drive and pointed out a secret cubbyhole investigators had missed where Chakalos had kept his collection of vintage World War II guns. Nathan claimed that no one else in the family had knowledge of the weapons.

Detectives grilled Nathan as to the whereabouts of the Sig Sauer rifle, but he refused to talk.

"Before invoking his Fifth Amendment rights, he had admitted to owning a shotgun but claimed that he didn't own any other weapons," recalled Chief Melanson. "He never mentioned that he had purchased an AR-style assault rifle, like the one used to murder John Chakalos. He never admitted that. How did that rifle go missing soon after he had purchased it?"

Police officers scoured the area where Nathan's horse Cruise was laid to rest, theorizing that he had buried the rifle next to his favorite animal. Their search of the location also turned up empty.

The missing weapon was not the only thing troubling investigators. They were also alarmed by the fact that Nathan had discarded the GPS in his truck and that he refused to show them the route he took to Glastonbury when he allegedly got lost on the morning of the murder. Because he had kept his cell phone shut off during the hour-long drive to meet his mother, investigators could not rely on cell towers to pinpoint his exact location. Nathan had also destroyed his computer at around the time of the murder.

Nathan later claimed that he would have cooperated fully with authorities if he did not feel like he had a target on his back.

"If they [Windsor police] had asked me, 'Nathan, can we look at your hard drive?' or 'Nathan, can we have your GPS?' at that time, when they were in my apartment, my answer would have been, 'Sure, gladly. You can take it.' But they didn't," he recalled. "I think the police saw me as the lowest hanging fruit after my grandfather died because they saw that I had been diagnosed with [autism spectrum disorder]."

The investigative team believed that it now had enough evidence to arrest Nathan Carman for the murder of his grandfather. Windsor police sergeant Bill Freeman drafted an arrest warrant and sent it off to the Connecticut state's attorney's office for approval. Freeman figured that an official sign-off would not take long. His team kept an eye on Nathan out of fear that he might flee the state. Investigators devised a logistical plan for how they would arrest the teenager at his Middletown apartment. Understanding that Nathan was adept at using firearms and believing that he had already killed once before, the key was getting him out of the apartment before he could barricade himself inside and before he could shoot himself, the arresting officers, or any innocent bystanders. While detectives wrestled with their approach, a state's attorney returned the arrest warrant unsigned with a demand for more evidence.

Most of the evidence gathered by investigators against Nathan was circumstantial, and without a murder weapon, state prosecutors believed they would not win a conviction against him for first-degree murder. Prosecutors also had the matter of Detective Russell Wininger to consider. His decision to withhold phone records relevant to the case would be dissected by Nathan's defense attorneys and picked apart at his trial. Windsor police chief Don Melanson believed that Wininger's actions made the case unprosecutable at the time.

"It's not like Wininger could tamper with phone records. Phone records are phone records," Chief Melanson pointed out. "But it was definitely something that did impact the investigation."

While prosecutors within the Connecticut State's Attorney's Office felt they would not be able to convince a twelve-member jury that Nathan

Carman had murdered John Chakalos, some members of the family were satisfied that investigators had identified the right man. Linda's younger sister Charlene Gallagher shared her suspicion with Clark Carman in a text.

You know your son killed my father, she told him.

In September 2014, ten months after the murder of John Chakalos, Nathan petitioned the court for the return of his tactical shotgun, his pellet gun, and the boxes of ammunition that investigators had seized from his apartment. Judge David P. Gold of Middletown, Connecticut, denied the request, stating there was a high standard of proof that Nathan posed "a risk of imminent personal injury to himself…and other individuals."

What had happened to Nathan's Sig Sauer rifle remained a mystery.

CHAPTER THIRTEEN

Months after his grandfather's murder, Nathan received $550,000 from his estate. The first $150,000 came from a trust fund that had been set up by John Chakalos to pay for Nathan's college education, while another $400,000 was given to him from what financial advisors had called a "beneficiary on-death" account, which allowed the family patriarch to name which family members would receive large payouts upon his death. Feeling harassed and hounded by investigators in Connecticut, Nathan used a chunk of his inheritance, $70,000, to buy a historic four-bedroom colonial home in Vermont that had been built more than a century earlier, in 1850. Now twenty years old, Nathan moved from Middletown to the small town of Vernon, which was a straight ninety-four-mile shot up Interstate 91. The house, which was in need of major repairs, was only a twelve-mile drive from his grandfather's mansion in West Chesterfield. Nathan's goal was to modernize the historic home and flip it and sell it for at least double his purchase price.

Nathan got to work right away, handling all the repairs himself, adding another floor to the home, and expanding its square footage from 1,938 to 6,207 square feet.

Vernon, Vermont, was a rural community, safe and quiet. Local dairy farms churned out world-famous Vermont cheddar cheese, and Nathan's historic home on Fort Bridgman Road, which came with a rustic old barn, had plenty of New England charm. But to the dismay of his neighbors, Nathan transformed the quaint property into an eyesore, leaving junk on the lawn as he haphazardly worked to add more space to the inside. He had no training as a carpenter and performed most of the remodeling with the assistance of do-it-yourself videos on YouTube. The result resembled a stack of Jenga blocks teetering on collapse.

Seventy-six-year-old Maynard Rounds watched the ruckus from his house next door. Rounds was an experienced woodworker and had spent years working for the Smead Lumber Company in town. Rounds monitored Nathan's progress and questioned his technique as he tore off the second story of the historic farmhouse and attempted to build three new stories without any help. The front door had no knob, rooms were in a state of disrepair, and building materials were tossed in piles around the yard. "I'd hear him pounding nails from daylight to dark," Rounds recalled. "He was not one to carry on a conversation. He kept his head down and said very little."

Rounds said that Nathan slept in his truck while he remodeled his house and that the two neighbors had a falling-out after he called the local sheriff to check on Nathan when he had not seen him tinkering around the farmhouse for more than a week.

"The first thing that come to mind was maybe he'd finally had that accident," Rounds explained. "Maybe he's over there laying on the ground dead as a crow."

The sheriff investigated and found out that Nathan was away at the time. When he returned, Nathan scolded his elderly neighbor for asking the Vernon police to conduct a wellness check.

"I'd like you to keep your nose the hell out of my business," Nathan shouted at the old man.

Rounds later described the confrontation to a local news reporter.

"He told me he was a big boy and could take care of himself," Rounds recalled. "I said, 'Well, I've been around for quite a while; we're a bunch of senior citizens around this neighborhood and we look out for each other. And if you don't want to buy into that crowd, then you have to look out for yourself!'"

With her father dead, Linda Carman hoped to spend more time with her son. Using some of her own inheritance money, she booked cruises and fishing trips with Nathan, including one excursion to Ontario, Canada. After being flown into Red Lake, 332 miles northwest of Thunder Bay, they stayed in a remote outpost cabin where they fished every day for walleye and northern pike. During one fishing trip out in the lake, their small boat capsized, and both had to swim through frigid water to get back to the shore.

Despite the mishap, Linda gushed about her time alone with her son. In a Facebook post promoting Canadian fishing, she wrote, **Fabulous outposts for some "mom and son" bonding time. No better way to connect than to unplug, drop a line in, and enjoy the peace and quiet and great conversation.**

After the fishing trip, Nathan returned to work on his ramshackle home in Vermont while Linda went home to Connecticut to attend another memorial service for her father, this one marking the one-year anniversary of his brutal death. Although Linda believed that her son had no involvement in her father's murder, her sisters remained steadfast in their conviction that Nathan was the true culprit. "This person killed at least once that we know of," Valerie Santilli said, referring to Nathan. "This person has gotten away with murder, and chances are it will happen again."

In 2015, the investigation of the murder of John Chakalos was handed over to members of the Connecticut Division of Criminal Justice Cold Case Unit.

The transfer of the case marked a bitter defeat for Windsor police sergeant Bill Freeman and his investigative team. They believed they had found the murderer but still could not locate the murder weapon. After more than a year of following up on hopeful leads and stumbling down blind alleys into dead ends, it was time for a new team of investigators to lay fresh eyes on the case and all the evidence that had been compiled thus far. Cold case detectives believed that if they could somehow locate Nathan's missing rifle, they would be able to match it to the ballistics report that was developed at the state police crime lab. They studied the timeline of the murder and read notes from ATF agent Kellie Senecal's interview with gun seller Jed Warner. Maybe the rifle was still in New Hampshire, possibly buried somewhere on his grandfather's estate? Or perhaps the murder weapon had been tossed in the ocean during Nathan's fishing trip with Linda on the morning of the murder?

When asked about the firearm, at first Nathan denied that he had purchased the Sig Sauer, then told investigators that he could not remember what had happened to it. After that initial conversation, Nathan clammed up, invoking his Fifth Amendment right against self-incrimination.

The Chakalos sisters had little faith that the Cold Case Unit would be any more successful than the Windsor police investigative unit had been in bringing their father's killer to justice. As the case dragged on without Nathan being charged with the murder, Valerie Santilli, Elaine Chakalos, and Charlene Gallagher brought their plea directly to the public. In a scene reminiscent of the Oscar-winning film *Three Billboards Outside Ebbing, Missouri*, the sisters paid for a massive billboard to be erected along Interstate 91 in Connecticut where thousands of motorists passed each day. The billboard showed a photo of Chakalos, the same image of him half smiling that they had used for his obituary. The murdered millionaire developer could now stare down at drivers on the highway as they studied his photo next to a banner headline that read *UNSOLVED MURDER,* printed in white lettering against a blood-red backdrop. The sisters also put up a $250,000 reward for "information leading to the arrest & conviction of person(s) responsible." The billboard included the date of the murder, December 20, 2013, along with the telephone number for the Connecticut cold case tip line. With microphones in hand, local television newscasters broadcast live reports in front of the giant billboard. Reporters also revisited John Chakalos's old neighborhood in Windsor and interviewed residents there.

"Maybe it'll lead to something," Joe Zotter, a neighbor and twenty-year friend of the dead man, told a reporter from Connecticut's NBC affiliate. "He always had a nice word to say about everything so you know it's tough. It was a real shock to have something like that happen not only to John [Chakalos], but a neighbor across the street."

The advertisement did not generate any leads, and the case grew even colder. Frustrated investigators could not have imagined what was about to happen next.

CHAPTER FOURTEEN

Brian Woods had grown up around boats, but he did not enjoy boating. He would much rather spend his time riding his motorcycle across the South Shore of Massachusetts, but on this day in late 2015, he was working at his boat yard in Kingston, near the historic town of Plymouth, getting one of his vessels ready for sale. He had named the thirty-one-foot pleasure craft the *Chicken Pox*, an homage to *Goose Bumps*, a boat that was once owned by his parents, who had been boatyard proprietors in the coastal town of Marion, Massachusetts, during his childhood. The *Chicken Pox* was a forty-five-year-old plug vessel that had once operated as a lobster boat. Woods bought it and then spent two years refurbishing it. He installed new bulkheads, added a Cummins 6BTA engine and an aluminum pilothouse, and made extensive external repairs to the hull as well as replacing part of the boat's deck with aluminum. By the summer of 2015, the *Chicken Pox* was seaworthy once again. Woods took out advertisements on Craigslist and on South Shore Dry Dock Marine's website and had fielded a few inquiries before Nathan Carman called his boatyard in late November. Nathan asked the boat builder a few questions regarding the asking price of the *Chicken Pox*, which Woods had listed for sale at $60,000. They made plans for Nathan to see the boat on a Saturday in early December. Woods met him at the boatyard and thought he was dealing with someone much older than twenty-two years old.

"My first impression of him was that he was a forty-five- or fifty-year-old guy, the way he was dressed and held himself," Woods remembered. "He wore a pair of overalls under a long snorkel jacket, a big furry hat, and had a very long beard. It looked like he'd just come out of the north woods."

Nathan told Woods that he was a builder, likely referring to his DIY home project in Vernon, Vermont.

The boat builder put very little effort into trying to sell Nathan the boat. "I was busy that day. I just told him to look around the boat, which was shrink-wrapped, for as long as he wanted."

Woods returned to work, and Nathan inspected the *Chicken Pox* for the next few hours before heading back to Vermont in his pickup truck. Nathan called Woods again the next week, and they scheduled another tour of the boat. "At that point, I thought he was a serious buyer," Woods recalled.

After spending more time with the *Chicken Pox*, Nathan offered Woods $50,000 for the vessel, which the boat builder agreed to. The sale was contingent on a survey from an independent boat builder.

"Excellent. That's the right thing to do," Woods told Nathan. "What are you planning on using the boat for?"

"I plan on taking my mom fishing."

Nathan wanted to take the *Chicken Pox* on a sea trial, but the boat had already been winterized.

"If you want to do that, you'll have to pay for it," Woods said.

Nathan argued with the boat builder about the cost of dewinterizing the vessel.

"That's how it works," Woods explained. "Everybody who buys a boat knows that it's the buyer who pays for the inspection. It's just like a home inspection. That's the way it goes."

At that moment, Woods said that he began to suspect that Nathan knew very little about boats.

The *Chicken Pox* now had to be unwinterized, put on a trailer, and hauled to the ocean and launched. "He [Nathan] didn't understand it. I wasn't sure that this was going to go anywhere at that point," Woods recalled.

Nathan sent Woods a check for $2,000 as a deposit for the boat.

"If I don't buy it, you can keep the money to pay for hauling and getting the boat into the ocean," Nathan told him.

The Chicken Pox, *a fishing boat purchased by Nathan Carman in December 2016. (United States Coast Guard Handout)*

Woods peeled the shrink-wrap off the *Chicken Pox* and brought it down to Brewer Marine at Safe Harbor in Plymouth.

Nathan hired a local surveyor named Bernard Feeney, who conducted an external inspection of the vessel and then joined them for a sea trial in Plymouth. It was a bitterly cold day in mid-December 2015 when Nathan took his first ride on the *Chicken Pox*. Woods brought them out to Duxbury Pier Light, known to the locals as "Bug Light" because it was shaped like a water bug. The eighteen-foot-high lighthouse had been protecting mariners from a perilous nearby shoal since 1871. The trio had the entire harbor to themselves on this day, as temperatures had dipped into the low twenties, and the windchill made it feel even colder.

"Nobody else was on the water. The wind was howling," Woods recalled. "There was no way that we were taking that boat outside the harbor. We just stayed in the bay."

They left the dock and went out through the breakwater with Woods at the helm. Nathan wanted to see how fast the boat could go, so Woods gunned the engine to twenty-one knots. The *Chicken Pox* picked up speed and bounced along the ocean like a stone that had been skipped across a pond. Midway to Bug Light, they heard a loud bang, and all three men lurched forward. The boat had hit something.

Holy shit, what the hell was that? Woods asked himself. At first, he thought they had hit a log.

Woods went below to inspect the bilge for damage and ordered Nathan and the surveyor to stay in the channel, as the water was now running high over the mudflats.

"Just follow the channel. Don't deviate," Woods ordered.

The engine was idling, but there was no apparent leak in the boat. Woods quickly located the problem, which was a four-inch hose that had come loose from the turbo. He reconnected the hose, and the engine roared back to life. Woods pulled his head out of the bilge and noticed that Nathan had steered the *Chicken Pox* straight into the mudflats. The boat builder feared that the vessel would run aground.

"You fucking moron, we're half in the middle of the mudflats," Woods yelled to Nathan. "Get outta my way."

Woods pushed Nathan aside and took control of the steering wheel.

"I was beside myself," Woods later recalled. "I thought that I'd be spending the next twelve hours in the freezing cold stuck on a mudflat with that fucking idiot. I realized quickly that Nathan didn't know a thing about boating. He didn't know shit."

Woods got the boat back to the dock, and the surveyor gave the *Chicken Pox* his stamp of approval. Nathan offered Woods $48,000 for the boat, along with the $2,000 he had already provided as a down payment. Woods took the deal, and Nathan then offered him more money to perform additional work on the boat. Nathan wanted Woods to install a transducer, which would allow him to measure the depth of the water; add cockpit lights to the back of the pilothouse; make him a radar stand for his new radar; and build him a cradle for a life raft. Nathan wanted all the work done before Christmas.

Woods hauled the boat out of the water and into the parking lot on a hydraulic trailer. The boat builder put the transducer in and welded the other equipment onto the boat before placing it back in the ocean. Nathan had promised to pay Woods after the work was completed. He also told the boat builder that he planned to sail the *Chicken Pox* to Rhode Island.

"I don't think that's too smart," Woods replied. "This boat has never been out of the harbor."

Although the boat had been built in 1974, the refurbished vessel only had twenty hours of ocean experience. The boat was equipped with some electronics, including radar and a GPS system, but it had no life jackets and no life raft.

"I'm taking my boat to Point Judith," Nathan told Woods.

The boat builder was flabbergasted. Nathan was an inexperienced sailor, and he was now planning to take the *Chicken Pox* over sixty nautical miles down Massachusetts Bay and through the Cape Cod Canal into Long Island Sound toward Point Judith, a small village on the coast of Narragansett, Rhode Island—a challenging journey for a novice sailor.

"This isn't a good idea," Woods warned him. "Don't you have somebody to go with you?"

Nathan said that he would be making the journey alone. Woods tried to get Nathan to reconsider and later expressed his concerns about the young man's safety to his wife. But once Nathan Carman had his mind on something, there was no talking him out of it.

"He was a grown man. I was beating a dead horse every time I told him that taking the boat that far was a bad idea," Woods remembered.

The two men agreed to meet at Brewer Marine on the morning of

Nathan's planned trip to Point Judith. They scheduled the meeting for 6:00 a.m., but Woods arrived early, just after 5:00 a.m., to find that Nathan was already there. He had brought a ramp truck with him, and Woods watched as Nathan loaded his own pickup truck onto the ramp truck and then ordered the driver to transport the vehicle to Rhode Island. Nathan had promised to pay the boat builder the money he owed for the additional work he had performed on the boat, but Woods had the suspicion that his customer had planned to leave him high and dry.

"Where's my check?" he asked Nathan.

"I forgot my checkbook."

"Oh, here we go," Woods shot back angrily.

"I'm not gonna screw you," Nathan insisted before he climbed into the boat.

Woods scanned the vessel once again and did not see any life preservers on board.

"You're making a big mistake taking the boat out like this," he warned once again.

Nathan did not respond. Instead, he released the dock lines, flipped the ignition switch to start the motor, and then headed off out of Plymouth Harbor toward the Cape Cod Canal and on to Rhode Island.

At nightfall, Woods's wife urged him to call Nathan. "You need to see if he made it," she said. "You need to make sure that he's okay."

The boat builder grabbed his cell phone and punched in the digits. Nathan answered after a few rings, and Woods was surprised by his reaction.

"He [Nathan] was so indignant that I had called to check up on him," Woods remembered. "He didn't even thank me for calling. Instead, he was irritated that I'd called. It did not connect with him that another human being was interested in his well-being."

Once Woods realized that Nathan was okay, he asked him again when he would get paid for the work he had done on the boat. Nathan told the boat builder that he would get back to him.

Woods followed up with calls and texts, but Nathan never responded, and the boat builder never got paid. Nathan continued to duck him for months. Not only was Woods concerned about the unpaid debt, but the boat was still registered in his name. He had signed over the title to Nathan, but it had not been notarized, and the registration number, the MS number, still belonged to Woods.

"If anything happened to that boat or if he crashed into somebody else's boat with my plates, I was concerned that I would be liable," Woods said.

In the state of Rhode Island, a boat owner cannot register a vessel without a notarized title. Technically, it would be illegal for Nathan to operate the *Chicken Pox* in Rhode Island waters.

Again, Woods texted Nathan.

I want my plates back, he wrote in frustration. **You have my dock lines too. None of this shit belongs to you. I want it all back.**

Woods called the Office of Boat Registration in Rhode Island to confirm that Nathan could not register the boat without a notarized title. A registry employee assured him that it was true but also told him that Nathan had recently registered the *Chicken Pox* without Woods's knowledge.

"How's that possible?" he asked.

The registry employee told Woods that Nathan had found a loophole in the state law and had gone and registered the boat in New Hampshire first and then did the same thing in Rhode Island. The boat builder was outraged.

"So basically, you can take a stolen boat to New Hampshire, register it there, and then the next day register it anywhere you want?"

The employee told Woods that it was perfectly legal, as New Hampshire was a nontitle state.

"Now he's got my boat registered, he's got my plates that he's still using, and he's still got my dock lines," Woods later pointed out. "I was pissed."

In late May 2016, Woods hopped on his motorcycle and took a ride down to Rhode Island and searched for the boat, which he found docked at Ram Point Marina in the town of Wakefield, nearly twenty miles south of Newport. The *Chicken Pox* barely resembled the boat that Woods had sold to Nathan back in December. It was in shambles. The pilothouse was half open, and Woods could see that Nathan had jammed the boat's cylinder. The $600 compass that Woods had installed was now on the deck of the boat. He also noticed that Nathan had cut big holes in the boat's bulkheads, located under the deck, which made no sense to the boat builder.

Woods took his Massachusetts plates and his dock lines off the boat and left. Later, Nathan texted him and accused him of theft. He also reported the incident to local police. An officer called Woods and pressed him on the matter.

"What do you know about the theft on the boat?" the cop asked.

"I didn't steal anything," Woods insisted. "All the stuff I took was mine."

"Well, you really didn't have permission to take it."

"Listen, this guy [Nathan] has had all the time in the world to pay me back and send me my stuff. He went a roundabout way to register that boat, and he still hasn't put his new numbers on it. I took my stuff back. If you wanna press charges against me, go ahead!"

Woods never heard from the police officer and believed that he would never see Nathan Carman or hear from him again.

CHAPTER FIFTEEN

One month before Woods retrieved his property from the *Chicken Pox*, Nathan almost got stranded in his thirty-one-foot boat along the west break wall inside the Harbor of Refuge near Point Judith. Just after 7:00 p.m., on April 26, 2016, Nathan radioed the Coast Guard to alert them that a fire had broken out on board and that the vessel was now disabled and floating adrift about a half mile from shore. The Coast Guard launched a forty-five-foot rescue boat to the scene and notified the Block Island ferry to stay clear of the area. The crew reached the *Chicken Pox* quickly and boarded the vessel. They found that the engine had overheated but that there was no fire on board. The mishap occurred because Nathan had not opened a valve to allow water in to cool the engine. The crew cited Nathan for only having one fire extinguisher on board and for not having any identification number printed on the hull. As a precaution, the Coast Guard rescue boat towed the *Chicken Pox* back to the marina, and the case was closed.

"During that incident, he learned and demonstrated an understanding of how the search and rescue system worked, almost like he was testing it," retired U.S. Coast Guard captain W. Russell Webster said later.

Nathan filed a claim with his insurance company after the incident.

After the rescue, Nathan's mother, Linda, bought him an EPIRB, an emergency position indicating radio beacon, which is a satellite-synched device that sends out an SOS signal to rescue agencies in case of an emergency.

"Now, Nathan's nine-digit maritime mobile subscriber index was in a database where it would flash when a satellite passed on the system, and within forty-five minutes, the government would know that the boat was in trouble within a narrow circumference," Webster further explained.

Nathan had purchased the boat for fishing and had the appropriate safety beacon on board, but he still had no fishing equipment. He spotted an advertisement on Facebook Marketplace promoting tuna gear for sale. The asking price was $2,000. He called the number listed and connected with Shawn Sakaske, a sport fisherman from central Massachusetts, who had recently sold his boat and was in the process of downsizing and selling off his bigger fishing gear.

"I'm above Northampton, in Vermont," Nathan told Sakaske over the phone. "I'll swing down and take a look at what you have."

Nathan got into his green Ford pickup truck, drove an hour south to the town of Ludlow, and pulled into the driveway of Shawn Sakaske's home.

After brief introductions, Sakaske invited Nathan into his garage to check out the fishing equipment. The two men talked for thirty minutes about fishing, and for the first time, Nathan opened up during the conversation instead of being closed off to any interaction with another person.

"He was very talkative and liked the fact that I was really familiar with Block Island," Sakaske remembered. "We started talking about striper fishing, and Nathan seemed very interested in it."

Sakaske had been fishing for over a decade and loved to go out on the water with his brothers and a group of friends. He would supply the boat, while his buddies would chip in for fuel and supplies.

"Who do you like to go out fishing with?" he asked Nathan.

"I like to go out fishing with my mom," he replied. "I don't have any friends to go with. My mom is my best friend."

At first, Sakaske found Nathan's situation hard to believe.

"You must have some other friends, right, Nathan?"

"No, my mom is my best friend," he reiterated.

"Well, if you are ever looking for someone to fish with, I'd love to go fishing with you," Sakaske told him. "I don't have a boat anymore, but I still love to fish."

"I'd be interested in that," Nathan replied. "But I've only ever fished with my mom. Or I'd go by myself."

Sakaske then asked Nathan about his favorite fishing spots.

"I fished off Long Island when I had another boat," Nathan told him. "But now I have this newer boat [the *Chicken Pox*], and I'm up at Point Judith, and the boat is docked in the salt pond."

Sakaske was familiar with the area. Nathan mentioned that he had started to fish off Block Island and named a few of his prime locations, including an area he called Striper Rock.

"I know just about every fishing spot off Block Island, including Black Rock Point, North Rip, and Southwest Ledge, but I'd never heard of Striper Rock," Sakaske recalled. "I began to think that maybe he didn't know what he was talking about."

Nathan also told Sakaske that he liked to go fishing at night.

"Well, I don't recommend fishing at night out there, especially alone," Sakaske advised him. "I've been fishing out there probably a dozen times, and it's not the most comfortable feeling. There's good-size waves out there even in calm conditions, and if you're by yourself, it can be very dangerous."

Sakaske showed Nathan the tuna gear he had advertised for sale, which included four spreader bars, cedar plugs, and deep-diving plugs. He was selling the gear at a discount, as he was just trying to get rid of it. Sakaske had given up on tuna fishing and was focused now on fishing for stripers instead.

"Listen, I'll give you a good deal on the gear, as I just want to unload it," he told Nathan. "And if you wanna take me fishing some time, that would be awesome!"

Nathan agreed to the idea, took the deal, and paid cash for the tuna gear. They continued their conversation after the transaction was made, and while Nathan remained surprisingly chatty, he was still a bit reserved in his interaction with Sakaske.

"I'm pretty friendly and joke a lot, but when I'd crack a joke, Nathan wouldn't smile or acknowledge it. He was straight-faced and serious the whole time," Sakaske recalled.

Nathan continued to bring up his mother and how she was the only person who would go fishing with him. Hearing this, Sakaske began to feel sorry for him.

"It was really sad, and I felt that he was opening up and being honest with me," Sakaske remembered. "It wasn't like he was conniving with me. When he mentioned places that didn't really exist like Striper Rock, I think he was just confused and naive about those fishing spots."

Coming to the realization that Nathan was not an experienced boater, Sakaske again tried to warn him against fishing all by himself.

"You shouldn't be going out there at night alone, Nathan. That's a terrible idea. If you're new to Block Island and don't know your way around yet, don't do it."

Sakaske advised him to get familiar with the area during the day and then go at night, but only if he had a seasoned fisherman to accompany him.

Nathan then mentioned that his goal was to fish in Block Canyon.

"He definitely wasn't an offshore fisherman," Sakaske said later about Nathan. "I think he was an inshore fisherman, a striper guy who'd never been as far out as the canyons before."

Sakaske had never gone fishing in Block Canyon either. He had gone as far as thirty miles off-shore toward Tuna Ridge and Butterfish Hole, just south of Block Island, in his single-engine fishing boat, but the canyons were about seventy-five miles out and were the domain of more experienced fishermen with much larger vessels.

Running from Maryland to Cape Cod, the subsea canyons of the North Atlantic, twenty in all, are roughly a quarter the size of the Grand Canyon and thirty-six hundred feet deep from the rim to the bottom in some spots. President Barack Obama had recently designated the first marine national monument in the canyons in an effort to protect what the White House called "the fragile deep-sea ecosystems off the coast of New England."

Fishermen from up and down the East Coast descended on the canyons in July and early August each year when the combination of warm water off the Gulf Stream eddies, long daylight hours, and stable fronts offered ideal conditions for big-game anglers hunting for yellowfin tuna, marlin, sword-fish, and even sharks.

"It's a four- to five-hour ride just to get out there to the canyons, and then you gotta get back," Sakaske explained. "Most of the boats that make that kind of trip are big forty-foot sport fishing boats with cabins, so you can stay overnight. You might see a twenty-five-foot center console fishing boat go out there, but you gotta pick a dead calm, perfect day to attempt to fish for school tuna, like he had planned. You also need to be experienced at that sort of thing. Nathan was not."

Sakaske urged Nathan again to go out with an experienced fisherman who could teach him how to fish in that perilous area.

"What happens if you hit your head or accidentally fall off the boat?" he asked Nathan. "I've fished for fifteen years, and I've never gone alone."

Sakaske offered once more to go fishing with Nathan and show him the ropes.

"I know safety, and I know the weather that we should go out in and the weather we shouldn't go out in," Sakaske told him. "It can get rough in a minute out there, and if you're not paying attention to the weather, you can get yourself into some real trouble."

At the end of the meeting, Sakaske's wife pulled up and was introduced to Nathan as he loaded the fishing gear into the back of his green Ford pickup truck. Nathan nodded to her and then drove away.

During the summer of 2016, Nathan was a constant presence at Ram Point Marina, but he kept mostly to himself.

"I saw the boat passing by, and the guy never waved," said Narragansett harbormaster Kevin Connors. "Everyone waves to each other when they're boating. He just wouldn't interact with anyone else at the boatyard. The marina is a very tight-knit place where everybody knows everybody."

Those who did not know Nathan or his disorder labeled him odd and even potentially dangerous. A strong supporter of then-presidential candidate Donald J. Trump, Nathan joined a large crowd of MAGA disciples at a political rally in a sweltering high school gymnasium in Windham, New Hampshire. Wearing a shirt and tie, Nathan listened to the Republican presidential nominee rail against China, the Islamic State, and political foe Hillary Clinton, whom he called unstable.

As supporters chanted "Build that wall!" one attendee turned his focus to Nathan, who appeared to be highly agitated, walking in circles and talking to himself. The supporter flagged security and had Nathan removed from the rally, saying that he was "uncomfortable with his [Nathan's] demeanor."

Shortly after the incident, Nathan returned to the marina to tinker with his boat while his mother made plans for the two of them to get away during the holidays later that year. Linda Carman reserved two seats aboard the *Silver Galapagos* cruise ship for a tour through the islands. It was an expensive trip, each ticket costing $8,400. Linda's plan was to fly to South America and take a train to Peru, where they would get to explore Machu Picchu over Christmas before boarding the cruise ship. The trip added to the growing tension between Linda and her sisters, as it fell on the anniversary of their father's death, when the entire family had planned the annual traditional Greek Orthodox church memorial service in John Chakalos's honor.

Linda continued working on their vacation itinerary as Nathan urged her repeatedly to join him on board the *Chicken Pox*. She was now sharing her home with a male friend, Monty Monterio, and his three-year-old daughter. During her fishing trips with her son, Linda sent photos proudly holding the fish they had caught to her roommate. But she also confided in him that although it was the type of boat that Nathan had wanted, she was not fully comfortable going out on the *Chicken Pox* yet.

"She wasn't interested in fishing. She wanted to connect with him in any way possible," said Linda's longtime friend Jeannette Brodeur. "And when she found out that was what he enjoyed doing, she was all in."

Brodeur had been close to Linda since she had delivered a hot meal to her doorstep when Nathan went missing in 2011. A friendship blossomed from there. Linda was generous and giving to Brodeur, taking her on annual trips to Yankee Stadium so that Brodeur's son with special needs could watch his favorite major league baseball team. "She'd pile us all into her beat-up Chevy Suburban and drive us into the Bronx and relished in the fact that she could make my son, who hated loud noises and crowds, enjoy a ball game up close," Brodeur remembered. "I haven't met a person like her. She was so giving and kind."

Linda lived very modestly, and Brodeur had no idea that she came from a wealthy family until her own family was invited to the farm in West Chesterfield, New Hampshire, to see the annual Christmas light display. "Have the kids bring their swimsuits," Linda told her.

Linda drove Brodeur and her three kids to New Hampshire, and they were dumbstruck.

"It was this enormous house with all these Christmas lights, and the kids were just amazed."

Brodeur said that the inside of the Chakalos mansion was as decked out for the holidays as the outside was. "There was this enormous foyer with tables lined up to display a huge Christmas village, and my kids were like, 'Wow!'" Brodeur and her children also got to swim in the indoor pool. "We took pictures of the kids jumping in the pool and playing. It was just a really sweet time."

But while Linda grew close to Brodeur's family, she shielded them from her own son. Linda kept her relationship with Nathan private.

"I didn't want to push it, but I could tell that he didn't want to be around her, and it was heartbreaking to see that from a distance," Brodeur claimed.

She remembered one visit she paid to Linda at her home in Middletown while Nathan was living in the RV parked in her driveway. Linda nodded over to the vehicle. "He's not talking to me," she told her friend in a heartbreaking tone.

"She tried and tried but just couldn't connect with him," Brodeur said.

When her son emerged as a suspect in his grandfather's 2013 murder, Linda mentioned it to Brodeur but did not provide any details.

"She had asked me if I would share the billboard offering a reward for information about her father's killer on my Facebook page. Linda then told me that her family thought that Nathan was the killer. That was all she said. She kept her cards very close to her chest."

Linda did confide in her friend that she had had a falling-out with her sisters Valerie, Elaine, and Charlene.

"She felt that everyone was toxic, and the less she did with them or associated with them, the happier she would be," Brodeur claimed. "I know she was making an effort not to get sucked into any of the drama of that family."

On Sunday, September 11, 2016, Brodeur and Linda hiked together through the hills of Washington Depot, a picturesque eighteenth-century New England village in Litchfield County, Connecticut, accentuated by green rolling hills and a dense forest.

"We would always try to go walking when Nathan wasn't around," Brodeur said. "We'd make plans to go walking, but Linda always said that she would have to cancel our hike if Nathan agreed to see her."

Nathan would promise his mother that he would see her, but his plans often changed, which left Linda disappointed but eager to spend time with Brodeur.

During the hike in Washington Depot, the two friends walked, laughed, and discussed a trip to Ireland that they were planning to take together after the new year. Linda had also brought the young daughter of her friend, Monty Monterio, on the hike.

"We got lost for about four hours. We had no sense of direction," Brodeur remembered. "We talked about everything on that hike, and we taught the little girl how to 'skip to my lou.'"

Linda took out her phone and captured a video of Brodeur teaching the girl how to skip.

"Even though we were lost, we had such a great time that day. We smiled a lot."

The pair had such a good time that Linda promised Brodeur that she would hike with her again the following Sunday after she returned home from an overnight fishing trip with her son aboard the *Chicken Pox*.

"I'll call you if we've gone all night and I'm tired," Linda told her friend. "I'll let you know if we're gonna do it later or not."

"That's fine," Brodeur responded.

The two friends hugged, kissed each other on the cheeks, and went their separate ways.

CHAPTER SIXTEEN

Nathan left his house in Vernon, Vermont, on Saturday, September 17, 2016, and drove 146 miles south to Ram Point Marina in South Kingstown, Rhode Island, for the planned fishing trip with his mother. At some point before he left, he decided to get rid of his computer, which had long been his lifeline to the outside world.

At Ram Point Marina, Nathan spent much of the day working on his aluminum fishing boat. He had replaced the port bilge, and Mike Iozzi, a fellow boater, noticed him bending over the vessel, using an electric power drill to make one-and-a-half- and two-inch holes in the boat.

Iozzi kept his own boat, a thirty-six-foot Mainship sedan named *Fruition*, at Stone Cove Marina, just up the road in Wakefield, Rhode Island. Iozzi was enjoying a leisurely afternoon with two friends who owned the slip next to Nathan's.

The man watched as Nathan continued working, drilling four holes in the boat, including one that was as large as a Kennedy half-dollar, in the boat's transom. He used the drill to remove three screws at the top of the vessel's trim tabs, which are used to raise the windward side of the boat to block the spray that blows over it, resulting in a drier ride. Trim tabs also help with fuel efficiency and keep the boat from listing.

"What are you doing?" Iozzi asked him.

"Well, I'm trying to fix my trim tabs," Nathan replied. "They don't make the boat respond well."

"You can't fix the trim tabs while the boat's in the water," Iozzi warned him. "The boat could sink."

Nathan did not take Iozzi's advice and kept drilling. Iozzi, who made his living drilling holes in concrete, was concerned with the repair work but decided against pressing Nathan further.

Instead, he offered Nathan a snack of turkey meatballs, which he gladly accepted and gobbled up.

Iozzi continued his attempt to engage Nathan in small talk and asked him what his plans were for the day.

Nathan told the man that he was going to go fishing out at Block Canyon. Iozzi found this strange, because he did not see any fishing poles in the thirty-one-foot boat.

"You'd better not go all the way out there alone," Iozzi told him. "Night fishing is dangerous."

It was a warning Nathan had heard many times before.

In an effort to patch the holes, Nathan bought an epoxy putty stick and a fiberglass boat repair kit, but he paid little attention to the package instructions on how to repair the holes. He filled the holes with the epoxy putty but did not place the fiberglass fabric on the outside of the hull to seal the holes. Without the fiberglass backing, the epoxy could easily get pushed through the holes at sea, which could cause a serious problem and lead to the sinking of the vessel.

Nathan stretched the epoxy like bubble gum and got it all over his hands and clothes.

Iozzi watched Nathan work for a few more minutes before turning his attention back to his friends and thought nothing more of it.

Earlier in the day, Nathan had purchased a new bilge pump at a nearby

West Marine and installed it himself. He also had a rebuilt engine installed in the *Chicken Pox* that past June and complained to the marina about several issues after it was installed. The U.S. Coast Guard had given the *Chicken Pox* a passing grade during a random safety inspection the month before, and a marina technician conducted a visual inspection on the boat's engine just eleven days prior.

Linda Carman was still apprehensive about fishing aboard the *Chicken Pox*, but her son had assured her that they would not venture too far out and instead stick to the immediate vicinity of Block Island, about twenty-four nautical miles from Ram Point Marina. Nathan had wanted to go fishing later in the week, but his mother had to work, and he had promised not to go fishing without her.

"My mom and I had an agreement," he later said. "She didn't like me to go out on my own."

When Linda Carman arrived at the dock to meet her son, she texted their float plan to three people, including her best friend, Sharon Hartstein.

Heading out toward Striper Rock, Southeast of the windmills. Back by 9am. Call me 12 noon if you don't hear from me, the text message said.

Linda routinely sent text messages to her friends while she was fishing with Nathan: "where she was going, when she was due back, when to worry," recalled Hartstein. "If she pulled in and stopped to talk to someone else, she'd text that 'we'll be back in at such-and-such a time'."

Linda would also text Hartstein a photo of the boat and the registration number in case they got lost. Linda brought with her peanut butter and pasta, which she considered to be her "survival pack," because she didn't eat fish but would cook it for her son.

Surveillance cameras at Ram Point Marina captured video of Nathan and his mother preparing to board the *Chicken Pox*, which was tied to a slip that Nathan had recently rented for the season.

The boat departed the marina at around 11:00 p.m. on the evening of September 17 under starless skies and a light breeze. The temperature hovered around sixty-six degrees.

Linda then texted Jeannette Brodeur. **We're just leaving the dock**, she wrote.

Nathan steered the *Chicken Pox* slowly through the salt pond and across the breachway. Soon after, the bright lights of Ram Point Marina faded, and darkness surrounded them.

Within an hour of Linda's text to Brodeur, a fisherman spotted the *Chicken Pox* while on his way back from Point Judith. The vessel passed him on the right, going about twenty miles per hour and heading south toward Block Island, near the Southwest Ledge. The fisherman did a double take because the lights on top of the cabin looked odd and too close together.

"I couldn't really see anybody on board, since it was so dark," the fisherman remembered. "The seas were pretty calm that night and they were going pretty slow... It's a pretty unique boat. I have no doubt that it's the boat I saw."

Sharon Hartstein was expecting to hear from her friend on Sunday, September 18, and by noon, she was staring at her cell phone, wondering why she still had not heard from Linda Carman.

Jeannette Brodeur was also concerned when she had not heard back from Linda.

Maybe you're tired and it's raining, Brodeur texted her. She got no response.

Sharon Hartstein called Linda's cell phone but got no answer. Her mild concern grew to outright panic, and by late afternoon, she called Middletown police to report Linda and Nathan Carman missing. The U.S. Coast Guard was notified of the situation at approximately 6:15 p.m.

"It came in as a search and rescue case, an overdue boat with two people on board," recalled U.S. Coast Guard Search and Rescue Controller Richard Arsenault. "There was no distress beacon activated. When you get an overdue case, there is uncertainty, and you begin thinking about 'what if?' scenarios. You're not sure what's really going on."

Police in Rhode Island told Arsenault and his team that the missing boaters, whom they identified as Nathan Carman and his mother, Linda Carman, had intended to fish in the vicinity of the Block Island Wind Farm, which was located nearly four miles off Block Island itself. Authorities also stressed that the vessel had been scheduled to return to Ram Point Marina around 9:00 a.m. Arsenault did not believe that the Carmans had simply lost track of time, as they were now nine hours late returning to port. It was time to get to work with his two duty operators.

"The days are quiet until they're not," Arsenault explained. "It's like working in a firehouse, and you just hope that when the bell rings, you'll be able to answer the call."

From the watch floor at the U.S. Coast Guard First District in Boston, Arsenault and his team began to develop search models for the missing boat based on the last known cell phone reception from Linda's phone reported by Verizon Wireless. U.S. Coast Guard telecommunications specialists had been utilizing cellular technology in search and rescue missions for the past two decades with varying results.

"The Coast Guard has always looked at cell phone technology with a jaundiced eye," said retired Coast Guard captain and telecommunications expert W. Russell Webster. "Cell technology is point-to-point communication, and they're fragile in terms of distance and direction. But it does get you in the right area."

Oftentimes, cellular providers are not aware that Coast Guard officials have the right to gain access to customer information, even in times of duress. This can lead to lengthy negotiations between the Coast Guard and phone companies and impede rescue efforts. Fortunately, in the Carman case, Verizon allowed rescuers to analyze Linda's cellular data and identify the last known position of her cell phone at 12:45 a.m. on the south side of Block Island on Sunday, September 18, 2016.

Operational Watch Stander Richard Arsenault dubbed that part of the Atlantic Ocean Search Area Alpha. The Coast Guard search and rescue team mapped out probable areas where Nathan and Linda had gone fishing and then developed a drift scenario with their computer programming tools based on wind and ocean currents. Utilizing the Monte Carlo drift model, the program identified the last known position of the missing vessel and then allowed the environment to push it around based on the winds and the seas to create a probable search radius.

After identifying the search radius, the Coast Guard team developed four search models within that radius, covering 1,282 square nautical miles from Rhode Island Sound to the northern tip of Long Island.

At approximately 11:22 p.m. on September 18, five hours after the initial Coast Guard alert, operators on the watch deck in Boston contacted search and rescue mission coordinators across New England, and two aircraft were mobilized and deployed to lead the search and rescue effort.

"We did our search planning module, our simulation, to determine where the boat could be within our drift model," Arsenault explained. "Once we determined the datum, a position and a time to focus our efforts on, we then decided which Coast Guard resources would give us the best bang for our buck."

The first aircraft, a ninety-knot Sikorsky MH-60T Jayhawk helicopter, flew out of Air Station Cape Cod in Sandwich, Massachusetts, one hundred miles east of Block Island. The Jayhawk was the Coast Guard's medium-range search and rescue helicopter and could cover the distance quickly. Once over Search Area Alpha, the crew aboard the Jayhawk swept the area with an enhanced suite of electronics, including night-vision goggles and thermal cameras, but turned up nothing. The helicopter was forced to make an emergency landing on Block Island due to a mechanical issue. Fortunately, no one on board was hurt. The second aircraft, a Eurocopter MH-65 Dolphin helicopter, flew from Air Station Atlantic City in New Jersey with a three-member rescue crew aboard. Both helicopters combed the area for almost six hours for any sign of the *Chicken Pox*, a life raft, or a floating debris field. They found nothing.

The Coast Guard also launched a forty-five-foot medium-range response boat from Station Point Judith to search the vicinity of Block Island. Once again, there was no sign of the missing boat or its two occupants. It was as if the *Chicken Pox* had vanished into thin air.

CHAPTER SEVENTEEN

Nathan would later tell Coast Guard investigators that he and his mother drove the *Chicken Pox* out to Block Island and spent about an hour fishing for stripers. At around 1:00 a.m., he urged Linda to extend the fishing expedition and travel farther out with him to Block Canyon to hunt for tuna with the gear he had recently purchased from Shawn Sakaske. But once again, she expressed great trepidation about going that far out—seventy-five miles or so—in a small aluminum boat with her son, who had no experience with offshore fishing. She had planned to return to the marina later that morning and possibly meet up with Jeannette Brodeur for their weekly hike. A trip to the canyons meant that she would not make it back until nightfall.

"I almost felt like I twisted her arm," Nathan recalled.

Linda was concerned about their safety, and she was also worried about missing work. She had a new job taking care of children with special needs, feeding and bathing them in their homes. After struggling for years to keep a steady job, Linda felt that she had a real aptitude for caring for children with physical and intellectual challenges, and she did not want to let them down. The kids would not understand that Linda had missed work because she was deep-sea fishing with her son.

Nathan said they reached Block Canyon just as the sun was rising, and the weather conditions were near perfect, so neither of them had put on a life preserver. But the next moment, everything changed.

"I heard a noise on the belt on the engine. It was picking up water and kind of spinning it," Nathan claimed. "I knew that there was a serious problem [in the bilge], but I didn't think we were sinking. I thought I was going to diagnose the problem and that we were going to go back to shore."

He said that he closed the hatch and turned the engine off and ordered his mother to begin pulling in the fishing lines at the stern of the boat. Nathan did not want his mother to panic, so he gave her a simple task to perform instead.

"I treated my mother like a passenger," he later said. "She was more of a problem than a solution."

As Linda got to work on the lines, the *Chicken Pox* began taking on water—fast.

The deck felt spongy under his feet, so Nathan rushed to the pilothouse and grabbed three packages of survival gear or "ditch bags" and then moved to the bow of the boat to prepare the life raft. He had a functioning alert system on board the vessel, but he did not make a Mayday call. Nathan claimed that the emergency was unfolding too quickly.

"I was walking on deck, and it was there and then it wasn't," he said. "I knew that we had a problem, but I didn't know we were sinking until we sank."

According to Nathan, his thirty-one-foot boat just dropped out from under him, and he tumbled into the ocean. He suddenly found himself in the water, clutching a bag filled with safety gear. The plunge left him disoriented and fighting to reach the surface of the sea. He searched above the waterline but did not see his mother anywhere. He swam fifteen feet to the life raft, which had inflated automatically, and pulled himself aboard. Nathan said he did not hear his mother call out, and he feared the worst.

"I don't know if she got hit on the head. I don't know if she got tangled in the fishing lines," he said.

Nathan claimed that he then called out repeatedly for his mother and blew a distress whistle three times with three loud, short bursts.

"I assumed that if she had been on the surface and conscious that she would have been calling out and I would have been able to find her," Nathan later said. "But I didn't know why that hadn't happened."

Nathan did not leave the four-person, double-bottomed life raft and dive for Linda underwater. He saw debris on the surface and an oil slick where the boat had gone down, but his mother was gone. Nathan said at that point, his focus shifted away from his mother toward his own survival at sea.

After their initial search of the area where the *Chicken Pox* was last known to have been was determined to be fruitless, Richard Arsenault and his Coast Guard search and rescue team developed a new search model called Search Area Bravo, which expanded their coverage area from 1,282 to 1,875 square nautical miles, pushing farther north into southeastern Massachusetts and deeper south into Long Island Sound.

From noon to 4:00 p.m., the Coast Guard conducted five additional search patterns with the aid of an HC-130J Hercules maritime reconnaissance plane. The ninety-seven-foot-long aircraft flew at a cruising speed of 333 miles per hour over the expanded search area but found no trace of Nathan and Linda. Ram Point Marina was also a hive of activity as Coast Guard crew members walked up and down each dock, approaching boaters at each slip to see if they knew Nathan and when they had seen him last.

After each search, Arsenault and his team discussed what they could be doing better while trying to maintain some semblance of objectivity toward the mission. They could not get too close to the situation and let their frustrations and emotions take over. Arsenault had lost boaters at sea before, those who drowned or had succumbed to bad weather, but he refused to think about it now.

"What happens to folks in my position is that you get a prolonged exposure to stress. I had guys that worked with me years ago that had trouble sleeping," Arsenault explained. "That exposure to human tragedy over time clings to you. I learned to compartmentalize the job and not concern myself with the eventual outcome but with the immediate task at hand so I could perform my duties responsibly."

Arsenault reminded his team to "keep their saws sharp" and maintain a level of proficiency that was above par so they could do everything possible to bring Nathan and Linda home. The Coast Guard conducted a "probability of survival" analysis for the missing mother and son. With the water temperature at seventy-three degrees and the air temperature at sixty-nine degrees, rescuers predicted that they would only survive in the ocean without a life raft for about nine hours if they had something to hold on to.

But the hours and days began to stack up as ten additional search models, Charlie, Delta, Echo, Foxtrot, Golf, Hotel, India, Juliet, Kilo, and Lima, were established by the Coast Guard search and rescue team. In all, nine small boats, fixed-wing aircraft, helicopters, and Coast Guard cutters, including the USCG *Campbell* out of the Portsmouth Naval Shipyard in Kittery, Maine, the USCGC *Bonito* out of Montauk, New York, and the USCGC *Sitkinak* out of Bayonne, New Jersey, covered a massive area larger than the state of Georgia totaling 58,049 square nautical miles with forty-five search patterns over four days from the initial call on September 18 to midmorning on Thursday, September 22, 2016. Nearly fifty urgent marine information broadcasts were sounded from Cape Cod to the Carolinas. In total, about $1 million was spent by the Coast Guard during its search for Nathan and Linda Carman.

Still, it was not out of the realm of possibility that the mother and son were still alive and floating somewhere in the North Atlantic. There were several examples over the course of history to draw on, including the most improbable and dramatic castaway story involving a Japanese ship captain and his crew who had survived in a raft adrift at sea for an astounding 484 days, beginning in 1813, before they were rescued by an American ship off the coast of California in 1815.

Eric Gempp was working in his cramped office on the campus of the U.S. Coast Guard Academy in New London, Connecticut, when his telephone rang. A veteran agent for the U.S. Coast Guard Investigative Service, Gempp was informed by his counterpart in Boston that Coast Guard crews were searching for two missing boaters off Block Island. It was merely a courtesy notification that crews were active in the area. He thanked his Coast Guard investigative colleague for the heads-up and thought little about it after that and went about his day's work.

While he was working at the academy, Gempp's main focus was investigating any suspicious or criminal behavior involving eighteen- to twenty-two-year-old Coast Guard cadets. He had been working for the Coast Guard Investigative Service since 2003, with prior stints at the Rhode Island Attorney General's Office and with the U.S. Secret Service, where he specialized in welfare fraud cases and other financial crimes. When he began his work with the Coast Guard, Gempp's focus shifted to investigating incidents that violated the service's code of conduct as well as environmental crimes. He had played a major role in the successful prosecution of a pharmaceutical company that had discharged polluted wastewater from its New London factory into the nearby Thames River.

As he continued to receive courtesy calls about the attempt to locate Nathan and Linda Carman, the investigator was curious as to how their fishing boat could have disappeared.

"The Coast Guard has the best search and rescue operation in the

U.S. Coast Guard investigator Eric Gempp working out of his office at the United States Coast Guard Academy in New London, Connecticut. (Photo by Casey Sherman)

world," Gempp later explained. "Because of its success rate and the weather and time of year, it was very puzzling to me that they had not found something to that point."

Coast Guard rescuers found a sliver of hope in the Carman case when two local fishermen discovered floating debris off Block Island. The items included a marine deck box cover, a pillowcase, and empty engine coolant containers. Once again, a Coast Guard vessel was deployed to search the area around Block Island but to no avail. Investigators quickly determined for some unknown reason that there was a "high probability" the debris did not come from the *Chicken Pox.*

The previous day, Wednesday, September 21, 2016, the U.S. Coast Guard alerted the media that a search was ongoing for Nathan and Linda Carman after their fishing boat failed to return to Ram Point Marina in Rhode Island. Petty Officer Third Class Nicole Groll told reporters that weather and sea conditions were not factors in the *Chicken Pox*'s disappearance and that the search was now focused on Hudson Canyon, which was 115 miles south of Montauk, on the eastern tip of Long Island.

The story received little attention in the Carmans' largest hometown newspaper, the *Hartford Courant*, which ran a short article in its back pages under the banner "Police Briefs Connecticut." Local television stations covered the story and described the type of boat that was missing. Shawn

Sakaske watched a TV news segment and turned to his wife.

"Wait a minute—that rings a bell. Where did I hear that before?" he asked her.

Sakaske thought back to his meeting with the unusual, inexperienced fisherman in his garage a few months before.

"Shit, I think that was Nathan. That's the kid I sold the tuna gear to."

Brian Woods, the man who had sold Nathan the fishing boat, received a call from the Coast Guard asking for more information about the *Chicken Pox*.

"You'd better make your search area bigger, because that thing will go eleven hundred miles on a tank full of gas," Woods told rescuers. "It's got an incredible range."

Linda's friend Sharon Hartstein told a reporter that the idea that Linda and Nathan would suddenly decide to fish the canyons made no sense to her.

"I know she would never decide to extend the trip without letting someone know, and she also wouldn't *not* show up to work without letting someone know. This is not normal," she said.

Nathan later claimed that during all this time, he was battling the elements at sea in his tiny life raft. He said that he had spent the first two days calling out desperately for his mother. When it was clear that Linda would not answer, he prayed in the morning and again at night that somehow he would be saved. Nathan opened his survival kit and drank several one-ounce fresh water packets to stay hydrated. He had also purchased a device that allowed him to convert seawater into drinking water. He rationed his food bars, limiting himself to just one a day. His ditch bag was also equipped with smoke flares, a flashlight, seasickness pills, and a mirror to signal oncoming ships. The smoke flares were never used.

Nathan claimed that his two biggest concerns were that he would starve to death out on the ocean and that a large wave would roll in and topple his life raft and kill him. During most days, the seas were calm, but they sometimes turned violent at a moment's notice with wave heights reaching thirteen feet. When rough weather hit, Nathan said he zipped up the small opening of his life raft and rode out the turbulent waves. Since he was alone in a raft designed to hold four people, he had very little ballast and flopped around inside his floating tent like a pair of socks getting tossed in a clothes dryer.

The search and rescue team officially suspended its mission on September 24, 2016, after one of the largest operations in the history of the service. At the Coast Guard First District in Boston, the disappearance of the *Chicken Pox* gnawed at Arsenault and his team. He discussed the situation with his superiors, and they racked their brains to determine if there was something they may have overlooked. "There are always lessons to be learned, so we dissected the critical incident regarding the *Chicken Pox* to determine what we could do better in the future," Arsenault recalled. "This stuff isn't learned in the classroom. It comes from real-life experience."

Were they looking at the wrong thing at the wrong time while evidence snuck by them?

"We didn't have any more threads to pull. We pulled all the threads that looked like they were attached to something," Arsenault said. "And we wondered, why isn't there any evidence out there, no flotsam, no oil spill? It's scratch, nothing. There is something missing. Our result wasn't appropriate for such a massive effort."

Sharon Hartstein organized a vigil at Linda Carman's home in Middletown. She called it "Hope and Hugs for Linda," and the event was attended by twenty friends who knew her best. The group placed two empty folding chairs on the lawn, one red and the other blue, to symbolize Linda and Nathan. They tied yellow ribbons and formed a circle around the empty seats to pray for their safe return.

CHAPTER EIGHTEEN

What had begun as a search and rescue mission for a lost mother and her son quickly morphed into a criminal investigation while both Nathan and Linda Carman were still missing.

When Coast Guard investigators reached out to Linda's next of kin, they got a tutorial about the complex dynamics of the Chakalos family. Instead of showing concern for her missing sister and nephew, Valerie Santilli launched into a vitriolic diatribe against Nathan, calling him the "town freak" and accusing him of murdering her father in 2013. She also told investigators that he had plenty of reason to kill his mother, as Linda stood to inherit her father's mansion in West Chesterfield, New Hampshire, in a probate court settlement meeting that was scheduled the following week. If Linda was gone, she said, the farm would go to Nathan. Valerie did not know that Linda had already cut Nathan out of her will.

The Coast Guard called several law enforcement agencies, including the South Kingstown, Rhode Island, police, who scrambled a cruiser and two tow trucks to Ram Point Marina to impound Nathan's pickup truck and his mother's car so that he could not escape if and when he made it back to dry land. Investigators also began working to track the credit card records for both Nathan and Linda, fearing that he may have killed her and ditched his boat and was now traveling on foot. Detectives in South Kingstown grabbed surveillance footage from the marina security cameras. They watched as Linda arrived at the marina and began loading supplies into the boat. At no time did she appear to be under duress.

Linda's sister Valerie, her husband, Larry Santilli, and Sharon Hartstein gathered around the kitchen table at Valerie's house in West Hartford to receive a solemn update from the Coast Guard. Delivering the news that the search was suspended was Marcus Gherardi, the Coast Guard's chief of response for Sector Southeastern New England. Gherardi had driven down to Connecticut from his office on Cape Cod, dreading the eventual discussion with each passing mile.

"When you deliver this news, your heart feels like lead," Gherardi later recalled.

On Sunday, September 25, 2016, two days after the U.S. Coast Guard had called off its search, the Chinese cargo ship *Orient Lucky* left Providence, Rhode Island, and sailed south to exchange ballast water before making its run to Boston, Massachusetts, for refueling. The ship was now positioned about one hundred miles off Martha's Vineyard. The ship's captain, Zhao Hengdong, and a crew member spotted what looked to be an orange ball bobbing up and down on the choppy waves. When they realized it was a life raft with a person inside, the crew launched a rescue mission, tossing a life ring to Nathan as he swam and kicked his way through the rough waters toward the giant freighter.

Once Nathan was pulled up onto the ship's accommodation ladder, he paused and took deep breaths as he stabilized himself on solid ground. After floating around at sea for what he later claimed was seven days, it took him a few moments to orient his body and his equilibrium back to a surface that was not rocking as violently as the ocean. But Nathan did not need any assistance as he climbed the long accommodation ladder up to the deck of the *Orient Lucky* as his $400 life raft, an important piece of potential evidence in the unfolding case, was left floating in the sea.

Nathan was given water and food, was allowed to shower, and was then handed a white crew suit before he spoke about the ordeal to Richard Arsenault, calling from the Coast Guard's First District in Boston.

Nathan Carman shows little signs of fatigue as he makes his way up the accommodation ladder of the Orient Lucky. *(United States Coast Guard Handout)*

Arsenault figured that he would hear distress and fatigue in Nathan's voice after having been adrift for so long. "To sit in a raft in that position with salt water beating your body for days, he should have been in a much worse condition than he was," Arsenault said. "We had rescued some people off Haiti that had been in a boat for four days at sea, and some of them were severely dehydrated to the point of being unconscious and immediately needed a couple bags of saline to get them back on their feet. Now here's a guy who has supposedly been out at sea for a week plus, and he's right as rain."

When the ship's doctor gave Nathan a cursory examination, he noticed that his lips were not cracked to the point of bleeding, which is normally the case for anyone surviving in salt water for days. He also had no loss of muscle control and was not dehydrated despite minimal water intake.

Nathan also did not appear to be disoriented. He answered Arsenault's questions in his typical direct, matter-of-fact manner, as if he'd spent seven days on a cruise ship instead of being adrift at sea.

Inside his cabin aboard the *Orient Lucky*, Nathan grabbed a pad of paper and a pen and wrote two letters to Captain Hengdong. The first note was full of melancholy as he described his newfound loneliness without his mother. "If my mom is lost, which I fear is likely, I will have no one on Earth who will welcome me sincerely into their home," he wrote. "So I appreciate the efforts you and your crew have made to make your ship a home to me while I have been aboard." Also in the letter, Nathan offered to show the ship captain around if he ever returned to New England as a tourist on holiday.

After this rescue, Nathan Carman wrote a letter to the captain of the Orient *Lucky. (United States Coast Guard Handout)*

In the second letter, he took a more spiritual approach, expressing his thoughts about God and holding on to his faith. "When you are on a ship at sea, from your vantage point you cannot see him yet not believing in him does not make him any less real," he wrote. "When the world takes everything from you, there are several ways in which you can respond. The best way is to use the experience as an opportunity to see and be grateful for what you do have and what you are given."

Nathan left his cabin and walked up to the bridge, where he spoke to Captain Hengdong.

"How many miles can you see out into the ocean?" Nathan asked.

"About three nautical miles," the captain replied, feeling that the rescued castaway was still looking for his mother. Nathan then walked down to the deck of the *Orient Lucky*, leaned against the railing, and stared out to sea for two hours as the ship sailed toward Boston.

Clark Carman had been closely following news reports of the Coast Guard search for his son and ex-wife from his home in California. When Nathan was picked up by the crew of the *Orient Lucky*, Sharon Hartstein called him immediately to share the bittersweet news that Nathan had been saved but that Linda was still missing.

"I immediately flew back there to New England and rented a car," Clark recalled. "I got a call from Valerie's husband [Lawrence Santilli] saying where Nathan was and when he was coming in, and that's the last I ever heard from them."

Clark drove from the airport to the Coast Guard First District in Boston to await the arrival of the *Orient Lucky*.

Coast Guard investigator Eric Gempp was standing near the bow of the Block Island ferry as it cut through the waters back to the mainland at Narragansett, Rhode Island, when his cell phone rang. He was informed that Nathan Carman had been rescued by a passing Chinese cargo ship. Gempp knew those waters like the back of his hand. He had grown up in the small town of Warren, Rhode Island, but had spent twenty-six summers on Block Island with his brother, sister, mother, and father, who had worked for sixty years as a commercial fisherman.

"Working the boats with our dad was a rite of passage in our family," Gempp recalled.

His father, Herman "Bo" Gempp, had owned a traditional Downeast forty-foot lobster boat and then downsized to a twenty-three-foot center console in his later years. Bo Gempp had passed away that previous April, and his son was returning from a memorial service for him on Block Island when he learned that Nathan had been found alive, drifting in the continental shelf, but there was still no sign of Linda Carman. Gempp was told by his counterpart in Boston that Nathan had been fishing for tuna with his mother when his boat suddenly sank.

Gempp stared down at the sea and saw pods of tuna swimming just below the surface of the ocean off the port side of the ferry. It was the perfect time of year for tuna fishing, but there were so many questions swimming around in the investigator's mind. Still, he had to adhere to protocol and not try to jump ahead of the situation.

"We were just monitoring the case at this point, because it was still considered to be a search and rescue and recovery situation," Gempp recalled. "But we started talking to the South Kingstown Police Department and the Rhode Island Department of Environmental Protection just to make sure that we were staying engaged."

Gempp was told that Nathan was en route to Boston, and he wanted to make sure that he was there when the *Orient Lucky* arrived at port.

Meanwhile, Sharon Hartstein had serious questions of her own, and she demanded answers.

"I don't know how one got on the raft without the other," she told a reporter. "Where did it happen? Did they even reach their destination? Did they have the right equipment? Did they have the right fishing gear for tuna or just stripers?"

Hartstein was also frustrated that it was taking so long for Nathan to get to Boston.

"It seems like a long time," she added. "I understand that it's a big freighter ship and it's hard to get around the Cape [Cod]. But I'm surprised the Coast Guard didn't just go out and get him… I don't know the statistical hope at this point, but Linda is very strong. If there is any way she can survive, she will. If not, we still want her home. We want closure."

Sharon Hartstein called Jeannette Brodeur with the news about Nathan's rescue.

"I was at work and had to leave. It was just shocking," Brodeur remembered. "I was so stunned and scared. All I could ask was, where's Linda?"

Word quickly spread about Nathan's miraculous rescue at sea, and media outlets across the country and even overseas seized on it and treated it as one of the biggest "feel good" stories of the year, many comparing Nathan to Tom Hanks's character in the hit movie *Cast Away*.

"They spotted what they thought was someone adrift in a raft Sunday afternoon," Coast Guard Petty Officer Second Class LaNola Stone told reporters. "They brought him on board and after a quick phone interview, we learned the boat had been taking on water and the vessel began going down. Nathan deployed the four-person life raft on board and called out to his mother, but received no response."

Stone went on to say that Nathan was reported to be in good health and that the Coast Guard looked forward to conducting a debrief with him when he arrived in Boston. When asked about Linda Carman, Stone told reporters that it was no longer a rescue mission but a recovery mission. "We want to find out anything he can add to help locate his mother," Stone said. "Because of the survival window, we didn't commence a search for [Linda Carman] because there was only one life raft on board. Taking into consideration the water temperature, her age, fitness level—all that goes into trying to figure out if she's within that survival window. She was well outside of that by Sunday evening."

Reporters from major newspapers and television networks huddled with local journalists, all waiting eagerly for their first glimpse of Nathan as he was transported from the *Orient Lucky* at anchorage by boat and brought to Coast Guard headquarters in Boston for a forty-five-minute debriefing on Tuesday, September 27.

Christina Hager, a veteran television reporter at WBZ-TV in Boston, left the newsroom with her videographer and rushed over to the Coast Guard station.

"He's coming in, and we can see him staring out the window of the small Coast Guard boat," Hager recalled. "There was no expression on his face at all. It also did not look like he had endured any physical trauma for being out at sea that long. It was surprising how well composed he was."

Still wearing the white crew suit that had been given to him by his Chinese rescuers, Nathan stared blankly at Hager and the throngs of reporters, videographers, and news photographers who were lined up at the dock taking his picture and shouting questions his way.

He spent nearly an hour behind closed doors being interviewed by Coast Guard officers for a search and rescue debrief where investigators asked him questions in an effort to elicit information that could lead to improvements in future rescue efforts. They were perplexed by his account of his rescue and the disappearance of his mother.

"If he had been in that life raft during that length of time, we would have found him," said retired Coast Guard captain W. Russ Webster, who had overseen thousands of search and rescue missions. "There's no possible way with the technology we had, including forward-looking radar, that a person who wanted to be found could slip through our nets."

Coast Guard officers had serious questions regarding the spot where Nathan claimed his boat had sunk and the location where he was plucked out of the ocean by the *Orient Lucky*. The location had directly contradicted all Coast Guard drift models, as the currents would have pushed the life raft in the opposite direction.

"He showed up thirty-five miles east of where he should have been," Webster added. "In that general area, the currents flow from east to west. In his retelling, the currents somehow pushed him west to east, which is not at all possible."

Eric Gempp drove up to Boston with Detective Lieutenant Alfred Bucco of the South Kingstown Police Department. Gempp got his first close look at Nathan while Bucco interviewed him in the presence of his lawyer.

Gempp also interviewed crew members of the *Orient Lucky* and reviewed the ship's video footage and several photos taken of the rescue.

"There were some observations that were made based on the video that raised more questions," Gempp recalled. "If we take it in sequence, the *Orient Lucky* is in position to recover [Nathan]. He's in the life raft, and he's waving a flag. If you're in a life raft for seven days with limited water and food, are you physically able to move, manipulate, and hold a flag?"

Gempp continued to study the video and the photographs. In a sequence of photos, Nathan is seen jumping off the raft into the ocean, fighting the current and swimming to the *Orient Lucky*, and using his physical strength to fend off the ship to prevent himself from getting sucked under the massive hull.

"I began questioning that whole sequence. Because then he puts his arm through a life ring and manages to get up the accommodation ladder with little or no resistance," Gempp said. "And then he refused any real medical attention on the ship. I found it all very troubling."

Clark Carman had hired a Connecticut attorney and his team to represent his son at the Coast Guard briefing.

"We cooperated fully," said attorney Hubert J. Santos. "It was a tragic accident."

Santos wasn't just any lawyer; he was a legendary litigator in Connecticut. Known as Hubie to his friends and foes alike, Santos sat in the lead chair in many high-profile criminal cases and trials. At the time, Santos was representing convicted Kennedy cousin Michael Skakel in his bid to overturn his conviction in the infamous Martha Moxley murder case. The lawyer enjoyed the limelight, and he knew that the Nathan Carman case was a big one.

Nathan told authorities that he had only seen one other ship at a distance during his seven days at sea. After his debriefing with Coast Guard officials and his grilling from Detective Bucco, Nathan snuck out the back of the building and climbed into his father's blue rental car, and the two drove back to Nathan's house in Vernon, Vermont.

"We didn't discuss the actual sinking of the boat," Clark said about the ride home. "He just kept asking if anyone had found his mother."

When they arrived at Nathan's house, the area was crawling with reporters. Clark did not stop. Instead, he drove his son to a local motel for a few hours of rest. When they returned to the house, it appeared that the gaggle of media had doubled.

Wearing the same red shirt that he had been rescued in, Nathan stepped up to the crowd of microphones and addressed the media and the public for the first time.

"I just want to thank the public for their prayers and for the continuing prayers for my mother," he said. "I feel healthy. Emotionally, I've been through a huge amount."

WBZ-TV reporter Christina Hager spoke with neighbors in the small town of Vernon, where news did not travel quickly.

"Some people didn't know that he was missing or what he'd been through. He didn't socialize with his neighbors much either," Hager recalled. "When we told townspeople about what had happened, they were very sympathetic to him. They told us that he seemed like a good kid and how hardworking he was."

Hager herself looked over Nathan's remodeling job of his home and could not believe that he had done the work himself with no formal training.

"It was a big job. I also asked myself how a kid with no income that we knew of could pay for such a project," she recalled.

Hager and other reporters filed their stories with common themes of courage, survival, and painful loss. But just hours later, a seismic shift occurred in the overall narrative of the story when South Kingstown Police Detective Alfred Bucco issued a search warrant for Nathan's home.

The search warrant affidavit read that police "believe that evidence relating to the crime of RIGL 46-22-0.3 [operating so as to endanger, resulting in death] will be located at 3034 Fort Bridgemon [sic] in Vernon, Vermont."

Detective Bucco wrote up the application for the warrant, stating that investigators were looking for books, computers, documents, handheld electronic devices, global positioning devices, and maps that may provide clues to Nathan's true destination when he first boarded the *Chicken Pox* with his mother and where he had intended to fish. Detective Bucco was also searching for receipts for boat parts and repairs for the ill-fated vessel.

"This investigation revealed that Nathan's boat was in need of mechanical repair and that Nathan had been conducting a portion of these repairs on his own volition which could have potentially rendered the boat unsafe for operation."

The search warrant also claimed that Nathan was "capable of violence" based on his past behavior, which included an allegation that he held a child hostage with a knife when he was a kid.

At least eight police cars, including officers from the local sheriff's department and state police, searched each level of Nathan's four-story home with flashlights. They seized an Xfinity modem with cable, a Garmin SIM card, and a letter handwritten by Nathan. Police did not find his computer.

Detectives also searched Linda's home in Middletown, Connecticut.

To gain access to the home, officers walked past yellow ribbons attached to a nearby fence and fastened to porch railings with posters handwritten in blue Magic Marker that read *Never Give Up*, *Come Home Safe*, *Pray for My Mom*, and *God Bless Linda and Nathan*. Investigators spent hours inside the home, eventually hauling out several bags and boxes of evidence along with a computer and three big jars filled with handwritten notes.

"She [Linda] filled the first jar with notes that made her happy, the second about things she wished would get better," said her friend and occasional roommate, Monty Monterio. "The third jar was for the problems she was leaving up to God."

The police search led reporters to dredge up Nathan's potential connection to the 2013 murder of John Chakalos. Soon, the image of the shy young man who had tragically lost his mother transformed into a characterization of a sinister, criminal mastermind who was hell-bent on murdering his family members in a diabolical effort to seize the Chakalos family fortune.

CHAPTER NINETEEN

In the days following Nathan's rescue at sea, his father kept him busy running around town, getting him a new copy of his driver's license and other items that were lost when the *Chicken Pox* went down somewhere in the north Atlantic. Nathan also began planning for a memorial service in October 2016 to honor his missing mother at St. Thomas the Apostle Church in West Hartford, Connecticut.

"Nathan has not given up hope for his mother's rescue," his attorney, Hubert Santos, told reporters. "However, he also understands the difficult realities of the situation and that the Coast Guard stopped search and rescue operations last month. He believes that now is an appropriate time to begin the mourning process."

Nathan and Clark Carman worked the phones, calling family members and friends of John and Rita Chakalos and inviting them to attend. Nathan also wrote a rambling letter to his family to explain why he was going ahead with the memorial service.

"I hope beyond words that my mom will be recovered; however, I under-stand that is highly unlikely," he wrote. "I know if I had died at sea, I would want someone to hold a service for me promptly once it became certain that I was deceased. As difficult as it is to acknowledge that there is no longer any probability of my mom being alive, I feel that I have a responsibility to her to ensure that a service is held honoring her memory at which all who knew her are welcome. I also feel a service is something which I need to help me attain a sense of emotional finality which I hope will allow me to exit the state of purgatory-like uncertainty I am now in."

Linda's sisters, Valerie, Elaine, and Charlene, were shocked to hear that their nephew was planning such an event, especially as they shared in the belief that he killed his mother. They hired an attorney from Boston who expressed their disdain for the memorial service with members of the press.

"Linda's family and friends want to make clear that they are not involved in this event," attorney Dan Small said in a statement. "They believe that it is premature and inappropriate to stage this kind of event when there is an ongoing investigation into Linda's disappearance."

Linda's sisters refused to attend the service, as did all other members of the Chakalos family. Nathan's father, Clark, supported him and helped deliver bright yellow and orange mums, the colors of fall, to the church for the memorial, which took place just days before Halloween. The Catholic Archdiocese of Hartford was quick to point out that the mass was not a funeral or a memorial service because there was still an ongoing investigation into the disappearance of Linda Carman and a death certificate had not been issued. The planned service at St. Thomas the Apostle Church was abruptly cancelled because of pressure from the Chakalos sisters, and Nathan had to scramble to find a smaller venue, St. Patrick-St. Anthony Church in Hartford.

A smattering of Linda's friends did show up at the chapel, including Sharon Hartstein and Jeannette Brodeur. It was the first time that Brodeur had spent any time with Nathan.

"I met him, and I just got chills. I've never had that feeling about somebody," she recalled. "He just came across as very cold, like there was nothing, no kindness, nothing."

Brodeur approached Nathan inside the church and offered her condolences.

"I'm sorry for your loss," she said as she tried to hug him.

But Nathan did not reciprocate the heartfelt greeting. Inside the chapel, he stood rigid and stared back at his mother's close friend with a blank expression.

"The whole service just seemed bizarre to me," Brodeur remembered. "There was nothing in it that Linda would have liked. I thought that I was being used and that Nathan had created the memorial for the media. It just felt like a big show."

Other attendees felt uneasy as well. When the priest asked mourners if anyone would like to approach the altar and share their memories of Linda Carman, no one moved.

"I think we were all stunned," Brodeur said. "I think we all felt like the whole thing was ridiculous."

Nathan sat quietly and did not get up and speak about his mother during the hour-long church service.

The memorial was closed to reporters, but that did not stop a group of television and print journalists from gathering outside the church. As Nathan left the service, he was besieged by reporters sticking microphones in his face as he walked down the street toward his pickup truck.

Without breaking stride, Nathan told them, "I'm very grateful to the friends and family who attended in memory of my mom."

"How was the service?" one reporter asked him as he reached his truck.

"The whole family was invited," he replied. "I'm glad that many of my mom's friends chose to attend. And I think the service was a good time for us to come together and support one another."

"Are you sad your aunts didn't show?" another reporter asked.

Nathan closed his eyes and sighed before answering. "I wish very much that my whole family could have come together to pray for my mom," he replied, his voice cracking. "I made sure they were invited and that they had an opportunity to come."

Nathan was then asked if he had been informed by police about the status of their investigation into the sinking of his boat and the disappearance of his mother. He did not answer. "I wish desperately that my mom was rescued," he replied instead. "I hope that she will be found. As difficult as this is, I'm glad that family and friends came together to remember my mom and to support each other in this very difficult time. Now, I'm going to drive off."

He shut his door, turned on the ignition, and drove away with his father in the passenger seat of his pickup truck.

After the service, Sharon Hartstein visited Linda's home and found a small gift-wrapped box addressed to Jeannette Brodeur's middle-school-age daughter, Jilly. Linda had always joked to Jilly that she would buy a pet duck for her because the girl loved waterfowl. Hartstein brought the box to Jilly, who opened it and found a toy duck inside. The girl hugged the stuffed animal and burst into tears.

"It just reminded us of how considerate she was of others," Brodeur said.

Weeks later, Hartstein made a surprising move to gain control over Linda's financial affairs in an attempt to block Nathan from drawing money from Linda's bank account. Hartstein filed a five-page petition with the Middlesex Probate Court to seek temporary approval to manage, supervise, and protect her friend's property. Linda had appointed Hartstein as her durable power of attorney in 2013. Hartstein's attempt to take control of Linda's estate was backed by her three surviving sisters.

"Linda's family fully supports Sharon Hartstein's motion because they are respectful of their sister's decision to make her friend her power of attorney," their lawyer, Dan Small, said in a statement.

Small was getting pulled deeper into the complex issues surrounding the Chakalos family. A graduate of Harvard Law School and a former prosecutor,

Small had represented a number of high-profile clients, including Virginia governor Bob McDonnell, who was convicted of receiving improper gifts and loans from a Virginia businessman and sentenced to two years in prison. Small won an appeal before the U.S. Supreme Court. Now, he represented the Chakalos sisters, who were devising their own plans for litigation against their nephew.

As the trustee of Linda Carman's estate, Sharon Hartstein would maintain authority over her finances for seven years, the time determined by the court that Linda could officially be declared dead due to her drowning. At that time, Linda's estimated net worth was $6.5 million, her share of the family company, Chakalos Manor LLC, with an additional $305,000 available in cash and property. The small fortune did not include the millions more Linda stood to inherit from her father's estate. A judge would later deny Hartstein's request and instead appoint a local lawyer named Glen Terk to manage Linda's finances.

––––––––

Coast Guard investigator Eric Gempp did not spend any time trying to untie the complicated knots that had been wrapping themselves around the Chakalos family for several decades. Instead, he focused on closing the gap in the timeline of Nathan's ill-fated fishing trip with his mother.

"We would ask questions of Nathan, and we did not get many answers, which led us to more questions," Gempp explained. "We were trying to narrow down the timeline between the evening of September 17 when they left the dock and the eighteenth. After that, there was no timeline until Nathan was rescued."

During his initial interview with the Coast Guard, Nathan told officials that he and his mother had gone fishing just south of the wind turbine farm off Block Island in a relatively small area known as Southwest Ledge before heading deeper out to sea to fish for tuna. Gempp learned there was a fishing tournament going on, the Billy Carr Midnight Madness Striper Shootout, at Southwest Ledge during the same weekend that Nathan and his mother had gone missing.

"There were probably anywhere from thirty or forty boats out there fishing Southwest Ledge, and we interviewed every fisherman we could, but nobody saw Nathan," Gempp recalled. "So we didn't know whether he went down the east side of Block Island or the west side."

The investigator began exploring his options. He knew the Spring House Hotel on Block Island had a webcam facing east out into the ocean, and upon his review of the video footage, he did not see the *Chicken Pox* go by at any time on September 17. He also reviewed surveillance footage from a security camera that had been set up at the wind turbine farm off Block Island and found that there was no boat in the proximity of the windmills at the time that Nathan was alleged to have been there. Gempp then returned to Ram Point Marina and reviewed the video footage there that captured Nathan and his mother walking past a stationary surveillance camera and another camera that caught a boat that was consistent with the *Chicken Pox* leaving the dock. He also conducted follow-up interviews with several witnesses, including Mike Iozzi and his wife. Gempp found a fisherman who had seen Nathan on the night of September 17 in the Harbor Refuge.

"He was a participant in the fishing tournament," Gempp said. "He readily identified the boat and was close enough to see that there were two people on board. They were traveling toward Block Island in a southeasterly direction."

The Coast Guard investigator also scoured social media, particularly online fishing forums, and noticed a couple of posts from fishermen who claimed to have seen the boat. Gempp was trying to exhaust all the logical leads that he could in an effort to piece together this baffling jigsaw puzzle.

There was one point after Nathan's rescue where Gempp and his team almost recovered the life raft.

"I made a request to go and recover the life raft for safety and security reasons, because we don't need some boat to run into it or somebody seeing it and Coast Guard assets being deployed unnecessarily as if it was a new rescue," Gempp explained.

He had learned that the canopy of Nathan's life raft had deflated moments after he was recovered by the crew of the *Orient Lucky*. "I wondered how and why the canopy had been deflated."

A Coast Guard helicopter was dispatched to the area one hundred miles off Martha's Vineyard where Nathan was rescued, and crews spotted the life raft still drifting east to west. A Coast Guard cutter was then diverted to the scene, but bad weather had closed in and lasted three long days, and the search was suspended.

Gempp believed the life raft may have washed up on shore, so he took a group of investigators to Block Island and walked the beach from Southeast Light to an area called Dory's Cove. He had done this countless times with his family as a kid while hunting for seashells and hermit crabs. But now Gempp was looking for the life raft, any debris from the *Chicken Pox* that may have washed up on shore, and possibly even the body of Linda Carman.

"We spent a day there walking the beach, but we found nothing of evidentiary value, only large pieces of driftwood, lobster pots, and buoys," Gempp said.

He also wondered whether Nathan could have been hiding out with his boat during the days of the exhaustive search and rescue operation, so Gempp reached out to Coast Guard intelligence centers from Maine to Virginia, but there had been no sighting of the *Chicken Pox* anywhere along the coast of the north Atlantic.

The mysterious circumstances surrounding Nathan's rescue reignited the investigation into the murder of his grandfather, which had been dormant for a couple of years.

"It was a circumstantial case and an uphill battle for investigators. We began looking back at John Chakalos's financial records and saw that Nathan had tried to get names changed on trusts and other documents that would give him an avenue to gain access to funds," said Don Melanson, chief of the Windsor, Connecticut, police. "That was the financial motive to kill his grandfather. He was the last one to see his grandfather, and his phone was shut off during the early morning hours of December 20, 2013. There was a gap in his timeline where he wasn't able to be tracked."

The FBI joined the investigation and worked together with Melanson's detectives and members of the Connecticut Division of Criminal Justice Cold Case Unit as they studied existing clues and tried to unearth new evidence to firmly tie Nathan to his grandfather's slaying.

Investigators renewed efforts to find the murder weapon used to kill John Chakalos. In December 2016, members of the FBI Evidence Response Team, all wearing hazmat suits and some breathing through ventilators, searched a deserted property in Spofford, New Hampshire, that had been owned by the Chakalos family. Caretaker Joy Washburn escorted investigators onto the property. Agents searched inside multiple buildings that had once been used as a substance abuse treatment center known as Spofford Hall that John Chakalos had built in 1980. Investigators had no idea what they would find inside the abandoned buildings and wore the hazmat suits as a precaution.

The road leading to the site was blocked off by police while agents used rakes and shovels to dig and sift through dirt and search the woods across the sprawling complex. Investigators also focused their attention on a section of the adjacent Spofford Lake, which spanned 732 acres, believing that Nathan might have dumped his Sig Sauer rifle in the water. Authorities remained tight-lipped about the search, but a spokesperson for the Windsor police told reporters that the investigation was ongoing and that Nathan Carman was considered a person of interest in the case.

An FBI agent also reached out to Shawn Sakaske. The agent left brief voice mail messages on Sakaske's phone, along with his wife's phone.

"Why is the FBI calling me?" Sakaske asked his wife.

"I don't know, but you must be in real trouble, because they called my cell phone too."

Sakaske called the agent back and learned that the FBI wanted to go over the fisherman's interaction with Nathan. The federal agent drove to Sakaske's house in Ludlow, Massachusetts, for a tape-recorded interview.

"I told him that I had a different view of things compared to what I had seen in the media," Sakaske remembered. "If Nathan killed his mother, he had me duped. He just didn't feel like a murderer to me. It just seemed to me that he didn't know common sense."

The fisherman shared his doubts with the FBI.

"Why would he sink his boat and play with his own life? There's gotta be an easier way to do it," he told the FBI agent. "That boat could have sunk at the dock, the way he fiddled with it. How could he have timed it all out? He didn't seem like a criminal mastermind to me. He loved his mother. I could see it when we talked. She was his fishing partner. Who the hell would kill their only fishing partner? Also, no one in their right mind is gonna take the chance of floating around at sea for that long, hoping that someone picks them up."

The FBI agent was not interested in listening to Sakaske's theories.

"We don't care what you think," the agent told him sternly. "We just want to know what you know."

Sakaske believed the FBI agent was just going through the motions and wasn't interested in learning anything new about Nathan.

"I spoke with Nathan longer than most people had ever done," Sakaske claimed. "But the FBI didn't want to hear it. At that point, I think they were just trying to pin a murder on the kid."

CHAPTER TWENTY

Despite the whirlwind of suspicion that surrounded him, Nathan refused to keep a low profile after the disappearance of his mother. In November 2016, he filed an insurance claim asking for $85,000 for his sunken fishing boat. The insurance companies refused to pay. The National Liability & Fire Insurance Company and Boat Owners Association of the United States hired a naval architect and a marine surveyor to investigate the alterations that Nathan had made to the vessel. They determined that Nathan knew that the *Chicken Pox* was not seaworthy when he left Ram Point Marina. The findings led both insurance companies to cancel Nathan's policy and refuse to pay his claim.

But Nathan vowed to take his insurers to court. A month after his claim was rejected, Nathan was deposed by the insurance company's lawyers. Under oath, he told them that he had arrived at Block Canyon at around 7:00 a.m. on September 18 and fished with his mother for about five hours until he discovered that the bilge aboard the *Chicken Pox* was flooded. Nathan told the attorneys that by the time he turned off the boat and powered it down, the seawater was up to the battery boxes and only about three inches below the deck. He said that he asked his mother to bring in the fishing lines, which she acknowledged, but he never spoke to her or saw her again.

Lawyers questioned Nathan as to why he did not call for help.

"You began moving safety and survival gear to the bow to prepare for the possibility of abandoning ship," one attorney pointed out. "However, despite entering the cabin three times, you didn't make a distress call on your VHF radio."

Following the deposition, lawyers for the insurance companies asked for a declaratory judgment in the U.S. District Court in Rhode Island, where the vessel had reportedly gone down.

"Your boat's sinking was caused by your incomplete, improper and faulty repair," lawyers for the insurance companies wrote in a letter filed with the court. "The sinking was caused by your intentional acts."

Undaunted, Nathan looked forward to the opportunity to state his case in open court and began to prepare for a civil trial. But he was also losing his case in the court of public opinion after a series of headlines and stories that connected him to the murder of John Chakalos.

ABC news reporter Linzie Janis had been monitoring the case since it broke in September. Both she and her producer Michael Mendelsohn immediately began gathering elements for a story, which included search warrants.

"Why would anyone sabotage their own boat?" Janis asked herself. "Were police suggesting Nathan had killed his mother?"

They also spoke to Sharon Hartstein over the phone. She eventually gave them Nathan's cell phone number. Janis called but got no answer. She then got into her car with her producer and a videographer and began driving from New York City to Vermont. During that ride, she received a text from Nathan, who said that he was now willing to talk. They spoke on the phone twice. and Nathan agreed to a sit-down interview with the ABC News correspondent and told her that he wanted to set the record straight.

They agreed to meet at a park bench in downtown Vernon. Nathan showed up to the interview wearing his favorite red button-down shirt and a vest while clutching a cup of apple cider in one hand and a pad of paper in the other.

He had scribbled some thoughts on a yellow legal pad and shared it with Janis.

"I'm not sure how best to say this," he told her as he pointed down at something he had written on the pad.

Before beginning the interview, Nathan folded his hands together, closed his eyes, and prayed out loud. "Oh Lord, may you help us to...ah... to me, to accurately and effectively express what I've been through."

Janis then asked Nathan to go over the story, beginning with the night he motored out of Ram Point Marina aboard the *Chicken Pox* with his mother. Under the spotlight and in front of the news camera, Nathan appeared nervous, and he could not put together his thoughts in a cohesive manner. As the correspondent attempted to engage him, Nathan would shut her down.

"I'm not going to get into that now," he responded as Janis asked questions. "I'm not going to answer that. I'm not going to go there."

Nathan did tell the reporter that he and his mother fished together every other week.

"These fishing trips, you would often leave at night or in the early hours of the morning?" Janis asked, probing gently.

"Yes, that's correct," he replied in a soft, monotone voice. "We met at the marina in Rhode Island, got all of our gear on board, [and] pushed off from the dock."

When asked about taking his mother all the way out to Block Canyon, Nathan answered honestly. "I have experience boating. I have experience fishing. I did not have experience offshore fishing."

He told the ABC news reporter that he was comfortable making the trip because the seas were calm and the day in question was perfect for fishing. He described what happened when the engine sounded "different" and the boat took on water. Nathan told Janis that he was going to figure out what the issue was and then head back to Ram Point Marina, but at that point, the boat started to sink.

"Any sign of your mother?" Janis asked.

"No, not at that point."

As the interview continued, Nathan turned from the reporter and looked directly into the video camera.

"I love my mother, present tense," he said, showing emotion for the first time. "I love my mother."

Janis then asked Nathan if Linda Carman had been concerned for her safety and if she'd needed coaxing to go on the fishing trip.

"That's correct," he said with a nod. "It was not an argument. I was kind of pestering my mom. She had always been kind of skittish."

Suddenly, Nathan finished talking and waved his arms. "I'm stopping right here with that question. We're stopping right here."

He ended the interview after ninety minutes, and Janis followed him home and then headed back to New York City. The reporter now had more questions about him than answers.

"Wasn't Nathan's motivation in talking to me to tell his entire story?" she asked herself. "And in doing so, show people he had nothing to hide?"

The correspondent continued to text Nathan every couple of days, hoping for a second interview. The newsroom at ABC kept humming as journalists covered a deadly train crash in New Jersey and Hurricane Matthew, which blew through the Carolinas as the most powerful storm of the year. Time went on, and Nathan finally responded to Janis's texts and agreed to speak with her on the record again in Vermont, 193 miles away from ABC News headquarters.

When they sat down inside a local hotel and turned on the camera, Nathan told Janis that he had not received any calls from his three aunts since his ordeal. "It makes me feel like I have no family. I want to have [a] family. I want them to be my family."

Later, when the reporter spoke with the aunts' attorney, Dan Small, he told her, "It's a terribly upsetting and difficult time. Their focus is not on relationships but on getting answers to questions."

As part of the interview, Nathan gave Janis a tour of his property, which included a century-old barn, and drove her around the small town of Vernon.

"I'm not someone who understands relationships or who's good about talking about emotions," he told her.

The second interview appeared to be going much more smoothly than the first. He opened up briefly about his mother.

"What was she like?" Janis asked him.

"She was a good person, a warm person. We did have a challenging relationship at one point in my life," he replied. "But she was the only family who I really had, and now I don't have her, and that's a tremendous loss."

"You feel alone."

"Yes, and when I had her, I didn't feel alone."

Janis felt that she was finally connecting with Nathan. He told her he didn't understand why he ran away in 2011 but that it was something he felt he had to do at the time. But he refused to get into his personal health records with her and would not talk about his brief hospitalization that same year. "I can't answer that question," he told her.

When their conversation turned to the unsolved murder of his grandfather, he said there was zero proof to support allegations that he was involved.

"My understanding is that if you lie to the police and they prove that you lied, they can arrest you," he said in the interview. "And they haven't done so."

Later, when asked by Janis to discuss the police search of his mother's home in Middletown, he grew furious.

"We're done here," he said as he got up from his chair. "We're done for this evening, period."

Nathan took off his microphone and stormed out of the room.

He was coaxed back to the interview chair twenty minutes later to discuss the water packets and food bars that he relied on to survive at sea.

Janis finished the interview and took the footage back to ABC News. She fleshed out her pending *20/20* exclusive with interviews of legal experts, veteran boaters, and even a mental health expert who provided a play-by-play analysis of Nathan's interview.

Just before airing the story in early February 2017, Janis learned that Nathan's two insurance companies had refused to pay his claim. She immediately called him to get his reaction, but the cell phone was disconnected.

CHAPTER TWENTY-ONE

The *20/20* episode aired nationally in early February 2017, but it did not have the effect Nathan had hoped for.

"Was it missing at sea, or was it murder at sea?" ABC news anchor Elizabeth Vargas asked in her voice-over to open the show. "Targeted because of his diagnosis? Or because something suspicious is going on?"

The program was slickly produced, with *Psycho*-style music and overflowing with jarring twists and turns that one would find in a Hitchcockian thriller.

Over the course of the hour-long television special, Nathan was cast as the likely villain of his own story.

Shawn Sakaske watched the *20/20* episode with his wife.

"I thought it was bullshit, the way he was treated in that show," Sakaske observed. "Here's a kid who can't even keep his head straight, and now he's on TV, and nobody's really helping him as they're hammering him with questions from a professional interviewer. When I spoke with him, it didn't seem like he had the ability to lie. He was stone-faced honest."

For the millions of Americans watching the program who did not know Nathan, his behavior was off-putting. He rudely and repeatedly cut off the ABC correspondent's tough line of questioning. Instead of editing those moments out and leaving them on the cutting room floor, producers baked them into the program several times during the duration of the broadcast. Nathan's quirky behavior made for good TV.

After viewing the program, amateur detectives and armchair sleuths flocked to websites like Reddit and flooded chat rooms with comments like **I love it when the bad guy gets caught because they're stupid**, and **It's so sad in those cases where a mother gives everything to her troublesome son his entire life and then he repays her by killing her**, and **My gut reaction is he killed them both... I do think his motive was money, or he was enraged.**

Shawn Sakaske pored over comments on another website dedicated to boaters called the Hull Truth, where he read comments like **Not good that he [Nathan] is the last person to have seen two family members in recent years... Does he think he's smart enough to play dumb?... Definitely an interesting and odd story.**

"It was just so toxic, how everyone was crucifying this kid without ever having the chance to talk with him like I did," Sakaske said.

Much was also written about Nathan's diagnosis. Nearly every article about the case made reference to Asperger's syndrome, now known as autism spectrum disorder. Just as reporters and bloggers had done in the wake of the Newtown, Connecticut, massacre in reference to gunman Adam Lanza, they once again put the autism spectrum under the microscope.

The question raised: Could a young man with Asperger's Syndrome possibly have contrived to kill his mother by...luring her out on a fishing trip 100 miles offshore? asked blogger Charles Doane on the website Wavetrain.net.

During the *20/20* episode, psychologist Rebecca Sachs attempted to explain why Nathan refused to answer some of reporter Linzie Janis's questions.

"People with Asperger's [autism spectrum disorder] may seem evasive," Sachs said in the broadcast. "They're trying to process information, and they order their thoughts in ways that others might find unusual."

Sachs also defended Nathan's choice to order his mother to haul in the fishing lines when their boat was sinking. "Picking out what is the most important piece of information is often really difficult [for someone with autism spectrum disorder]."

Coast Guard investigator Eric Gempp watched the *20/20* episode closely.

"His recollection of events was similar to those he gave during his initial Coast Guard debriefing," Gempp recalled. "But we were hoping that Janis would help us get more answers to the questions we had, but just when we thought we were about to hear something new, Nathan would shut down the interview."

Gempp then made a request to ABC News for the entire video footage from the Janis interview, but he was denied access to it by the network's lawyers.

Despite his public plea claiming his innocence in the *20/20* episode, Nathan felt that he was still under heavy scrutiny from the media for the murder of his grandfather and the disappearance of his mother. In April 2017, Nathan's lawyer asked a judge to seal a 2014 warrant that implicated him in the murder of John Chakalos.

"During the course of their investigation, investigators learned from various sources that Nathan Carman was capable of violence when his coping mechanisms were challenged," Windsor Police Detective Bill Freeman wrote in the original warrant. "Information was obtained by investigators that Nathan had several episodes demonstrating this while attending Middletown [Connecticut] High School. Family members also make investigators aware of an incident in which Nathan, as a child, held another child 'hostage' at knifepoint."

The warrant also stated that Nathan was familiar with firearms and that he had concealed the fact that he had purchased a .308-caliber Sig Sauer rifle a month before his grandfather was killed with three rifle blasts to his body and skull.

"The facts contained [in the warrant] would seriously threaten Mr. Carman's reputation and his ability to seek and maintain employment," argued his attorney, Trent A. LaLima, Hubie Santos's law partner. "Mr. Carman is a very young man. These documents, if not sealed, could be discovered by potential employers, business partners or others, for decades to come."

Nathan's remodeling project was still unfinished, so he could not flip his historic Vermont home and sell it for a profit as he had hoped. Since the disappearance of his mother, he had been living off credit cards and racking up thousands of dollars in unpaid bills after having blown through $400,000 in a joint bank account owned by him, his grandfather, and his mother.

Nathan's attorney called the allegations in the search warrant "extremely serious" and said that they lacked any vetting from the court system.

"While Mr. Carman has been in the news over the past year, the effect of these articles may fade," LaLima stated in his filing. "In contrast, the continued public nature of this affidavit would allow unsubstantiated, negative rumors to persist or be re-raised at any time."

Nathan, now clean-shaven with a fresh haircut, attended a hearing on the matter in Connecticut only to learn that a judge would deny his lawyer's request. A state attorney argued successfully that Nathan's demand to have information sealed was ironic since he had willingly appeared on *20/20* and made public comments on several other news stations.

The lawyer for Nathan's aunts also weighed in on the judge's decision.

"The warrant has been public for over two years, and a motion to seal at this point is unnecessary," said attorney Dan Small.

Dejected, Nathan returned to Vermont, while his aunts Valerie, Elaine, and Charlene prepared to make a stunning chess move against him.

CHAPTER TWENTY-TWO

The surviving daughters of John Chakalos remained discouraged by the lack of progress made by police in arresting Nathan for his murder. The billboard they had put up on I-91 in Connecticut had been pasted over without generating any strong leads, and now their sister Linda was missing and presumed dead while her son had gone on a media campaign in an attempt to clear his name.

The criminal case appeared cold to the point of frozen, so Nathan's aunts decided to take action themselves. They huddled with their lawyer, and in July 2017, they petitioned a court in Cheshire County, New Hampshire, to declare Nathan Carman his grandfather's killer.

Their petition was filed under the controversial "slayer rule," which stops a person from inheriting property from a person they murdered. The sisters wanted to block Nathan from gaining any access to his grandfather's $42 million fortune.

In their slayer rule petition, Valerie, Elaine, and Charlene alleged that Nathan had committed the "heinous act" of gunning down their father out of "malice and greed."

"In 2013, four sisters suffered an unthinkable tragedy when their father John Chakalos was murdered in his own home," Dan Small, attorney for the sisters, said in a statement. "Less than three years later, one of those sisters, Linda Carman, disappeared at sea under highly suspicious circumstances. The last person to see both of these family members alive was Nathan Carman. The details and evidence in the death of John and the disappearance of Linda all point to Nathan as the prime suspect. Yet he now stands to inherit millions of dollars from their estates."

In the slayer rule petition, the sisters and their attorney also poked holes in Nathan's account of his ordeal aboard the *Chicken Pox*.

"[The boat] would have returned very slowly with each roll [when it started taking on water]. This very noticeable change would have alerted Nathan that something was wrong," the petition said. "Nathan could have issued a distress call long before the water reached the necessary level to sink the *Chicken Pox*."

The lawsuit also refuted the direction that Nathan had claimed his life raft had drifted after the sinking of his fishing boat. Regarding the murder of their father, the sisters and their lawyer claimed that Nathan and his grandfather had argued about money and issues regarding the future of the family mansion in West Chesterfield, New Hampshire.

The sisters feared that Nathan could gain access to his mother's so-called dynasty trust, or $7 million from her father's final estate, which was still being probated in a New Hampshire court. They did not know that Linda had omitted Nathan from her will, which he could have contested if and when she was declared dead.

Still, the Chakalos sisters claimed that their legal attack against Nathan had nothing to do with money.

"[The Chakalos sisters] cannot stand idle while their father's killer, and perhaps their sister's killer also, profits from his actions. It is about justice," said Small. "If the Chakalos sisters win this lawsuit and any money that would have gone to Nathan instead goes to the surviving sisters individually, they pledge to use those funds exclusively to pay for expenses incurred relating to the investigation relating to their father and disappearance of their sister, and any remaining funds will go to charity."

Small told reporters that the sisters continued to support the government's criminal investigations and that they hoped authorities would bring someone to justice in both cases.

"We understand that these things can take a long time," he added. "John Chakalos was murdered in his bed with three shots from a .308-caliber rifle. We are concerned that there is a killer on the loose and we want to do everything we can to get answers."

The sisters would have an uphill battle on their hands, as critics in the legal community believed the slayer rule dangerously straddled the borderline between private civil law and public criminal law. Most slayer rule cases required a criminal conviction before a probate judge could rule against a killer. Nathan had not been charged with his grandfather's murder. And since the sisters filed the petition in New Hampshire, they would have to prove that John Chakalos had lived full-time at the farm in West Chesterfield and not at his home in Windsor, Connecticut.

In an effort to expedite the proceedings, the case was quickly moved from the town of Keene, in New Hampshire's Cheshire County, to Concord, the state capital.

Meanwhile, Nathan continued to fight on a second front against his insurance companies for the $85,000 payout for his sunken boat. In August 2018, attorney David Farrell, representing both insurance companies, filed a petition in Rhode Island's federal court arguing that Nathan's alleged "criminal wrongdoing" could wipe out his insurance claim.

"His actions/inactions regarding his mother's death are within the scope of discovery as relevant to the sinking…as is his grandfather's homicide," Farrell wrote in his court filing.

This meant that what was supposed to be a minor legal dispute over an insurance claim could escalate into a de facto murder trial for Nathan.

For this case, Nathan hired David Anderson, a tenacious Boston attorney who was also an expert in maritime law.

"You have not alleged that Nathan intended to sink his vessel and/or kill his mother," Anderson fired back in response. "Or that he killed his grandfather several years ago."

Investigators for the insurance companies were also digging into Nathan's past, seeking information about his gun ownership and his mental health history.

Anderson filed his own claim in an attempt to quash the inquiry because the insurance companies had not alleged that Nathan had "committed insurance fraud, intentional sinking or murder" in its own court papers. "[Nathan's] brain works differently than the general population and this difference can affect the way in which he communicates with, and is perceived by, the average person," Anderson wrote in his petition to deny both of the insurance companies discovery motions in the case. The attorney referred to the opposing side's tactics as "discovery abuse."

Anderson also pushed back against Farrell's request to depose Nathan again, this time on video.

"I told you that just because he had Asperger's and the tabloid press has had a field day with him, I was not going to agree to have him be treated any difference [sic] than any other litigant."

A judge ordered Nathan's deposition anyway.

That same month, Nathan was involved in an accident on Interstate 91 in Vernon, Vermont, when his pickup truck was rear-ended by a tractor trailer. Although he was not hurt and little damage was done to his vehicle, the story involving the so-called Murder Boy still made news across New England.

CHAPTER TWENTY-THREE

Nathan Carman, the socially awkward, painfully shy loner, surprised everyone including his three aunts when he petitioned the court to represent himself in the slayer rule case, in which the Chakalos sisters were trying to declare him a cold-blooded murderer and cut him out of his share of the family fortune.

Nathan had taught himself how to be a carpenter and how to be a boat repairman. Now he would teach himself how to act as his own lawyer in a case that was worth millions of dollars.

He filed a one-page document in New Hampshire court, notifying the judge that he would be representing himself in the high-profile lawsuit. Nathan was strapped for cash, and he had initially tried to raise money to hire a lawyer, but his aunts blocked him from collecting any money from the Chakalos family estate.

Connecticut attorney Hubert Santos finally agreed to represent Nathan again, this time in the slayer rule case. His first order of business was to file a motion to get the lawsuit thrown out of court. Santos argued that New Hampshire was the wrong venue to hear the case since John Chakalos was not a legal resident of the Granite State, although he had owned property there. But through their lawyer Dan Small, Nathan's aunts contended that their father was a longtime resident of West Chesterfield, New Hampshire, and a beloved, "well-known, active member of the community."

"He loved the home that he and his wife Rita had built and which they shared with the surrounding community every Christmas," Small said in a statement. The lawyer also noted that Chakalos had given "generously" to the town library and West Chesterfield's police and fire departments. Chakalos's daughters also felt they were on solid ground legally since their parents' probate estate had been filed in New Hampshire.

In December 2017, four years after the murder of John Chakalos, the two sides went to court in New Hampshire to argue complex questions surrounding Linda Carman's legal status. Was she still missing and presumed drowned? Or was she legally dead? Both sides also fought over the venue for the case. Was John Chakalos a legal resident of New Hampshire or Connecticut, where he had operated his family business out of the modest, mustard-colored home he had owned for decades?

No rulings were made in court that day. "I'll see you back here in the spring," Judge David D. King told both sides.

The delay did not stop the sisters' lawyer from holding court with reporters outside the courtroom as he continued to hammer away at Nathan in the press.

"The sisters brought this case in the belief that Nathan is a murderer and that he killed his grandfather and that he should not profit by that murder," Small said. "They do not want blood money and they don't want Nathan to have blood money."

Small did manage one small victory by getting the judge to agree to seal several documents in the case until the next hearing, which was scheduled for May 2018.

As the calendar turned to January, the sisters again expressed their frustration with detectives working the criminal side of the case. They filed a Freedom of Information Act request with both the Windsor and

Middletown, Connecticut, police departments demanding documents concerning DNA samples taken from Nathan and ballistics reports on the bullets used to kill their father. Both departments had denied initial requests for information because the case was considered to be open and active. Attorney Small argued that police detectives had been sitting on their hands now that the investigation had been relegated to the Connecticut Division of Criminal Justice Cold Case Unit.

The police departments continued to stymie the Chakalos sisters, but they managed to catch a break when Nathan decided to fire his legal counsel and again represent himself in the lawsuit. It was another unpredictable move from a young man whose enigmatic behavior continued to confound both the public and those close to him. When asked to comment on his curious decision, Nathan sat down and wrote another rambling statement that resulted in a word salad that made little sense.

"I plan to aggressively pursue all legal avenues available to me for rectifying the injustices which have already been perpetrated and obtaining a just outcome in the matters that are ongoing," he wrote.

Nathan also claimed that Hubert Santos was not devoting much time to his case, as the Connecticut lawyer was just months away from a career-defining victory in overturning the conviction of Michael Skakel, Ethel Kennedy's nephew, in the murder of his Greenwich, Connecticut, neighbor Martha Moxley, who was bludgeoned to death with a golf club in 1975.

Nathan believed that a do-it-yourself approach in his own case would yield similar results.

"I am confident that through my hard work and determination alone if need be, the truth will prevail, I will be vindicated, and perhaps my grandfather's true murderer will be uncovered."

He then turned his attention away from his attorney and back toward his family. For the first time, Nathan took direct verbal shots at the Chakalos sisters.

"I did not kill my grandfather or my mother," he reiterated. "Nor did I engage in the violent behavior in my childhood that has been reported. It is my aunts who are being driven by malice and greed to make the vexatious, false and insupportable allegations which form the basis of their probate lawsuit in New Hampshire."

It seemed like every week, Nathan was engaging in a new battle in a two-front legal war.

In the insurance case, lawyers asked the judge to force Nathan to discuss what happened to his missing rifle, the weapon that Connecticut police suspected he had used to kill his grandfather. It was an odd request considering that the insurance case was focused solely on the sinking of the *Chicken Pox* off Martha's Vineyard.

Both cases were now merging together in the media and in the courts, and the walls were closing in fast on Nathan Carman.

Chapter Twenty-Four

Nathan showed up alone for his first court appearance relating to the slayer rule case after Judge David D. King ordered him to provide answers as to why he failed to offer information to his aunts' attorneys about his purchase of a Sig Sauer rifle, his tax returns, credit card and bank statements, and cell phone records. The judge called for an emergency hearing on the issues in early April 2018 in Concord, New Hampshire.

As Nathan entered the courthouse, reporters did a double take, as he had transformed himself from the scruffy ragamuffin who routinely wore a red button-down shirt, vest, cargo pants, and galoshes into a clean-shaven, well-groomed young man in a brown suit and tie.

He sat by himself at a lawyers table just a few feet away from Judge King and opposite attorney Dan Small and his co-counsel, Robert Satterly. The chair next to Nathan was empty, and it presented a stark reminder to reporters that Nathan had chosen to fight a David-versus-Goliath battle against his wealthy aunts and their high-powered attorneys without any help.

At the outset of the hearing, the judge wanted to make sure that Nathan understood the gravity of the situation he was in.

"I'm a little bit concerned that you're here this morning without an attorney. This is a serious case," Judge King told him. "It's a murder case, and even though you can't go to jail as a result of what happens here, obviously the stakes are pretty high for you financially."

The judge then told Nathan that unlike in a criminal case, he could not assert his Fifth Amendment rights in the civil case that was before them.

"I'm urging you in the strongest way that I can to get counsel in this matter," Judge King advised. "If you were a lawyer, I'd be telling you to get a lawyer in this case. You have important rights, and I want to make sure those rights are protected."

"I am not comfortable here either. I do not want to be representing myself," Nathan responded while seated. "However, there were substantive disagreements and long-standing concerns that I had with Mr. Santos. Two weeks ago today, I put my house on the market, and I'm hoping that it will sell quickly, and my intent is to use those funds to finance an attorney as my first priority, even before seeking housing for myself." Nathan admitted to the judge that he did not understand the legal issues surrounding how the Fifth Amendment can or cannot be used in a civil case. "I don't have a solid grasp of those details," he said.

Nathan said that he hoped to hire a new attorney to help him navigate the issue moving forward but that he would take the responsibility of representing himself for now.

"It's not the money. It's not so much my freedom. It's my reputation and seeing that I have a future going forward," he told the court. "That is what's in jeopardy here, and I'm very concerned about protecting my future."

Judge King then turned his attention to a filing from Small stating that Linda Carman was "constructively dead" and questioned whether the term had been used in another jurisdiction. Small's co-counsel, Robert Satterly, said no. The judge then asked the sisters' lawyers about family trusts that had listed Nathan as a beneficiary.

"He already has beneficiary status with one trust and is a contingent beneficiary on others," Satterly said. He pointed out that Nathan's status as a contingent beneficiary would change to present beneficiary once his mother was declared dead by the courts.

At this point, Nathan jumped in. "That's news to me. Let me state that I have never been informed at any point in my life that I am a present beneficiary of any of the trusts."

Small complained to the judge that Nathan had refused to comply with their requests for information and documents pertaining to his grandfather's murder.

"You can't just ignore what the other side files, even if you think it a frivolous motion," Judge King told Nathan. "You still need to file a response."

"I understand the importance of these proceedings," Nathan replied as he stirred in his seat. "It's also a challenge for me to face every day." He then began to stutter while searching for the right words. "With the emotional things that I'm still going through, it's a challenge. I understand that deadlines can't be flexible, but that is what I'm going through."

Reporters furiously tried to jot down Nathan's words on their notepads, as it was the first time that he had shown any emotion during the proceeding. But Small had zero sympathy for Nathan.

"My discovery has been badly delayed and grossly inadequate. And the family has been frustrated by it," Small argued. "We've bent over backward to accommodate, providing multiple continuances, providing multiple letters seeking to resolve these issues without any enforced court intervention."

According to Small, the most egregious example of Nathan's refusal to cooperate centered on his purchase of the Sig Sauer rifle.

"In our discovery, we have sought to obtain details and documents pertaining to what we feel is the murder weapon, which [Nathan] claims he somehow managed to lose."

Small and his team were seeking purchase and sale information about the weapon, but at the time, they had no idea which gun store had sold

Nathan the rifle, because members of law enforcement had refused to share that information with them.

"There are six hundred licensed gun dealers in New Hampshire. We could subpoena every one of them," Small told the judge. "But that obviously would be an absurd waste of time and resources."

The sisters' lawyer shared his frustration that a Freedom of Information Act request that had been issued to police departments had been recently denied due to the ongoing criminal investigation.

"We are trying to get that information in a number of ways, but one of them, the easiest way, is to get them directly from [Nathan]," Small argued. "You can't exercise your Fifth Amendment rights that selectively. You can't weave your responses around things you don't like and provide responses to things you do like."

Small also questioned why Nathan had not turned over copies of his tax returns, cell phone records, credit card records, and bank statements.

Nathan told the court that he did not pay taxes because he had never had a job. He also claimed that his grandfather had paid all his bills and that he had no access to any of John Chakalos's financial records. Nathan also took umbrage with Small's claim that he had lost the Sig Sauer rifle.

"I've never claimed that," he shot back. "I never claimed that I had lost the weapon."

Nathan insisted that he had pleaded the Fifth regarding questions about the rifle because Connecticut had "harsh laws" relating to firearms.

"Those are totally unrelated to their homicide statute," he explained to the judge. "I drew a line when asked whether I purchased the weapon and chose to invoke my Fifth Amendment right."

The question now buzzing in the heads of many court observers was why Nathan was so concerned about Connecticut's gun restrictions, especially if he had not taken the Sig Sauer rifle over state lines from New Hampshire to murder his grandfather.

In the course of asking questions about the standard of proof regarding the shooting of his grandfather and the drowning of his mother, Nathan asked the court why both cases were getting tied together, and then he turned the tables and directly attempted to implicate the Chakalos sisters in the murder of their father.

"What the petitioners are trying to allege and what you may ultimately be asked to rule on is whether I murdered my grandfather. [His] death is an event that occurred in December 2013," Nathan told Judge King. "Petitioners are asking about modifications that I made to my boat in September 2016. Are we trying two murder cases here, or are we trying one? Even if you did conclude that I killed my mom, how would that relate as to whether I killed my grandfather years earlier? … Who did have motive to kill my grandfather? I'll say that some of the petitioners had an awfully substantial motive, and I had very, very little."

There it was in open court. Nathan was accusing members of his own family of murdering John Chakalos.

The next day, the headline in the *Boston Globe* screamed, "Slay Suspect Points at Aunts."

Small did not challenge Nathan's charges during the court hearing, but outside the courtroom, he expressed contempt. "It's completely outrageous," Small told reporters. "Nathan refused to take a lie detector. Everyone else in the family agreed. Nathan refused to cooperate with police. Everyone else in the family agreed. Nathan wants the blood money. The family does not."

CHAPTER TWENTY-FIVE

Nathan stepped up his verbal attack against the Chakalos sisters after another hearing before Judge King in Concord, New Hampshire, a month later. Standing under a flag pole outside the courthouse, the normally reticent accused killer told reporters that investigators had the right family but the wrong man in the murder of John Chakalos.

"At least two of my aunts had a strong economic motive to kill my grandfather. My aunt Valerie, for example, has told me several times that she is the person that profited most from his death," Nathan alleged. "The petitioners are the people who have accused me of a murder I didn't commit."

Judge King had called both sides back to court to express his frustration at the slow progress of discovery motions, and he was disappointed to learn that Nathan had still not hired an attorney to defend him in the slayer rule case. The attorney for the sisters was planning to depose Nathan, so the judge appointed a special referee to intervene if and when Nathan attempted to plead the Fifth. Judge King vowed to move this case along to trial within a year.

During the hearing, Nathan refuted any claims that he bought a Sig Sauer rifle. In a questionnaire pertaining to the lawsuit, he also stated that he did not benefit financially from his grandfather's murder and instead lost money, because John Chakalos had showered him with nearly unlimited amounts of cash and gifts during his lifetime. Nathan also asked Judge King to throw out the case, which the judge said he would take under advisement.

Afterward, in front of the courthouse, Nathan seemed disinterested in the minutiae of the hearing and instead spent several minutes railing against his family, accusing a cousin of turning to sex and drugs after their grandfather's death. He also delivered a softer message to Linda's sisters.

"I want my aunts to know that I don't hate them," he said while shaking visibly. "Part of me can sympathize with them and how difficult it has been to deal with my grandfather's death. I just wish they could see how difficult it is for me too."

When asked what his aunts thought of him, Nathan grew more angry.

"My aunts hate me," he said matter-of-factly. "And they hated me long before my grandfather died."

Nathan said that he was now relying on his deep faith, which he hoped would help him become the person who his grandfather wanted him to be.

Once again, the sisters pushed back against their nephew's allegations through their legal mouthpiece, attorney Dan Small, who continued to tow the family line with his rhetoric.

"The idea that any of them would do this just to get money is abhorrent," Small countered. "Unlike Nathan Carman, his aunts have taken lie detector tests, fully cooperated with the investigation into John Chakalos's murder, and promised to donate Linda Carman's inheritance to a charity in her name if they win the slayer action case."

A month later, Judge King announced that he would not dismiss the case and, instead, scheduled a 2019 trial date in New Hampshire, which he expected would take ten days. Nathan emailed reporters saying that he did not agree with the judge's decision but that he felt extremely confident as he continued to prepare for the trial.

I expect to prevail at trial this coming January, he wrote in an email. **I am at peace with myself because I know that the truth is on my side.**

Nathan's version of the truth was further called into question by Dan Small and his legal team when they uncovered an old Facebook account they believed had belonged to him. The account, which had been deleted, had a list of Nathan's favorite things, such as "equestrian" under the heading *sports* and "losing stuff" under the heading *favorite interests*. When prompted by Facebook to supply his favorite quote, Nathan reportedly wrote, **My fam is only alive cuz I allow it.**

The sisters' attorneys raised the Facebook post as a serious issue with Judge King. The problem was that Nathan did not write or speak in that manner, and the last name on the Facebook account was misspelled. The account reportedly belonged to Nathan Carmen, not Carman, and the user claimed to have lived in Atlanta, Georgia, not Vernon, Vermont. Still, the Chakalos sisters' attorneys wanted to know if Nathan had opened and then closed a dummy account on the social media site to express his supposed rage against his family. Dan Small would later file a motion to compel Nathan to confirm that the deleted social media account was indeed his own, with the argument that many Facebook users used pseudonyms and that the posting about horseback riding was consistent with Nathan's background. There was also a question regarding the Facebook user's favorite interests. Did the words "losing stuff" refer to what Nathan allegedly did with the Sig Sauer rifle after the murder of Nathan's grandfather?

Nathan never admitted to having created the Facebook account.

Nathan faced off against his aunt Valerie Santilli for the first time a few weeks later at the town hall in West Hartford, Connecticut, where he asked a judge for an emergency order to transfer $150,000 in a family trust directly to him. The trust, which was worth $270,000, had been opened in Nathan's name by his grandfather before he was killed, but the money was now controlled by his aunt Valerie. Nathan told a probate judge that he needed the small fortune to hire an attorney to fight his aunts in the slayer rule case. Nathan had not seen his aunt in more than two years. They did not speak to each other in court, but in his filings, Nathan accused Valerie of being extremely hostile toward him. She walked into the probate hearing, smartly dressed and flanked by her lawyer, her accountant, and her husband, Larry Santilli, while her nephew showed up alone, wearing a crumpled gray suit. A uniformed police officer stood nearby to deter any eruptions of violence between the two estranged relatives.

Valerie and Small did not believe that her nephew was flat broke, because he refused to share any of his financial information. Valerie had already approved giving him $25,000 so he could buy a truck and had allowed him to take $175,000 out of the trust to pay for his lawyer, Hubert Santos, whom he later fired.

"He's hiding assets and has plenty of money to hire a lawyer," Small told the judge. "He may even be a millionaire."

"You're a professional liar," Nathan shouted in response, his loud voice echoing through the town hall. "I need to hire an attorney to defend me in New Hampshire to ensure a just result. What am I supposed to do? I do not have the financial resources to hire an attorney."

Small, who had been fighting with Nathan for information pertaining to the slayer rule case, saw an opening. He offered Nathan "all the money he wants" in exchange for honest information about his own financial status.

"Nathan Carman has a long history of playing fast and loose with the truth," Small said in the hearing. "He has never answered the simple questions of 'what are his income and his assets?' It would be irresponsible of the trustee to squander the majority of the trust's assets without backup information."

The judge did not rule on the matter at the hearing, and Nathan left the town hall empty-handed and was chased into the parking lot by reporters tossing out a number of questions. He jumped into his truck and said that he was leaving for a long-overdue vacation at an "undisclosed location."

No one knew where Nathan was headed, but it certainly was not his mother's house in Middletown. The home was vacant now. The roommate she had been living with when she disappeared had moved out with his young daughter. Her friend Sharon Hartstein stopped by the address on Hendley Street occasionally to check on the house and do a little landscaping. There was concern that the property would fall into disrepair and become a prime target for looters and squatters, so Linda's court-appointed executor allowed one of her relatives, a local school teacher, to move in and keep an eye on the place. Nathan never visited his mother's home and instead kept to himself at his property in Vermont, where he had put up a "No Trespassing" sign along with a handwritten note to the media: *Please stay off my property, I will not grant any impromptu interviews.*

The sisters' legal team had yet to discover how much, if any, money Nathan had stored away, but they did finally learn new details about the Sig Sauer rifle believed to be at the center of their case. The information was a gift from attorneys who were battling Nathan in the insurance case in nearby Rhode Island. Private investigators working for the insurance companies were able to unearth details that Nathan had purchased the weapon in November 2013 at Shooters Outpost in Hooksett, New Hampshire. This information had not been disclosed by law enforcement to any attorneys. Lawyers for the insurance companies filed a motion in U.S. District Court in Rhode Island that included a statement that Nathan had paid cash for the Sig Sauer 716 rifle, one that used .308-caliber bullets, the same caliber used to kill John Chakalos. But investigators were unable to test the ballistics of Nathan's weapon because it had disappeared.

"How do you lose a gun like that?" attorney Dan Small asked a reporter covering the case. "How do you forget about it when the police ask you? But how do you lose it? Do you leave it at the Dunkin' Donuts or something? The story is nonsense and it is deeply disturbing."

Small was still neck-deep in depositions in the slayer rule case in New Hampshire. He needed to establish that John Chakalos was a resident in that state and not in Connecticut, or the case could be thrown out of New Hampshire court.

In his will, Chakalos had claimed that he was a resident of West Chesterfield, New Hampshire, although the document was drafted, executed, and notarized in Connecticut. The millionaire developer had also filed his estate in New Hampshire, which Nathan claimed he had done because he was "a savvy businessman who did not like paying taxes."

But Small's case was hindered by his own client, Valerie Santilli, who had told Windsor police after her father was murdered that he "never ate at home" and that on his last night alive, he "slept alone at home." If the word *home* referred to Chakalos's house on Overlook Drive in Windsor, Connecticut, and not the farm in New Hampshire, Small's case was sunk.

Small had tried coaching Valerie later for her deposition by Nathan's lawyer in the boat insurance case. When she was asked about her involvement in her father's business affairs at his home in Windsor, Connecticut, Small intervened quickly. "Object to the word 'home.' Home was in New Hampshire," he stated.

"Well, I worked in my father's office prior to his death," Valerie told Nathan's attorney David Anderson.

"Where do you consider your father's home to be?" he asked her.

"Oh, New Hampshire," she replied while Small looked on.

Valerie went on to say that her father slept at his *home* in West Chesterfield while his wife, Rita, was in the late stages of breast cancer and living in Windsor, Connecticut.

"Why did he sleep there while your mother was in hospice care?" Anderson asked. "I'm sorry to get into this."

"Do we have to get into personal family dynamics?" Valerie replied.

Judge David King later reviewed Valerie's police interview and her deposition in the insurance case in formulating his decision about whether the slayer rule petition in New Hampshire was valid.

Valerie's lawyer Dan Small also had to contend with information provided to police by William Rabbitt, who had worked for years as John Chakalos's financial adviser. Rabbitt claimed that Chakalos did not want to file taxes in Connecticut but that he had no choice.

"We didn't want John and Rita to live in Connecticut," Rabbitt said under oath. "We wanted them to be from New Hampshire [where they have to live six months and a day], and they were skirting it big time. It was gonna be a problem. We knew it was gonna be a problem. You have to live in New Hampshire, and if you own a house in Windsor, that looks bad, right? There was no hiding the fact that he lived in Connecticut. He lived in Connecticut."

Nathan returned to probate court in West Hartford a month later in September 2018, the two-year anniversary of his mother's death. This time, he spoke directly to his aunt Valerie Santilli, who was seated just a few feet away from him, in a heated exchange over the money that Nathan believed was rightfully his in the trust fund bearing his name.

"Do you believe that my mother is alive?" he asked his aunt.

"I don't know where she is," Valerie replied.

Nathan then discussed the fact that his aunt had already given him money from the trust to pay his previous lawyer, Hubert Santos, when he was first identified as a "person of interest" in the slaying of his grandfather.

"Did you believe I was guilty of the murder then?"

"Yes."

Nathan then turned to the judge. "She is trying to punish me for something which she thinks I did," he complained. "Which police haven't said I did and in fact that I didn't do!"

As Nathan tried to wrestle funds out of a family trust to pay for a new lawyer, David Anderson, his attorney in the boat insurance case, was ready to drop a bombshell. He told a judge in federal court in Rhode Island that he had evidence that would exonerate Nathan in the murder of his grandfather.

CHAPTER TWENTY-SIX

Attorney David Anderson believed there were major discrepancies in the Windsor Police Department's claims that Nathan was the last person to have any contact with John Chakalos on the night of the murder, and he also questioned their assertion that he had been gunned down in his bedroom at 3:00 a.m. on December 20, 2013.

Anderson told the judge that Chakalos had engaged in a lengthy phone conversation with a woman about money after Nathan left his grandfather's home in Windsor. He also said there was a witness who lived next door to Chakalos who swore that they heard a loud gunshot coming from 52 Overlook Drive at 2:00 a.m., a full hour before investigators claimed the man had been shot. Anderson told the judge that there was surveillance footage that showed that Nathan was in his apartment until 2:40 a.m. on the day of the shooting.

It was the first time anyone in court or out in the public had learned about the contradictory evidence in the high-profile case. Could this have been the reason why the criminal arrest warrant against Nathan Carman still remained unsigned?

Outside court, David Anderson declined further comment and instead allowed these stunning revelations to hang in the air. Reporters seized on the story, and for the first time, newspapers generated headlines that appeared to favor Nathan Carman. The *Record-Journal* in Meriden, Connecticut, ran an Associated Press story with the headline "Lawyer: Evidence Could Exonerate Man in Windsor Grandfather's Death."

A few weeks later, Anderson introduced Chakalos's twenty-five-year-old girlfriend, whom he dubbed "Mistress Y" in court filings, and suggested that there was strong evidence that she was involved in the murder of the millionaire developer. The news sent shock waves throughout New England and tore into the well-crafted image of John Chakalos as a beloved and benevolent family patriarch who had supported his community generously that had been presented to the media by his daughters.

Nathan's lawyer claimed that Mistress Y knew that Chakalos had a lot of money in his house and that she had spoken to him on the phone just hours before he was killed.

"Testimony from 'Mistress Y' is likely to establish facts from which one could reasonably conclude that Mr. Chakalos' lifestyle and activities prior to his death made him a target of robbery and/or murder by some unknown person(s)," Anderson wrote in his filing.

Anderson asked the judge for permission to depose the woman for the boat insurance case, despite her lack of any involvement in the sinking of the *Chicken Pox*. Her name had been redacted from Windsor police files to protect her identity as a possible witness in the criminal case. But court filings by Anderson went into great detail about Mistress Y and her tryst with Chakalos at the Mohegan Sun Casino just days before his murder.

"While they were at the casino, he gave her $3,500, which she felt he was assisting her for paying for the [breast enhancement] surgery and she showed him her boobs," the Windsor police report stated. "The two made out, but she did not have sex with him."

The report also confirmed that Chakalos had visited the Hartford sex shop Luv Boutique on the day of his murder.

BLOOD IN THE WATER · 181

Anderson hinted that Mistress Y had motive and opportunity to kill her "sugar daddy" because she was aware that Chakalos carried around large wads of cash and that when Nathan left his grandfather after dinner, Chakalos would be alone at his home on Overlook Drive for the rest of the evening.

Although Nathan and his lawyer had raised legitimate questions about Mistress Y, the attorney for the Chakalos sisters accused him of trying to smear their father's reputation, ruin his legacy, and deflect attention away from missing evidence that was key to the case.

"Nathan's shameful attack on his grandfather shows there is no depth to which he will not sink to avoid producing his gun, which is the probable murder weapon. Now he is trying to cast blame on his own aunt, even though she willingly took and passed a police lie detector test...while Nathan lied repeatedly, including about this very gun," Dan Small said. "Every day that passes in these legal proceedings shows even more clearly that Nathan's behavior is calculated, evasive, and ultimately, guilty."

Small and his team of lawyers mobilized quickly. Since they had been left out of the boat insurance case, they tried to compel the judge in the slayer rule case to seal twenty-two thousand pages of investigative records, especially those pertaining to Mistress Y. Attorneys for the sisters claimed that Nathan had violated a protective order when he allowed his lawyer to reveal that Chakalos had spoken to his mistress on the telephone on the night of his death. But Nathan objected to the idea that records that could possibly exonerate him both in court and in the public's eye be kept confidential. His lawyer David Anderson said the records were fair game. A First Amendment rights group urged the judge to unseal the documents.

"Courts are presumptively open," argued attorney Justin Silverman from a group called the New England First Amendment Coalition. "We don't live in a country where there are secret trials. This is a probate court we're dealing with. Generally speaking, we don't operate within secrecy in courts."

Nathan's lawyer also asked to depose a witness he called "Neighbor X" who had written to police, "On 12/20/13 at about 0200 hours, I was home and in my Mom's bedroom; located in the northeast corner of our house. I heard a loud bang coming from the direction of my neighbor's house located at 52 Overlook Drive. My Dog [sic] began barking at about the same time, which I thought was unusual for the hour. At about 0300 hours, I was laying in my Mom's bed and heard traffic out in front of our house. I heard multiple cars driving by. I heard one of the cars either brake or turn hard and it made a squealing noise."

Anderson also raised serious questions about the ballistics report in the Chakalos murder. He pointed to the state police crime lab report, which he claimed "doesn't indicate that the murder weapon was a .308 firearm or that the gun everyone wants to keep asking questions about could have been the murder weapon."

The 2014 report, written by Connecticut State Police forensics experts, stated that at least one bullet fired from the murder weapon was a hollow-point bullet, while at least two other bullet fragments came from a ".30 caliber class boattail jacketed bullet." They went on to write, "if any .30 class firearms are developed in this case they should be submitted to the laboratory."

A Sig Sauer rifle like the one Nathan owned fires either .308-caliber bullets or a 7.62 mm cartridge.

"Nowhere in the CT State Police Forensic Lab Report is there any mention whatsoever of a .308 caliber bullet and/or 7.62 mm bullets," Anderson concluded in his court filing.

There were several other rifles that used .30-caliber class boattail jacketed bullets, including the 300 Winchester Magnum and the 300 Remington Ultra Magnum. Nowhere in the 2014 state police crime lab report was there a direct reference to a Sig Sauer rifle, only the caliber of bullets that were used to kill John Chakalos. Anderson claimed that several different firearms could have been used in the murder.

The Chakalos sisters' lawyer promised to produce a weapons expert who would testify conclusively that the bullets used to kill John Chakalos could only have come from Nathan's missing Sig Sauer rifle. Dan Small also chastised Nathan and his lawyer for making the ballistics report public, suggesting that they violated a court order.

Judge David King refused to sanction Nathan for releasing the confidential records. In a thirty-seven-page response to the sisters' lawyers, Judge King ruled that their pleadings were without merit. The judge also chastised attorney Dan Small for his own attempt to release Nathan's medical records. Judge King called the move "uncivilized, bordering on unethical conduct."

Judge King announced that he had scheduled the ten-day civil trial for January 21, 2019, and told Nathan that he would have a month to disclose whether he would present any expert witnesses in the case. Nathan was still representing himself in the case after having fired Hubert Santos.

"I did that [fired Santos] with my eyes wide open," he said. "I hoped to hire another attorney, but I knew that it might be difficult."

Judge King also asked the sisters' lawyers if they planned to produce any evidence that Linda Carman was indeed dead. In Connecticut, where Linda was living at the time of her disappearance, a person cannot be legally declared dead until they have been missing for seven years.

"We are going to move forward and offer proof that we believe will lead you to conclude that Linda Carman is deceased," said attorney Robert Satterly.

Criminal investigators, including Eric Gempp, kept a close eye on both the slayer rule case in New Hampshire and the civil case in Rhode Island, hoping that any new evidence against Nathan presented in either one could help them in their effort to finally put him behind bars.

Chapter Twenty-Seven

Since Nathan had still not produced his Sig Sauer rifle, speculation continued to grow about its whereabouts. Attorneys for the insurance companies were convinced that he had ditched the so-called murder weapon after he killed his grandfather. In a court filing in Rhode Island, lawyers for the insurance companies claimed that Carman and "the Sig Sauer [rifle] were criminally involved in his grandfather's murder... The Sig Sauer was capable of firing the same caliber rounds that killed his grandfather, and Nathan Carman was the last known person to see him alive. In the morning, Nathan Carman went fishing on a boat headed out of Point Judith, Rhode Island, jettisoning his Sig Sauer, which now lies at the bottom of the sea."

The insurance companies' attorneys offered no definitive proof that the murder weapon was in fact a Sig Sauer rifle or that Nathan had tossed the weapon into the cold waters off Rhode Island. Instead, they claimed that he had executed a common theme with "striking, chilling parallel losses of evidence, omissions, concealments, misrepresentations, false testimony and fraud to procure a substantial inheritance by causing first his grandfather's murder and second his mother's death at sea."

But Nathan's supporters, most importantly his father, argued that lawyers for the insurance companies and those representing the Chakalos sisters lacked basic logic.

"Nathan had been given everything he had ever wanted by his grandfather, whom he probably loved even more than me," Clark Carman said. "Since he was born, [Nathan] was the favorite son. John [Chakalos] was eighty-seven years old and only had a few years left to live. Does it make any sense that Nathan would want to kill him when he stood to inherit the money naturally?"

Attorney Anderson blasted the opposing lawyers for floating the trial balloon that Nathan had sent his rifle to "the bottom of the sea" without offering any supporting evidence and accused them of using their "unlimited resources to string this case out and thereby wear down the Defendant and his counsel." Anderson also argued that the insurance case was now two years old, and neither side had even completed the first phase of discovery.

As Nathan prepared for the January trial date against his aunts in New Hampshire, the Chakalos sisters made a surprise move of their own to fire their attorney Dan Small and the rest of his legal team. The shocking announcement came during a routine hearing to clear up any outstanding motions before the trial. At the hearing, Small, who had represented the sisters for two years and had acted as the tip of their legal spear, sat with spectators in the small courtroom. This time, it was Elaine Chakalos who attended the hearing with her probate attorney, Robert Satterly, who had acted as Small's co-counsel in the slayer rule case.

Satterly told Judge King that they were stunned by his "devastating and critical review of their counsel" and that they were "displeased by the judge's loss of confidence in their trial counsel." In his lengthy ruling the month before, Judge King had accused Dan Small of trying to take advantage of Nathan's pro se status (representing himself) and his lack of legal training. Satterly asked for a ninety-day continuance to replace Dan Small's law firm, Holland & Knight.

Nathan objected to any delay in the trial. If he could represent himself, so could his aunts represent themselves in court.

"This has taken up the last five years of my life," Nathan told Judge King. "If I have to go to trial naked so to speak, I'd rather do it myself than hire someone who can just talk fancy. I don't care anymore. My reputation's been shot and it is never going to be recovered."

Despite Nathan's emotional plea, Judge King had no choice but to agree to a continuance of the trial, which he believed could help Nathan.

"My strong inclination is to postpone the trial, and quite frankly, you have the most to gain from that, Mr. Carman," Judge King told him during the hearing. "You need a lawyer in this case and now that you are able to get one I would strongly recommend that you do so."

Judge King's comments reflected the recent news that a West Hartford probate judge was set to rule in Nathan's favor and allow that at least $125,000 be taken out of his trust fund and allocated to him so that he could hire an attorney in New Hampshire. An additional $25,000 would be granted so that Nathan could hire expert witnesses for the civil trial.

The West Hartford judge would also later agree to allow Nathan to use the trust to pay off his credit card debts. Nathan had been living off credit cards and owed $30,000 dollars in unpaid bills.

The slayer rule trial was rescheduled for June 10, 2019, and it was expected to take three to four weeks. Nathan spent money on a new lawyer, Cathy Green, and a team of attorneys based out of a law office in Concord, New Hampshire. Green was a veteran attorney who had started her career as a public defender in the late 1970s. The sisters hired a new lawyer as well, Michael Connolly, from the Boston-based firm Hinckley Allen.

Both sides deposed Mistress Y and learned all the sordid details about her affair with John Chakalos and the illicit excitement he felt when she used sex toys on herself while he watched.

Nathan's new lawyers proved to be a worthy investment for him. In

April 2019, one of his attorneys presented evidence to Judge King in the hope of getting the case tossed out in New Hampshire. Attorney James Rosenberg supplied the court with sticky notes that Chakalos had kept on his desk in Windsor, Connecticut, and several years of credit card bills that were sent to the dead man's primary residence there. Judge King had earlier rejected the argument that Chakalos was a resident of Connecticut, but this new evidence was something that he had to consider.

"The records show that Mr. Chakalos spent nearly every day in Connecticut, regularly eating meals there, but rarely doing so in New Hampshire," Nathan's attorneys argued.

A few weeks later, on May 9, 2019, Judge David King announced that he would not bring the case to trial, and instead, he dismissed the sisters' slayer rule petition outright. The decision marked a major legal victory for Nathan Carman against his family and paved the way for him to inherit millions of dollars from his grandfather's estate. Most important to Nathan, the decision meant that he would not be declared a cold-blooded killer by the judge.

"The court determines that John Chakalos, although by birth originally a domiciliary of New Hampshire, established a domicile in Connecticut and never re-established one in this state," Judge King wrote in his forty-one-page decision.

King wrote that the millionaire developer had never intended to live outside the state of Connecticut. He also roundly criticized Valerie's former attorney Dan Small for "clearly coaching" her in a deposition. The ruling cited the deposition of Dr. Gheorghita Zugravu, a priest at St. George Greek Orthodox Cathedral in Hartford who claimed to be Chakalos's spiritual advisor. The priest stated that while Chakalos did not attend services, he kept a Bible at his home in Windsor and prayed "every morning and every night."

The judge also gave weight to obituaries for John and Rita Chakalos that read that they were from Windsor, Connecticut, along with Nathan's own statements that he and his grandfather would take day trips from Chakalos's "home in Windsor to New Hampshire."

Upon hearing Judge King's ruling, Nathan released a statement through one of his attorneys.

"I want to be clear that the underlying allegations in my aunts' dismissed petition that I murdered my grandpa and/or mom, are as false and meritless as my aunts' position on my grandfather's residence has been shown to be… In all my statements in court and under oath, I told the whole truth."

The Chakalos sisters strongly disagreed with Judge King's decision and were considering filing further actions in both New Hampshire and Connecticut.

"John immersed himself in New Hampshire where all of his adult and childhood friends live and where he constantly gave back to the community," the sisters said in a statement. "He especially felt a part of Keene, where he was from, and Chesterfield, where he built the home of his dreams, voted, and had many joy-filled occasions with family and friends."

Asked whether Nathan would take a victory lap and relish in the defeat of his aunts Valerie, Eileen, and Charlene, his attorney James Rosenberg said no. "There is no celebrating, because Nathan lost the two people in the world closest to him. His pain continues."

Nathan had won a bitter and drawn-out legal battle with his aunts over his inheritance, but he still faced a civil trial in Rhode Island in the case involving his $85,000 insurance claim for the sinking of his boat, the *Chicken Pox*. He had little time to savor his victory in the slayer rule case as a federal judge ordered the insurance case trial for late August.

CHAPTER TWENTY-EIGHT

In the weeks leading up to the civil trial, lawyers for the insurance companies filed a fifty-eight-page document with the court that contained a deposition from a Rhode Island lobsterman who poured cold water on Nathan's claim that his boat had sunk in Block Canyon in late September 2016.

Alex Aucoin captained an eighty-two-foot offshore lobster boat called the *Prudence*. Aucoin told insurance investigators that he was fishing that day in a spot just a few miles from where Nathan said his boat was and that he did not see any sign of a sinking boat or a life raft. According to insurance investigators, the automatic identification system on Aucoin's lobster boat placed it in Block Canyon "on the very day Carman claims to have sunk there and…confirms *Prudence* was within a few miles from where Carman says he was trolling [for tuna]. Aucoin did not see a boat or a life raft that day in Block Canyon."

The insurance companies' attorneys also included quotes from a Woods Hole oceanographer named Richard Limeburner, who said that his data contradicted Nathan's story of his seven-day drift at sea. Limeburner was in the middle of writing a sixty-three-page analysis of the drift path of Nathan's fishing boat. He collected data from the paths of two satellite-tracked surface-drifting buoys that had passed near Block Canyon during September

2016 and used collaborating information gathered from satellite sea surface temperature and OSCAR-derived ocean currents. OSCAR is an acronym for ocean surface current analysis real-time.

"It is my opinion, to a reasonable degree of certainty as a physical ocean-ographer, that assuming the *Chicken Pox* sank on September 18, 2016, the reverse drift analysis in this report indicates the *Chicken Pox* sank approximately 39 nautical miles east by south (102° True) from where the life raft was found adrift on September 25, 2018 by the *ORIENT LUCKY* and not at Block Canyon 42 nm northwest of the *ORIENT LUCKY* position," Limeburner wrote in his report.

During his deposition, Nathan had placed an X in Block Canyon at the break in the continental shelf where the ocean depths went from a relatively shallow 100 fathoms to a much deeper slope of 140 fathoms and said, "The boat sank when we started trolling north."

"The difference between the reported Block Canyon drift track and the known *ORIENT LUCKY* end position reverse drift track is 78 nm (nautical miles)," Limeburner explained. "This 78 nm difference is too large an error for the 7-day drift estimates in this report and this fact provides evidence in my opinion that the reported Block Canyon sinking location is not consistent with the known evidence and is suspect."

The Woods Hole oceanographer stated that if Nathan's story was true, he would have been drifting in the opposite direction from where he was found by the crew of the *Orient Lucky*.

Nathan's lawyer feared that Captain Aucoin's testimony and Limeburner's analysis could have a devastating impact on their case in the insurance trial.

"If I were Nathan and I didn't want to be found and the boat didn't really sink, I could have avoided Coast Guard searchers," retired Coast Guard captain W. Russell Webster explained further. "He could have hustled up close to the shoreline, or I'd head north somewhere off Cape Cod. I'd putter around for a while, because the Coast Guard didn't look there."

Attorney David Anderson did catch a break when the judge ruled that no evidence could be admitted at trial regarding the 2013 murder of Nathan's grandfather. The federal judge ordered that evidence should only focus on the exact language of Nathan's insurance policies with the National Liability & Fire Insurance Company and the Boat Owners Association of the United States and the reasons the *Chicken Pox* actually sank.

"Because the issues of Mr. Carman's alleged intentional acts have been severed from this trial, there is no need for any introduction of any evidence at this time about the death of his grandfather, or questions whether Mr. Carman intentionally caused the death of his mother," Judge John J. McConnell wrote.

Lawyers for the insurance companies had spent hundreds of hours developing their case, which would be highlighted by Nathan's alleged murder of his grandfather and the plot to kill his mother. They had planned to call Nathan's aunts as witnesses, along with investigators from the Windsor Police Department. But the judge had now taken the wind out of their sails. The judge's decision also came as a blow to Nathan's attorney David Anderson, who was prepared to call Mistress Y and Neighbor X to the witness stand in federal court.

Judge McConnell also set strict guidelines for the trial. Both sides were limited to fifteen hours of opening statements and closing arguments, direct and cross-examination, and objections. The judge promised to keep a chess clock on his bench to keep track of time.

The trial got underway on August 14, 2019. Nathan, dressed in a new gray suit and tie and sporting a fresh haircut, climbed the steps of U.S. District Court in Providence with his attorney David Anderson. Nathan stared straight ahead and avoided the questions getting thrown his way by reporters.

"How long were you in the life raft?" one reporter shouted. "They're saying it wasn't seven days."

Nathan did not respond. He held open the door of the courthouse for his lawyer, who lugged in several plastic bins filled with documents and evidence. They entered the courtroom and waited for the judge to open the proceedings. There would be no jury to hear the evidence. Judge McConnell would make his ruling from the bench.

During his opening statement, the attorney for the insurance companies said that it was unsurprising that the *Chicken Pox* sank to the bottom of the ocean after Nathan's dangerous alterations.

"He left Point Judith with holes in his boat and 12 hours later, it sank," attorney David Farrell told the court. He pointed out that Nathan had used an epoxy to fill holes that he made in his boat despite directions on the epoxy's label that warned against using it to fill holes. "The evidence will show the boat Mr. Carman bought was in great shape. It was seaworthy," Farrell added. "[But] when you add up all the ill-advised changes Carman made to his boat, it was perfectly predictable that it sank the next day."

Farrell promised to call several witnesses who would blow Nathan's story out of the water, including an expert who would testify that there was "little chance" that Nathan would not have suffered hypothermia if he had been drifting in a raft for a week before his rescue and a doctor from Massachusetts General Hospital who would testify that based on photographs of the young man taken by crew members of the *Orient Lucky*, Nathan looked surprisingly healthy and therefore must have been in the life raft for significantly less time than the seven days he had claimed.

Farrell showed photographs of Nathan inside the life raft and questioned how Nathan could look and act so strong after surviving on minimal food and water for so long.

"He would in no way be able to stand up on the life raft like he did here and wave a flag," the attorney for the plaintiffs argued.

During his opening statements, Farrell made no mention of Linda

Carman and what may have happened to her. Nathan listened intently to the plaintiffs' attorney and took several notes during his oratory.

When it came time for Nathan's attorney to address the judge in his opening statement, David Anderson tried to shoot down Farrell's theories and pointed out the fact that Nathan was not sure exactly where his boat sank as he did not have a fixed compass.

"Block Canyon doesn't have a clear boundary," Anderson argued. "It's not like the city limits of Providence [Rhode Island]. There are a lot of things that could have caused this vessel to sink and we're not here to prove what did [as that is the plaintiff's job]."

Anderson did attempt to lay some of the blame on Brian Woods, the previous owner of the vessel.

"There were real problems with the *Chicken Pox*. It looked pretty good on the surface, but underneath, it wasn't really a great boat," Anderson claimed. "That's not something Mr. Carman knew. That's not something the insurance companies knew, but it's a fact. He [Woods] couldn't sell the boat until Nathan came along, who had more money than experience, and he saw an opportunity to take advantage of him."

Woods was the first witness called to testify in the trial.

"He [Nathan] wouldn't look at me in the courtroom," Woods recalled. "He never made eye contact with me, as much as I tried."

Woods said he was shocked by Nathan's appearance and his actual age.

"He had to say his name and the age he was, nineteen, when this all started, and I almost fell out of my chair. I thought he was much older than he really was," Woods said. "He also looked like he'd gone through a car wash. He was much cleaner compared to when I last saw him. He looked like two different people."

Woods testified that he was deeply concerned that Nathan was alone when he showed up to pick up his boat in December 2015. "I didn't think it was very prudent that he take the boat from Plymouth to Point Judith by himself."

Woods also described his shock when he traveled to Rhode Island later to retrieve his license plates and found the *Chicken Pox* in complete disarray. The fishing boat was a big mess, and Nathan had removed a $1,200 compass from the center console. "I was concerned about his lack of respect for the ocean," Woods told the judge.

During cross-examination, Nathan's attorney questioned Woods about how he had installed the trim tabs on the boat, which Nathan later removed.

"I remember installing the trim tabs, but the exact fittings I used and how I installed them, I can't recall," Woods admitted. "I have a very good memory, so I'm stumped [as to] why I can't remember how I installed the trim tabs."

Coast Guard investigator Eric Gempp and his partner from the FBI, Special Agent Lisa Tutty, attended the trial each day, looking for more evidence that they could potentially use in a criminal case against Nathan. After working the case for more than two years, both Gempp and Tutty were now convinced that Nathan had killed his mother. The criminal investigators had spent much of their time focused on Nathan's purchasing timeline in early to mid-September 2016.

"He was purchasing repair items from a number of different marine stores," Gempp contended. "That was standing out to me as being unusual. Why wasn't he getting all of his stuff in one place? Or opening an account at one store and maximizing your purchases? We never got the answers to those questions."

Gempp also learned that Nathan had bought a bucket of live eels to use as bait for tuna fishing but that he had left the bait in the back of his pickup truck and never brought it aboard the *Chicken Pox* for the fishing trip.

Special Agent Tutty, who was assigned to the FBI's New Haven, Connecticut, office, had searched Nathan's Vermont home and found it suspicious that he had thrown out his computer just before the fishing trip with his mother. Tutty did find his cell phone. It was not a smartphone, just a rudimentary device that could only send or receive text messages. Tutty said that FBI behavioral analysts had worked up a psychological profile of Nathan Carman but admitted that agents never consulted with any outside psychologists to gain a better understanding of Nathan's autism spectrum disorder and how it may have impacted his decision-making. Tutty said that Nathan's diagnosis was not a major factor for criminal investigators.

"It informed the investigation, but it ultimately did not really influence the investigative steps that were taken," Tutty explained. "You can look at someone's behavior and their verbals and their nonverbals, but in a court of law and in terms of proving the case, we had to follow the evidence. He wasn't misunderstood because he had Asperger's. Everything we had in this case was driven by the evidence."

Tutty also believed that Nathan was grappling with other mental health issues at the time.

"Based on documents I read and witnesses I talked to, I believe that he was an undiagnosed schizophrenic," Tutty claimed. "He was in a very difficult place mentally. I think he was [also] having religious delusions."

Tutty and Gempp said they had no contact with attorney David Farrell prior to or during the civil trial because they did not want to give the impression that the U.S. Coast Guard and the FBI were colluding with the insurance companies. "They had their reason for doing what they were doing, and we had our reason for doing what we were doing," Gempp explained.

Still, Gempp and Tutty recognized the value of monitoring every moment of the civil trial from inside the courtroom.

"We didn't know what the testimony was going to be, but we knew that each side had experts, and there was going to be this proceeding that may have been helpful to our case," Gempp said.

On day two of the civil trial, Farrell called Bernard Feeney to the stand as an expert witness. It was Feeney who had originally inspected the *Chicken Pox* for Nathan before he decided to buy it.

"It was in good, serviceable condition, and that means pretty much turnkey. The boat was seaworthy when he bought it, but not seaworthy after. It was going to be in peril sometime," Feeney told the judge. "[Nathan] put four holes in the boat an inch or two above the water line. The boat was taking on water the whole time it was in the ocean and he never checked the bilge pump."

Feeney also testified that Nathan had damaged the boat's structural integrity by removing two bulkheads to create more room to store his fishing rods.

Under cross-examination, Nathan's lawyer got Feeney to admit that the *Chicken Pox* was an old boat that had been in the water for forty years and modified several times, first as a lobster boat and then turned into a racer before ultimately being transformed into a fishing boat. But the expert witness insisted that the trim tabs should have been repaired by a professional, not removed by an amateur.

Judge McConnell stepped in and asked the witness point-blank whether he believed that Nathan's work on the boat led to its sinking.

"The holes in the boat and the poor repair made it unseaworthy," Feeney replied.

The plaintiffs' attorney also called a boat designer to the witness stand to refute Nathan's claim that his boat dropped out from under his feet.

"I don't see any way this boat could rapidly sink short of striking a huge object in the ocean or a rogue wave going over the top of it," naval architect Eric Greene told the court.

Woods Hole oceanographer Richard Limeburner also testified, referring to his reverse drift analysis of the case.

"I don't see how a drifting life raft can drift upstream or drift upwind,"

Limeburner told Judge McConnell. "In my opinion, where Mr. Carman was found conflicts with my estimation of his drift plan."

During the first two days of the civil trial, plaintiffs' attorney David Farrell presented a number of credible witnesses who testified against Nathan. The cards were now stacked against the defendant, and his lawyer had to come up with a plan to gain the judge's empathy for his client.

CHAPTER TWENTY-NINE

Nathan's lawyer introduced his client's developmental disability into the trial when it came time for a boat insurance adjuster to testify as to when he made the insurance claim. Although Nathan had filed the claim within weeks of the sinking, the insurance adjuster delayed calling him to allow him time to grieve over the disappearance of his mother, Linda. The adjuster also hoped that she would get the opportunity to inspect the boat.

"Mr. Carman did say that it was not likely to be recovered because it was so far offshore," insurance adjuster Martha Charlesworth testified. "I just wanted to make clear that there was a potential issue with the claim."

At the time, she told Nathan that investigators would be looking into the reported sinking, somewhere in the vicinity of Block Canyon. Charlesworth explained to the judge that the insurance policy language allowed for cancellation if the risk of the boat's sinking was increased by faulty repairs.

Attorney David Anderson pressed Charlesworth about whether she had asked Nathan to provide documentation about all the repairs done to the vessel.

"He has Asperger's. He can't read your mind. If you need documents, you need to ask him specifically," Nathan's lawyer told her.

"I did," Charlesworth replied.

According to Anderson, Nathan tinkered with his fishing boat the same way that he had attempted to remodel his Vermont house, by pulling pieces apart and trying to put them back together again. Nathan thought he could do it, just as he had originally thought he could act as his own lawyer in the New Hampshire case without any formal legal training. At the crux of this trial was the idea of intent. Did he alter the vessel in a diabolical plot to kill his mother for her inheritance? It was time for Nathan to take the witness stand and try to convince the judge otherwise.

Attorney David Farrell felt like he had his hands tied behind his back as he developed his line of questioning for the trial's star witness. He was under strict orders from Judge McConnell to narrow his queries to the repairs that Nathan made to the *Chicken Pox*. McConnell was treating this like any other insurance case, but the reality was far from it. To the plaintiffs' attorney, this case was about deceit and murder.

Nathan took the witness stand on Thursday, August 22, 2019, in U.S. District Court in Providence. Dressed in a gray suit, white shirt, and striped tie, he sat uncomfortably as Farrell paced back and forth in front of the witness stand.

The plaintiffs' attorney began his line of questioning focused on the dangerous alterations Nathan had made to the boat.

Nathan admitted that he had removed trim tabs from the stern of the *Chicken Pox*. Farrell told the court that the removal of the trim tabs left four holes in the back of the boat, each about the size of a silver dollar, which Nathan later filled with an epoxy. Nathan disagreed with Farrell about the size of the holes, which he claimed were smaller, more like the shape of a quarter, and how he made them.

"I know for a fact the seals of putty I made were bigger than the holes," Nathan told the judge. "I did not bore a hole in my boat, period!"

Instead, he claimed that he may have used a saw or a drill bit to roughen the edges of the holes left when he removed the trim tabs.

When asked by Farrell why he removed the trim tabs, Nathan told him that they were making the boat drag.

"Removing the trim tabs was something I planned to do," Nathan explained. "It was a way to fill my free day."

Farrell then asked him to recount the moments before the fishing boat went down, presumably in Block Canyon. Nathan recounted the tale, as he had done numerous times before. He told the court that he had heard a funny noise coming from the engine compartment.

Farrell found it suspicious that Nathan had replaced the bilge pump just days before the fishing trip and accused him of not testing it before he left Ram Point Marina.

"You admit the pumps weren't working when the boat took on water?"

"I don't know if the pumps were pumping water at their full rate of capacity," Nathan replied. "Which means to me they were keeping the bilge dry, which clearly they were not."

Once Nathan heard noises coming from the bilge, he said that he rushed over to investigate, lifted the hatch, and saw water filling the boat just below the deck. Nathan said that he then asked his mother, Linda, to reel in the fishing lines while he collected their safety gear. She never asked him what was wrong. Nathan said that he viewed her as "kind of a problem" when the boat took on water. "I thought of my mom more like a passenger," he testified, stating that despite all their fishing trips together, she did not know her way around boats.

"At that point, the boat just dropped out," he testified.

Nathan said he never saw or heard his mother. He said that he plunged into the cold water holding a bag filled with safety gear.

"I did not hear her scream," he said unemotionally. "I don't think there would have been time to compose a sentence. I know when I got to the life raft, I was yelling out: 'Mom, Mom, Mom,' making sure to pause so if she was yelling out, I'd be able to hear her."

The insurance companies' lawyer did not believe a word of it. Farrell thought Nathan was telling a "fish story," a deadly one, and it was his job to bring the truth to the surface.

"Is the reason you didn't say anything to your mother [when the boat was sinking], is that because she couldn't talk, or she couldn't hear you? Was your mother even on board?" Farrell instigated.

Nathan straightened his body in the witness chair.

"I told you yes, she was on board," he replied emphatically. "And I asked her to reel in the lines."

"Is the reason your mother didn't say anything because she couldn't talk?"

The implication from Farrell was that Nathan had silenced her by killing her and tossing her body into the sea.

"I believe she could talk," Nathan mumbled.

"You didn't hand her a life jacket?" Farrell asked in an accusatory tone.

"Nor did I put one on myself," Nathan countered.

Farrell then asked Nathan why he did not activate the boat's emergency beacon, which would have notified the Coast Guard of his situation and identified his location.

"I actually have a strong aversion to pressing a button that is going to result in a helicopter coming out," he replied.

Nathan told the court that despite all the water filling the boat, he still thought he could fix the problem and get himself and his mother back to shore.

When he climbed aboard the life raft, Nathan claimed that he had filled it with enough food to last for at least two weeks, along with a dry bag of dry clothes. "I was cold, but not hypothermic."

He told the court that he had made the preparations after reading Nathaniel Philbrick's award-winning book *In the Heart of the Sea*, which recounted the true story that had inspired Herman Melville's classic novel

Moby Dick, in which a giant sperm whale rammed and sank the Nantucket-based whaleship *Essex* in 1820, leaving crew members adrift in the southern Pacific Ocean for ninety days, fighting for their lives.

Nathan told Judge McConnell that he remained standing on the life raft, looking for his mother and trying to spot floating coolers or an oil slick that may help him determine exactly where his mother might be. He testified that he thought Linda might have hit her head or been dragged underwater by their fishing equipment.

Judge McConnell then asked Nathan if he dove into the ocean to search for her.

"No, I didn't," he replied. Nathan claimed that his perch on board the life raft gave him the best view of the area in case his mother emerged from the ocean. He said that he continued to call her name into the night but only heard the sounds of the sea: waves lapping against his life raft, an occasional seabird, and blowing winds.

Under direct examination, the name John Chakalos was only mentioned one time when Farrell questioned Nathan about his limited work experience, slightly implying that he was dependent on the financial windfall he would receive from his mother's estate.

"He gave me the title of senior project manager," Nathan said proudly. "He wanted to call me VP, but I didn't think it was appropriate. The whole job was best described as an internship."

When later questioned by his own attorney, David Anderson, Nathan said that he wrote a message on his survival bag indicating the date and location of where his boat had sunk in Block Canyon. He said that he also kept a tally of his seven days drifting at sea.

Anderson then asked him why he chose to go out that far on the fishing expedition.

"I don't think I did anything wrong," Nathan replied. "I wanted her to go to the canyons with me. I know if I asked her, she would go."

Leaving federal court after his testimony, an exhausted Nathan was flanked by his attorney, who ran interference for him as media microphones were jammed into his face.

"He's not going to have any comments whatsoever while he's on the stand," Anderson barked at reporters. "I don't even think you're allowed to do that so it's going to be no comment whatsoever, okay?"

While Nathan and his lawyer kept mum, public reaction to Nathan's testimony was filled with vitriol toward the young defendant. Comments in the *Boston Globe* skewered Nathan.

This is one creepy dude. I wouldn't leave the dock with him at the helm, one commenter wrote, while another added, **There is no doubt in my mind that this kid killed his mother.**

Other commentators called him a **psychopath**, a **sociopath**, and **toxic**.

Of the forty-seven comments that accompanied the *Boston Globe* article about his testimony, Nathan had only a single defender, one who raised the issue of his autism diagnosis.

Nathan is on the spectrum, the commentator wrote. **It wasn't fair to be peppering him with pointed questions.**

Another reader took offense to the post and fired back their own retort.

Yeah, it wasn't fair for his mother or grandfather for him to kill them either, replied someone writing under the name some.nerd. **But they can't argue those points themselves, can they?**

The battle lines had been drawn in the court of public opinion, and most trial observers had now aligned themselves against Nathan Carman. But it would be the judge who would have the final say in this trial.

CHAPTER THIRTY

Judge John McConnell set closing arguments for early September 2019, nearly three full years after the *Chicken Pox* went down, presumably killing Nathan's mother, fifty-four-year-old Linda Carman.

The federal court judge kept a close eye on the fifteen hours that he had allotted for the civil trial and allowed both sides in the case just two more hours in total to convince him whether Nathan deliberately sank his boat back in 2016.

The plaintiffs' attorney addressed the court first, painting Nathan as a con artist and imploring Judge McConnell to "look at Mr. Carman's deep-rooted credibility problems, I'll say, lies."

Attorney David Farrell then pointed to Nathan's claim that he never heard a sound from his mother when the boat went down.

"Not one word or even scream from his ever-vigilant mother about what's going on?" Farrell asked. "We're now one hundred miles at sea in stunning silence. How can that be unless she's in a coma, already dead, or not on board?"

Farrell spoke for a total of thirty minutes. The plaintiffs' attorney placed much of the focus of his closing argument on Nathan's bizarre alterations to the *Chicken Pox*.

"The fact is he had holes in his boat, and he shoddily repaired it," Farrell told the court. "You don't run a boat with half-inch holes a hundred miles out to sea. No one can verify his scenario of how the boat sank."

He then pointed out that Nathan had not offered his mother a life jacket and that he walked by the boat's radio and emergency beacon three times without turning them on.

"He was looking out for his own skin," Farrell said. "And gets into the raft with his thirty days [of] supplies and never looks for her."

Although Farrell was ordered by the judge not to present evidence that Nathan may have murdered his mother, the sinister tone of his closing argument was implied.

Nathan sat motionless at the defense table, wearing the same suit he had worn during the duration of the trial.

It was now time for his lawyer, David Anderson, to address the court.

"This gentleman has been telling the truth from day one in this case," he said, pointing at Nathan.

"Something catastrophic happened on that boat. What it was, we'll never know."

Anderson then tried to blame the sinking of the *Chicken Pox* on its previous owner, Brian Woods.

"This thing was never designed to be a boat," he argued. "We know it was water-logged. I suggest to you that the hull was not sound. It never was."

Anderson pointed over at his client once again. "Mr. Carman would never go out there with his mom in the middle of nowhere if he felt the boat was going to sink. Something let go in that boat."

Regarding claims that Nathan drilled holes in his boat, witnessed by Michael Iozzi at Ram Point Marina, Anderson said that Iozzi was an honest witness who merely misinterpreted what he saw.

"He saw [Nathan] bend over the side of the boat and heard the drill and put it together that Nathan had used it to drill holes, but he never saw

206 · CASEY SHERMAN

him actually drill any holes," Nathan's lawyer contended. "What he saw was different from the conclusions that he drew."

During his testimony, Nathan said he had used either a saw or a drill bit to rough out the holes left when he removed the trim tabs but did not drill the holes himself.

Anderson then attempted to explain away the discrepancies between the location where Woods Hole oceanographer Richard Limeburner testified that the boat would have gone down according to his reverse drift analysis and where Nathan claimed his boat sank.

"Nathan had never used sea charts before. He was confused," Anderson told Judge McConnell. "When the vessel went down, it was significantly farther south in Block Canyon than what he thought, and that is why he wasn't seen for seven days. He was in a different area than the lobstermen were fishing and where the Coast Guard searched."

Nathan had been tight-lipped outside court throughout the trial, but he addressed reporters on the final day.

"I almost feel like I have a responsibility to my mom to make sure that the truth comes out," he said on the courthouse steps. "And [the plaintiffs] have made claims against me that are so tremendous, I don't feel like I can walk away from it."

Following Nathan out of the courthouse was witness Brian Woods. The boat builder was shaking with anger as he had just listened to attorney David Anderson question his workmanship and lay blame for the sinking of the *Chicken Pox* squarely at his feet.

"It was an excellent boat. The survey proved it was excellent," Woods told reporters. "He [Nathan] used it for many months before he had this problem. He altered the boat. Ultimately, he sank the boat."

Judge McConnell told both sides that he would issue a written opinion on the $85,000 insurance claim at a later date.

The civil trial had been the hottest ticket in town for court observers and true-crime aficionados in New England. The gallery was filled each day with reporters and spectators alike. All were fascinated by the case and the enigma that was Nathan Carman. Was he a calculated, manipulative, money-hungry killer? Or was he the ultimate victim of circumstance?

After the trial, Nathan retreated once again to his Vermont farmhouse and refused to give any more interviews as he awaited the judge's decision.

Judge McConnell evaluated the evidence for nearly two months before rendering his decision in November 2019.

"Based on all the evidence presented at trial, the Court finds that Mr. Carman's boat was unseaworthy when it left Ram Point Marina on September 17, 2016, because he improperly repaired the holes he created by removing the trim tabs, and he compromised the boat's stability by removing the bulkheads," the judge wrote in his sixteen-page opinion. "The unseaworthy state of the boat brought about by the faulty repairs at least indirectly caused it to sink. National appropriately denied coverage for the resulting property loss after a good faith investigation."

Judge McConnell pointed to the testimony of Brian Woods, who he deemed a credible witness. The judge said that Woods had built the *Chicken Pox* with "structural strength and integrity" by installing new bulkheads and two bilge pumps on the stern and the port cockpit hatch of the vessel. Judge McConnell said that Woods had also correctly installed trim tabs on the transom of the boat, which were consistent with the manufacturer's directions.

The judge also credited naval architect Eric Greene's trial testimony, in which he opined that there "was a high likelihood that water entering from the inadequately filled holes would gradually fill the bilge."

He then outlined Nathan's repair work: his removal of the trim tabs using an electric power drill and his sloppy attempt to patch the holes with putty without using a fiberglass mat fabric on the outside hull to seal the holes.

"The evidence shows that Mr. Carman's transom hole repairs were incomplete, improper, and faulty because he filled the holes with epoxy and did not use fiberglass as an exterior seal," the judge declared. "The removal of the trim tabs and the faulty repairs rendered the boat unseaworthy and in poor condition."

Although Judge McConnell rejected Nathan's $85,000 insurance claim, he made sure to note that his ruling had zero to do with the larger issues surrounding Nathan Carman.

"To be clear, the Court is making no determination of whether Mr. Carman intended to sink his boat or harm his mother," the judge wrote.

Nathan's lawyer appealed the judge's ruling, but a request for a new trial was flatly denied.

"Nothing raised by the defendant supports any amendments to the findings, or supports a new trial," Judge McConnell stated.

The judge's ruling came on the same day that Nathan's aunts dropped their appeal in the slayer rule case in New Hampshire, but the fight over the family fortune was still far from over.

Chapter Thirty-One

Nathan Carman was now a reported millionaire thanks to the fortune left behind by his grandfather for the entire family in his dynasty trust, but he had nothing to show for it. His aunts would continue to commit vast resources to tie up his inheritance in court. The Chakalos sisters filed new motions in the state of Connecticut, despite having claimed for the past few years that their father was a resident of New Hampshire upon his death. Without any money to support himself, Nathan took a job at a nearby Amazon warehouse, sorting packages on the overnight shift. He enjoyed the solitude of working overnights without many people around the warehouse. During the day, he would take catnaps in his truck while continuing to remodel the farmhouse, a project that was virtually never-ending.

One day, he received a text message from an admirer, an attractive young woman named Alicyn Patton, who had attended Nathan's civil trial in Providence.

"I had heard about the case and knew that he was coming this way," Patton explained. "I said to myself, 'This case seems interesting. I wanna go.'"

Patton sat in on the trial each day, feeling great empathy for Nathan and trying to make eye contact with him in court. A year after the trial was over,

Patton found his telephone number, and they started texting each other. She told him that she'd been following the case for several years and that she was the smiling face he saw every day at trial. But Nathan immediately put his guard up.

I don't mean this in a bad way, but why after nearly two years, are you still interested in me/supporting me? he wrote. **What is there about me that appeals to you? It is unusual that someone that I have never met would stand by me for this long after not hearing from me. On one hand, I appreciate it, yet on the other, I don't know what to make of it.**

It's just that a part of me thinks you shouldn't be living life in & out of courtrooms all the time, she texted back. **I will always stand behind you no matter what you decide to do. I really do care about you.**

Maybe it is inappropriate for me to ask this, but you have said you support me and there is something I really need so I think I should ask, he replied. **It [would] be life changing for the better if I had someone to help with paying attorney's fees. For example, I would like to sue my aunts for what they did in New Hampshire, but I cannot afford to. It is something where the outlay up front is in the 10's of thousands but I could pay it back with interest down the road. I was wondering if you are in the position to help with that and, if so, whether it is something you would consider. I would really appreciate it if you were to help.**

Patton was in no position financially to assist with such a request and instead offered Nathan her sympathy regarding how he had been treated by his aunts.

I know it's Terrible what your aunts did, she wrote back.

For the first time in his life, Nathan had discovered a true friend. He had always said that his best friend was his late mother, Linda, but he had never sought or received companionship outside his closest family members: his mother, his father, and his grandfather John Chakalos.

Nathan and Patton continued to correspond through text messages, and she told him that she was interested in driving up to New Hampshire from Rhode Island and visiting Ice Castles, a sprawling winter theme park in the town of Bethlehem, with caverns and archways, ice slides, snow tubing, and what park organizers called a "Mystic Forest Light Walk" through the woods.

They agreed to meet in early March 2021.

Hi Alicyn, Saturday March 6 for Ice Castles would work for me, Nathan texted her. **It sounds like that is when you have tickets for? Sorry about ignoring your messages sometimes. I am just really unsure what to do about a lot of things. I will definitely go.**

In one of her texts, Patton mentioned that she was also interested in skydiving but misspelled the word.

I have never heard of ski diving, he replied. **But I am looking forward to completing my sky diving certification which I started before COVID.**

Nathan told Patton that he would make his own hotel arrangements in New Hampshire, which likely meant that he would sleep in his truck for the night.

She booked a room at the Chandler at White Mountains Hotel in Bethlehem, just a short drive from the attraction. After Patton got settled in room 312 of the hotel, she texted Nathan in the lobby.

"He came right up to my room. He was so nice," Patton recalled. "He knocked at the door, and then we chatted for about an hour and a half. He told me that his mother, Linda, was the 'black sheep' of the family."

Patton was alone with Nathan, who had been accused by his family of double murder. Still, she never felt nervous or in any danger in his presence.

"I wasn't scared at all," she remembered. "He seemed pretty harmless and was very polite."

Nathan told her that he had stepsiblings, other children of his father, Clark, whom he had never spent time with. Patton had half siblings of her own whom she had never met.

"We're very much alike," Nathan told her.

He then talked openly with her about his legal battles.

"My concern right now is that I want to sue my aunts for what they did to me in New Hampshire," he reiterated to her.

They left the hotel and drove to the Ice Castles theme park.

The night was bitterly cold, and as they entered the winter wonderland, which was illuminated in bright colors of blue, purple, and red, Patton spotted a horse and carriage. She knew that Nathan had a love for horses dating back to the bond he had formed with his horse, Cruise, when he was a teenager.

"Nathan, look, there's a horse," she said.

They took a ride on the horse-drawn carriage and then walked together through the ice castle trail.

Afterward, Nathan and Patton walked over to the concession stand, where she bought herself a cinnamon roll. The cashier handed her the tasty roll, dripping with frosting, and looked at Nathan.

"Do you want one?" the female cashier asked.

"Not unless it's free," Nathan replied.

"We don't give out free things here."

Patton bent over, giggling.

The two decided to go for pizza, and Nathan got into his truck and followed his new friend to the restaurant. When they arrived at GH Pizza in Lincoln, New Hampshire, Patton could not help but notice that it was also a Greek restaurant.

"That's funny. I know you're Greek. You must love the food here," she told him.

Nathan nodded yes and cracked a slight smile. They could not dine in the restaurant because of COVID restrictions, so they brought the pizza to Patton's car. Nathan sat in the passenger seat while Patton kept the conversation light over slices of hot pizza.

"I didn't ask him any questions about the case," she said. "I didn't want him to think, 'oh, this is why she wants to spend time with me?' I just really did like our conversation."

But Patton did not want the night to end. "I just felt comfortable with him."

Nathan appeared comfortable too. For the first time in many years, the future seemed bright for him.

CHAPTER THIRTY-TWO

Following the civil trial, Coast Guard investigator Eric Gempp requested all the court transcripts and then began studying each document, reviewing every statement that was made and recorded to re-educate himself to see if there was anything he may have missed.

"At this point, we were never losing sight that we still had a missing person out there," Gempp recalled, referring to Linda Carman. "We have a boat that's out there somewhere, and we don't know where Linda is."

Gempp and FBI Agent Lisa Tutty made several requests to speak with Nathan through his attorneys, but those requests were always denied. Their investigation slowed during the COVID-19 pandemic, and they were limited in terms of what they could do.

"We initially had conversations about pursuing this case in federal court by the U.S. Attorney's Office in Connecticut," Gempp said. "They initially took the case for consideration but did not find the merit to move forward."

The investigation could have ended right there, but one day, seemingly out of the blue, Gempp received a call at his office at the U.S. Coast Guard Academy from the U.S. Attorney's Office in Vermont, the state where Nathan had been living for almost a decade.

"We would like to sit down and talk about this case with you because we consider it to be righteous for prosecution," a federal prosecutor told Gempp.

Gempp and Tutty drove up to southern Vermont and met with U.S. attorney Nikolas Kerest and assistant U.S. attorney Paul Van de Graaf at a state police barracks. The prosecutors wanted to know about any planning that Nathan could have done in Vermont, and the investigators informed them of some online purchases of boat repair equipment that Nathan had made, presumably from his home computer.

"They saw the merits of the case and were willing to further follow up on it," Gempp said. "And as we continued to follow up, we gained some traction."

Gempp stated that although prosecutors did not have a proverbial smoking gun in the case, there was enough evidence against Nathan to warrant criminal charges.

After several months of further investigation by the U.S. Attorney's Office in Vermont, an arrest warrant for Nathan Carman was issued on May 2, 2022, and executed on May 10.

Nathan was invited to come to a local state police barracks to discuss the case, and he went there willingly without being accompanied by a lawyer.

"When he got there, we informed him that he was under arrest," Gempp said. "He declined to answer any questions or have any further discussions with us."

The official charge was murder on the high seas.

As soon as Nathan was taken into custody, law enforcement initiated a search of his home.

The tranquility of the town of Vernon was shattered on that sun-drenched morning in early May 2022 when a fleet of police vehicles tore down Fort Bridgman Road with sirens wailing and pulled onto Nathan's property just before 11:30 a.m. Uniformed police officers, plainclothes detectives, and agents from the FBI all jumped out of their vehicles and climbed over a virtual obstacle course of stuffed trash bags, old tires, two parked boats, a gas grill and rusted propane tanks, and other debris scattered across the front yard as they entered the historic home. Federal agents spent the next several hours carrying out cardboard boxes filled with evidence from the house while officers from the local police department looked on.

By now, state prosecutor Nikolas "Kolo" Kerest had ascended to the position of U.S. attorney for the state of Vermont, having been appointed by President Joe Biden and then confirmed by the U.S. Senate six months before Nathan's arrest. Kerest had been recommended for the post by U.S. senator Patrick Leahy.

"Kolo is an exemplary prosecutor, dedicated to upholding the rule of law and putting the interest of Vermonters first, above all else," Senator Leahy, a Democrat, said at the time. "As a former prosecutor myself, I am confident that Kolo has just what it takes to keep our communities safe while honoring Vermont's values."

Kerest, a resident of Shelburne, Vermont, and a graduate of Cornell Law School, had been working in the criminal division of the U.S. Attorney's Office in Vermont since 2019 and would now lead an office of twenty-four attorneys and twenty-seven staff members. Before he took over as Vermont's top cop, Kerest's biggest legal victory was against an electronic health records vendor that had been accused of paying off clients with kickbacks to promote the company's products. Kerest's team won a $155 million settlement against the company. As U.S. attorney, Kerest hoped to make a big splash right out of the gate, and his eight-count federal indictment of Nathan Carman was explosive. It charged him with the September 2016 murder of his mother, Linda, and also publicly accused him of killing his grandfather in a scheme to obtain millions of dollars and property from his grandfather's estate.

"Beginning in or about 2013 and continuing until the present, in the District of Vermont and elsewhere, defendant Nathan Carman devised a scheme to defraud the Estate of John Chakalos, its executor, the Dynasty

Trust, and its trustees, and to obtain money from the Dynasty Trust by materially false and fraudulent pretenses, representations, and promises," the grand jury indictment read. "As a central part of this scheme, Nathan Carman murdered John Chakalos and Linda Carman. He concocted cover stories to conceal his involvement in those killings. As part of his cover-up, Nathan Carman misrepresented his involvement in and responsibility for those deaths to law enforcement, to his family, to others who made inquiries about the deaths and their circumstances, and to others who challenged his cover-up or challenged his rights to his grandfather's assets."

Although he was not being officially charged with the murder of his grandfather, the indictment provided a detailed timeline of events surrounding the slaying.

"In 2012 and 2013, Nathan Carman presented detailed questions to John Chakalos's trust attorney and financial advisor about Carman's financial interests in John Chakalos's assets and the operation of the trusts... On November 6, 2013, Nathan Carman, while living in a rented apartment in Bloomfield, CT, registered his truck in New Hampshire and obtained a New Hampshire driver's license. Carman listed his New Hampshire residence as the house built by John Chakalos in West Chesterfield, NH. On November 11, 2013, Nathan Carman used the New Hampshire driver's license to purchase a Sig Sauer rifle at Shooter's Outpost in Hooksett, NH," prosecutors wrote. "On December 20, 2013, Nathan Carman murdered his grandfather, John Chakalos, shooting him [three times] with the Sig Sauer while Chakalos slept in his Windsor, CT home. After Nathan Carman killed John Chakalos, and as part of his plan to cover up his involvement in that crime, Nathan Carman discarded his computer hard drive and the GPS unit that had been in his truck the night of the murder. These acts prevented law enforcement from reviewing the data on these devices.

"Between December 20, 2013, and January of 2014, Nathan Carman provided false information to the law enforcement agencies investigating

John Chakalos's murder. Among other things, Nathan Carman falsely denied involvement in the murder. He misrepresented his whereabouts between approximately 3:00 a.m. on December 20, 2013, when he left his apartment in Bloomfield, and approximately 4:00 a.m., when he arrived at the location where he planned to meet his mother to take a charter fishing trip. He also falsely denied purchasing the Sig Sauer in November 2013.

"After John Chakalos was murdered, Nathan Carman received approximately $550,000 as a result of Chakalos's death: $150,000 from the college account and $400,000 from the beneficiary-on-death account. Carman moved to Vermont in 2014. Carman spent much of this money between 2014 and 2016, during most of which he was unemployed. By the fall of 2016, he was low on funds."

After attempting to establish that Nathan had killed his grandfather for money, prosecutors then described Nathan's alleged plot to murder his own mother.

"In September 2016, Nathan Carman arranged to go on a fishing trip on the *Chicken Pox* with his mother, Linda Carman. Nathan Carman planned to kill his mother on the trip. He also planned how he would report the sinking of the *Chicken Pox* and his mother's disappearance at sea as accidents," the grand jury had concluded in the indictment. "Prior to the trip, Nathan Carman told his mother that they would be fishing in the immediate vicinity of Block Island, RI. Nathan Carman and Linda Carman left in the *Chicken Pox* from Ram Point Marina in South Kingstown, RI at approximately 11:13 p.m. on September 17, 2016. Linda Carman believed that she would be returning home by noon the next day, as evidenced by the float plan she left with friends.

"Prior to the trip, Nathan Carman altered the *Chicken Pox* in several ways, including removing two forward bulkheads and removing trim tabs from the transom of the hull. Prior to the trip, Nathan Carman removed his computer from his home, preventing law enforcement from reviewing the computer while he was away. After leaving the marina, Nathan Carman killed his mother, Linda Carman, and eventually sank the *Chicken Pox*.

"On September 18, 2016, when it learned the *Chicken Pox* had not returned from the fishing trip, the Coast Guard began an extensive search and rescue mission that continued until September 24, 2016. During that interval, Nathan Carman and the *Chicken Pox* avoided detection by the search and rescue team. On September 25, Nathan Carman was 'rescued' from an inflatable life raft by a commercial ship, the *Orient Lucky*. After being picked up by the *Orient Lucky*, Nathan Carman made false statements to the Coast Guard, to law enforcement investigating the disappearance of Linda Carman, and to others about what happened to Linda Carman and about what occurred on the *Chicken Pox*."

Federal prosecutors in Vermont had sought a murder charge against Nathan after analyzing more than twenty-two thousand documents relating to the case that were never made public. Although the evidence against him was highly circumstantial, U.S. attorney Kerest and his team believed they had a slam-dunk murder case.

The indictment also mentioned the slayer rule case that was brought unsuccessfully by Nathan's aunts as well as the boat insurance case.

"Between on or about September 2016 and in or about August 2019, in the District of Vermont and elsewhere, defendant Nathan Carman devised a scheme to defraud and to obtain money from Boat U.S. and the National Liability and Fire Insurance Co. by materially false and fraudulent pretenses, representations, and promises about what occurred between the time the *Chicken Pox* left the Ram Point Marina and the time Nathan Carman was picked up by the *Orient Lucky*," the indictment read. "On or about June 10, 2017, in the District of Vermont and elsewhere, defendant Nathan Carman, having devised the scheme to defraud and to obtain money by materially false and fraudulent pretenses, representations, and promises described above, transmitted and caused to be transmitted by means of wire communication in interstate commerce an email that attached his narrative about the sinking of the *Chicken Pox*, for the purpose of executing the scheme."

Following his arrest, Nathan was taken from the police barracks, placed in the back of a police car, and brought to a local jail, the Marble Valley Regional Correctional Facility, to await his arraignment the following morning in federal court in Rutland, Vermont.

"When I heard that Nathan had been arrested, I couldn't believe it," his father, Clark Carman, remembered. "First, he would never kill his mother, and second, he was never charged with murdering his grandfather. So why did they call him John Chakalos's killer in the indictment? It was totally irresponsible."

Reporters descended on the little city of Rutland, the ancestral home of John Deere, with quaint antique stores, coffee shops, clothing boutiques, and even a curiosity shop that sold collectibles, quilts, and salvage items. A police car pulled up to the back of the large federal courthouse on West Street in Rutland, and an officer reached into the back seat and helped Nathan out of the vehicle. He had handcuffs on and was wearing a dark sweater, dark pants, and a mask to protect himself from COVID-19.

"Do you have anything to say, any reaction to the charges?" one reporter asked.

Instead of avoiding the media on his way into the courthouse, Nathan shouted his answer in their direction.

"Not guilty," he said angrily as officers whisked him inside.

CHAPTER THIRTY-THREE

Nathan repeated himself before the judge, pleading not guilty to the murder and fraud charges that, if proven beyond a reasonable doubt, would send him to prison for life. Prosecutors read all the counts from the murder indictment in court and then asked the judge to keep Nathan behind bars until his trial.

The U.S. Attorney's Office filed a motion with the court to detain Nathan, claiming that he was a flight risk.

"For an individual who would kill his own family members, nothing is off the table. Carman is alleged to have killed for money, and there is no reason to believe he would not also kill again to gain advantage in a criminal case, particularly to avoid the possibility of life imprisonment."

Prosecutors also stressed Nathan's autism spectrum disorder and his possibly undiagnosed schizophrenia as a reason to keep him locked up. "Carman's mental instability, which has gone untreated for the past decade, provides further reason to believe that he poses a danger," the motion stated. U.S. attorney Kerest and his team cited a mental health expert who claimed that Nathan had "exhibited a highly unconventional problem-solving style" that led him to murdering his mother and grandfather and might lead him to kill anyone else who got in his way.

"He has limited human connections and little personal interaction with other people," prosecutors wrote. "Carman's history and characteristics include the obvious fact that, in addition to having little or no human connections, he has little or no empathy for others."

Nathan was assigned two public defenders, who argued successfully to postpone the hearing about his incarceration until the trial for sixty days while they conducted their own investigation. Nathan left the courthouse in handcuffs and was returned to the Marble Valley Regional Correctional Facility, where he was kept in a single cell away from other prisoners.

While many inmates might have feared the isolation that came with imprisonment, his father said that Nathan was conditioned for it. "If anyone could have survived prison, it was Nathan," Clark Carman theorized. "He had spent all of his time alone anyway. He had no friends, so that wasn't an issue. He liked to read and had access to the library, so he really had all that he needed in there."

Still, his court-appointed attorneys, Mary Nerino and Sara Puls, fought for his release. In July 2022, they filed a motion for Nathan's bail, calling the evidence against him "weak" and "tenuous at best." The public defenders also insisted that the U.S. attorney's claim that Nathan was a risk to others was nothing but thin gruel, as he had been battling his aunts in court for nearly a decade.

"At no time during that lengthy period has Mr. Carman ever attempted to threaten a witness, contact a witness inappropriately, or sought to influence a witness in any way," Nathan's attorneys argued.

The lawyers painted a vastly different picture of the accused double murderer than had been presented by federal prosecutors and members of the press. They said that Nathan had lived a quiet life for eight years in Vernon, Vermont, where he participated in town forums and attended church services. According to his attorneys, Nathan was a pillar of the community. This characterization was also supported by several people from the accused killer's past who wrote letters to the judge.

"He came to our church because it was a traditional Latin rite service, the closest he could find to the Greek Orthodox rite he enjoyed so much with his grandfather," wrote Middletown, Connecticut, businessman Richard Sabato. "While in church, Nathan was quiet, respectful and prayerful." Sabato had met Nathan when he served in the Boy Scouts as a child and later reconnected with him at church. "It is my opinion, based on the interactions with the family, that Nathan had no motive to kill his grandfather who provided for him, loved him and whom Nathan cared for very much."

In another letter, a former riding instructor stated that Nathan had never been prone to aggressive outbursts while receiving riding lessons as a teenager in Glastonbury, Connecticut. Renee Scarpantonio, president of the Hunters Run Stables, also noted that John Chakalos had paid for Nathan's riding lessons and his beloved horse, Cruise.

"I see no financial motive for Nathan to kill his grandfather because he seemed to give Nathan everything he wanted," Scarpantonio wrote the judge. "He and Nathan seemed to have a very special relationship."

Nathan's father also weighed in with a letter to the court claiming that his son was "a responsible young man who poses no ongoing mental health issues" and only wanted the truth to come out that he was innocent.

Alicyn Patton wrote to the judge and offered to take Nathan in should he be freed on bail. "Unfortunately, I don't have a house to put up for him as a bond for Home Confinement, if I did I would," she wrote. "But if he needs to stay with someone, if you should decide to let him out, And if you don't feel comfortable releasing him back to his house, He is more than welcome to stay with me in Warwick RI while in home confinement. As I do Not believe he is a danger to the community or a flight risk. I live alone with my Kittens… I care about him a great deal, and it is extremely concerning to me that he is being held. If you could find it in your heart to give him a chance, and let him out on Home confinement since he's never been in trouble with law before, would mean a great deal. It breaks my heart that he is in there. As I get emotional writing this letter, I truly believe with all my heart he should be given a chance."

The Chakalos sisters wrote their own letter to the court, stating that they feared for their lives.

"We are very concerned that Nathan has nothing to lose if he is allowed out of jail at this time and will seek retribution against the family," the letter stated. There was a family trust that was about to be dissolved, and the sisters were also concerned about what would happen if Nathan got access to the trust if he was let out on bail. "[Money from the family trust] would allow him significant ability to flee the jurisdiction of the court and allow him sufficient funds to carry out further acts of violence to the family."

As conditions of his release, Nathan had agreed to surrender his passport and wear an ankle bracelet to monitor his movements. Nathan was also willing to hand over $10,000, all the money he had, for bail. Prosecutors filed their own motion reinforcing their narrative that he was a dangerous flight risk in an effort to block Nathan's release.

One federal prosecutor, Nathanael Burris, supplied a new potential motive for the murder of John Chakalos. Burris claimed that Nathan had received straight Fs on his college report card in late 2013, which had disheartened his grandfather. According to Burris, Chakalos had threatened to cut Nathan off financially if he flunked out of school.

"Two days after Carman got his grades, his grandfather was shot to death at this home...by the same kind of rifle that Carman had recently purchased, lied about buying, and later claimed to have lost," Burris told U.S. District Court Judge Geoffrey Crawford during a hearing.

For years, court observers had questioned whether Nathan had any motive to kill his grandfather, who was eighty-seven years old and doted on him as his first male grandchild. Authorities had never come up with any reason for Nathan Carman to kill John Chakalos until now, nearly nine years after the murder. The alleged heated argument between the grandfather and grandson over Nathan's grades is also contradicted by the fact that the two of them shared a cordial dinner and Nathan drove his grandfather home on the night he was murdered.

Judge Crawford, a graduate of Harvard Law School, ruled in favor of the prosecution at the bail hearing. He cited "the seriousness of the charges," Nathan's "lack of strong family, employment or community connections," and "his involvement with firearms and the ongoing feud with his family over his grandfather's estate" as the main reasons to keep him in jail without bail. Judge Crawford referred to the "acrimonious dispute" between Nathan and his aunts and his purchase of a Sig Sauer rifle as "evidence that this is a volatile situation."

The U.S. Attorney's Office now had one legal victory under its belt against Nathan Carman, but federal prosecutors still had a long way to go to win a conviction in a case that was highly circumstantial. A question for many observers centered on why the charges were filed in Vermont if the murder of Linda Carman took place on the high seas off Rhode Island or Massachusetts. Why did prosecutors boldly insist in the criminal indictment that Nathan had also murdered his grandfather although he had never been arrested or charged with the crime? Linda Carman's body had never been recovered, and she had still not been declared officially dead by the state of Connecticut, where she lived when she presumably drowned in 2016. Could prosecutors win a conviction against Nathan Carman without a body?

Tad DiBiase prosecuted several homicide cases during his twelve years as assistant U.S. attorney in the District of Columbia and has consulted with police departments on fifty "no-body murder cases" across the country. According to a study he published in 2023, DiBiase found that prosecutors won 86 percent of all murder trials where a body had not been recovered with only a small number of dismissals, mistrials, or reversals on appeal. But in the majority of these cases, there was some trace evidence of the crime, such as blood found in a hotel room, or witnesses or accomplices who testified they saw a victim being shot or strangled.

Federal prosecutors had none of these types of evidence at their disposal in the alleged murder of Linda Carman. There was no evidence of any struggle aboard the *Chicken Pox* because the fishing boat was now at the bottom of the ocean. There were no witnesses who could testify that Nathan killed his mother, and there was no confession, as Nathan had maintained his innocence since getting plucked out of the ocean by the *Orient Lucky*.

"What you find in these cases is the difficulty in bringing them to trial," DiBiase said. "You can't find the body. You don't know how Linda Carman was allegedly murdered. But the rules are much more generous in federal court than they are in most state courts, and that allows the government to put in more allegations, like Nathan perhaps killing his grandfather, into their indictment. Without any trace evidence that a murder took place on the boat, federal prosecutors had to frontload the idea that Nathan also murdered his grandfather to get it in front of the grand jury."

DiBiase said that U.S. Attorney Nikolas Kerest must have believed that he had more than a 50 percent chance that his office would win a conviction against Nathan. "Or they would not be allowed to bring the case forward," he added. "Those rules are strictly enforced at the federal level."

DiBiase said that the very first "no-body murder" cases in the United States resulted from victims being lost or buried at sea. One story appeared in the January 16, 1880, edition of the *New York Times*, detailing the murder of a crew member aboard a ship called *Archer*, during a voyage from Amsterdam to Red Hook, New York. The crime was the result of an argument between an Irish sailor named Daniel Leonard and a Russian crewmate named Anton Klowitonski. "Klowitonski picked up a tar stick and struck [Leonard] with a single blow on the head. Leonard, without thinking what he was about, plunged the knife into the assailant's abdomen, inflicting the fatal wound," the article read.

The victim's body was buried at sea, which was a maritime custom during that era. Leonard was given a speedy trial where he was convicted and eventually hanged. Although the prosecutor had no body to inspect in that case, he did have corroborating accounts from the ship's captain and fellow crew members aboard the *Archer*. But what had occurred more than a century later aboard the *Chicken Pox* was vastly different. There were no witnesses to the drowning of Linda Carman, and the dead could not speak.

While prosecutors still had their legal work cut out for them, Nathan was being tried and convicted in the court of public opinion. Reddit.com users flooded group chats, sharing their opinions on the case. **Kill me once, shame on you**, one poster wrote. **Kill another, you're going to jail—the law, probably.** Another Reddit user compared Nathan to notorious killer Robert Durst. Kevin Cullen, a veteran columnist for the *Boston Globe*, called Nathan's alleged plot "an elaborate, almost Shakespearean conspiracy to gain proceeds from his grandfather's estate."

CHAPTER THIRTY-FOUR

Alicyn Patton was worried. She had no idea where Nathan was being held after his detention hearing, as he was no longer housed at the Marble Valley Regional Correctional Facility. After writing a letter on Nathan's behalf, she asked the public defender's office where her friend was being detained and said that she would like to speak to him.

Nathan received the information from his lawyer and telephoned Patton in September 2022 from the Northwest State Correctional Facility in St. Albans, Vermont, a short distance from the Canadian border.

"I can't really talk to you about the case," Nathan told her.

"After Ice Castles, I didn't hear from you," she said.

"Well, Ice Castles was cold. It wasn't my type of setting."

"Well, you're supposed to Google things before you go," Patton replied jokingly. "It's supposed to be cold there. I'd like to come visit you."

"Well, it is a five-hour drive up here to St. Albans," he replied. "It's almost into Canada."

"I don't mind. I can drive up every two weeks." Patton heard the voices of other inmates in the background. "How is it over there? Is anyone bothering you?"

"Unfortunately, I can't call you from a private room. But it's pretty laid-back over here."

"What are you going to do?" she asked.

"I want to get a private attorney," he told her.

"Nathan, just because you get a private attorney, that doesn't mean that you'll be released on home confinement," Patton replied.

"I think a private attorney will do a better job."

Nathan was upset over the fact that his public defenders could not convince the judge to let him out on bail or home confinement until the murder trial, which was still more than a year away. He reached out to a lawyer he knew in Connecticut named Paul Spinella, who was seriously ill at the time, and asked him to recommend a seasoned defense attorney, one who had experience with high-profile murder cases. The attorney came up with the name of Martin "Marty" Minnella, a defense lawyer based out of Middlebury, Connecticut.

Gray-haired, mustachioed, and heavily jowled, Minnella was known as a pit bull in the courtroom. He was also familiar with the media scrutiny that often came with big murder cases. In 1981, Minnella represented an accused killer from Brookfield, Connecticut, named Arne Cheyenne Johnson, who was charged with stabbing his landlord to death on the front lawn of a local kennel after a drunken argument over a woman. Local police called it a classic open-and-shut case. But days after the murder, famed paranormal investigators Ed and Lorraine Warren, whose exploits would later inspire the hit horror movie franchise *The Conjuring*, claimed that nineteen-year-old Johnson's body had been inhabited by a demonic spirit when he stabbed the victim, forty-year-old Alan Bono, several times in the chest and the stomach. Minnella offered to take the case for free and made a bold attempt to put the devil on trial for the first time in an American courtroom. Johnson had taken part in three exorcisms of his girlfriend's younger brother conducted by the Bridgeport Diocese several months before. According to the Warrens,

"Johnson leaped up and cried to the demon, 'Come into me. I'll fight you, come into me.'"

Minnella attempted to use demonic possession as an insanity defense for the accused killer, but the judge would not allow it, calling demonic possession "irrelevant, unprovable and needlessly confusing to a jury."

Johnson was later convicted of the murder, and the case was chronicled in a 1983 NBC television movie called *The Demon Murder Case*, with Kevin Bacon playing the possessed murder suspect and Harvey Fierstein providing the gravelly voice of the demon. Interviewed by a reporter years later, Minnella stood by his defense. "If you believe in God, you gotta believe in the Devil," he said in an interview with the *Hartford Courant*. "And what I saw in Arne as a young guy has profoundly affected me the rest of my life. There's a lot of crazy people out there that have contacted me to represent them with the same idea, 'the devil made me do it.' But our case was based on fact, not fiction."

Nearly forty years later, Minnella was ready to try another case that was making national headlines. The attorney and some colleagues drove north and met with Nathan for four hours at his jail. Minnella listened intently as Nathan provided detailed background information about the case. At the end of the meeting, Minnella stood up and addressed Nathan. "You're the real victim here."

"Please do not refer to me as a victim," Nathan told him.

The defense attorney obliged. "But I could still feel his pain," Minnella said later. He jumped at the chance to defend Nathan, but he knew he could not do it alone, especially with the fraud charges that were also being leveled against the young defendant. Minnella contacted a friend and sometime nemesis, attorney David X. Sullivan, to serve as his co-counsel. Minnella and Sullivan had litigated cases against each other for more than thirty years. Sullivan was a sharply dressed former federal prosecutor turned defense attorney who brought with him decades of experience working on white- collar crimes such as money laundering and asset forfeiture. In the fall of 2022, they took over Nathan's defense pro hac vice, meaning they also had to partner with a lawyer in Vermont, Robert Katims, where the trial was scheduled. But it was Minnella and Sullivan who handled nearly all responsibilities as Nathan's legal counsel.

"I read the indictment, and I wanted in. I don't do murder cases, but I was going to defend this young man for murder," Sullivan said. "This thing was being shopped from jurisdiction to jurisdiction. It was a very creative indictment. Because of the fucking bullshit mail fraud and wire fraud charges in his pursuit of insurance fraud alleged in the indictment, they were trying to bring John Chakalos's death into the trial, and we were going to have to defend him on two murders."

After his initial meeting with his new client, Sullivan said the idea that Nathan murdered his grandfather and then his mother in a macabre scheme to get rich just did not make sense to him.

"Nathan wasn't like one of the Menendez brothers," Sullivan said, referring to the siblings who were convicted of murdering their parents inside their Beverly Hills home in 1989. "He wasn't partying, didn't have girlfriends, didn't have fast, expensive cars. He wasn't drinking. He wasn't drugging. He wasn't Hunter Biden. This kid didn't even swear."

Sullivan began reviewing seventy hours of witness statements that were videotaped by police after the John Chakalos murder and said he was stunned by the lack of follow-up questions from investigators when it came to other potential suspects in the murder. Sullivan found himself providing color commentary while watching videotaped interviews and asking his own questions in frustration to police detectives. "I kept asking myself, 'Okay, are you going to pursue that line of questioning?' Because you've just accepted an answer that is incomplete or inconclusive," he recalled.

Sullivan was convinced that Windsor police and detectives from the Connecticut Central District Major Crimes Squad did not want to look beyond Nathan as their prime suspect. "Nathan had an unusual affect and could not read the room," Sullivan said. "And that rubbed people the wrong way. Nathan was either extremely bright or extremely stupid. I don't know how you can be both at the same time."

When the topic of his family feud was brought up, Nathan never spoke ill to Sullivan of his aunts. "Instead, he gave a clinical assessment of them. It wasn't harsh, but it was clinical," Sullivan recalled. "I think he loved them. When he got off the boat and nobody cared that he was alive, that really rocked his world."

Sullivan handled most of the discovery in the case and zeroed in on testimony from John Chakalos's neighbor, who placed the murder an hour before police claimed that Nathan killed his grandfather, and also on an interview that the family's longtime caretaker, Joy Washburn, gave to the FBI, which made its way onto a 302 report. The caretaker's claim that someone had allegedly asked her to kill Chakalos and make it look like a hunting accident would now be admissible in the murder trial.

"The fact that Joy's statement was memorialized in a 302 report was pretty damn compelling," Sullivan pointed out. "I went through the Chakalos family interviews and found that they had a high regard for Joy Washburn. They found her extremely reliable and very trustworthy. One sister said that they would trust their children with Joy."

Coast Guard investigator Eric Gempp had also interviewed the caretaker on three separate occasions. "She was very cooperative, and I believed her to be credible. She had a tremendous amount of institutional knowledge about observations regarding the family," he recalled. "Joy shed insight into things that maybe she did not want to shed insight into within the family. She was a trusted family employee for many years."

Gempp said that Joy Washburn had never given him a reason to place her on the list of unreliable witnesses during his investigation.

The defense lawyers also wanted to see the grand jury minutes that resulted in the eight-count criminal indictment against Nathan. A hearing was scheduled in federal court in Rutland, Vermont, in early February 2023.

Nathan was present at the hearing, as was his friend Alicyn Patton. "I drove up to see him in court and tried to get his attention," Patton recalled. "But he wouldn't look at me. I think he was embarrassed to be seen wearing his orange prison jumpsuit."

Attorneys Sullivan and Minnella were outraged that federal prosecutors had accused Nathan of murdering his grandfather in their indictment despite the fact that he had never been charged, convicted, or civilly held responsible for the 2013 slaying. "[The indictment] includes matter-of-fact assertions of uncharged and unadjudicated criminal conduct," they argued. They demanded to know what prosecutors had presented to the grand jury regarding Chakalos's murder, claiming any such evidence was "inaccurate" and "untrue" and that Nathan may have had grounds for a dismissal of the indictment. "These outright assertions are very troubling to the defense," Sullivan told Judge Geoffrey Crawford.

Prosecutors countered, insisting that information about the Chakalos murder was relevant to the fraud charges in the case. They told the judge that they planned to call several expert witnesses at trial, including a survival expert and an expert on drift analysis. They were working off the same playbook that the insurers' lawyers had used successfully in the civil trial, only the stakes were much higher now, as Nathan faced life in prison if convicted. Judge Crawford set a trial date for October 2, 2023, and both sides vowed they would be ready.

CHAPTER THIRTY-FIVE

Alicyn Patton had asked one of Nathan's attorneys for information as to where Nathan was being held, but for some reason, she claimed, they refused to give it to her. He was no longer incarcerated at Northwest State Correctional Facility in St. Albans, Vermont. She was desperate to make contact with him and reached out to a reporter friend, who told her Nathan was now behind bars at the Cheshire County Jail in Keene, New Hampshire, just sixteen miles from his grandfather's former mansion in West Chesterfield, which had recently been sold. Patton went online and found a list of prisoners incarcerated there, but Nathan's name was not on the inmate manifest.

She went back to her reporter friend, who dug deeper and learned that Nathan was indeed locked up at the Cheshire County Jail in a second-floor cell, D-204, at the end of the corridor next to a bank of telephones. There was no barbed wire fencing around the jail, but the warden had maintained a strict visitation policy, and the rules were now even tighter since the pandemic. The medium-security facility had the capacity to hold 136 prisoners, and all were stuck there until their trials, when they would either be acquitted or sent off to the state penitentiary.

Although the jail promoted the humane treatment of detainees in a rehabilitative setting where safety and security were a paramount concern, the facility was being investigated following the alleged beating of a prisoner named Antwaun Tucker, who, his lawyers claimed, had been Maced and tased and had one of his legs broken by prison guards during an incident in March 2022. Tucker, who was being held on drug charges, was later moved to another prison while pursuing $2.3 million in physical, emotional, and mental damages against administrators at the Cheshire County Jail.

Nathan was the most notable detainee at the Cheshire County Jail. He continued to be hounded by reporters from national newspapers and television networks with interview requests as he prepared for trial. Like his attorneys, Nathan was confident that he would win an acquittal in the case where the other side was relying heavily on circumstantial evidence. Much had been made over the fact that Nathan had been found responsible for making shoddy repairs to his fishing boat in the 2019 civil trial in Rhode Island. It was something that his attorneys planned to attack head-on in court.

"Nathan did all the repairs to that boat in broad daylight on a public dock with people around," said Marty Minnella. "If he was planning to murder his mother, he would have hauled the boat out of the marina and made the alterations under the cloak of darkness. He didn't do this, because at the time, he thought he was doing the right thing. Any juror would see that."

"He wasn't a skilled mariner and could not have purposely avoided Coast Guard planes and helicopters for a week," David X. Sullivan added. "It's ridiculous."

Sullivan did not dispute the fact that Nathan had made several inquiries about the Chakalos family trusts, but he argued that it was not done as part of a "scheme" as alleged by the prosecution. "John [Chakalos] was always there with Nathan, telling him to ask questions and be inquisitive, especially since his aunt Valerie's husband, Larry Santilli, was the trustee."

In 2023, Santilli was embroiled in investigations and a number of lawsuits regarding his company, Athena Health Care Systems. The company agreed to pay the Massachusetts Attorney General's Office $1.75 million, the largest nursing home fine ever in the state, for admitting people with substance abuse issues to its nursing homes without providing them with appropriate treatment. This lack of care led to numerous resident overdoses. According to the Massachusetts Attorney General's Office, "Athena was aware [of the problem], but still encouraged the Athena facilities to admit residents with histories of SUD [substance use disorder]." Santilli's company was also facing a wrongful death lawsuit filed by the family of a man who was bludgeoned with a walker by his roommate.

Although federal prosecutors had planned to mirror much of their strategy with insurance attorney David Farrell's reliance on ocean drift and survival experts, they would also have the opportunity to introduce Nathan's missing Sig Sauer to jurors. The accused killer still had not accounted for why he was so evasive about the weapon and what ultimately happened to it.

"We had experts ready to testify about the ballistics in the case," Minnella explained. "Our position was that it wasn't Nathan's rifle that killed John Chakalos, so we didn't really care what he did with the weapon."

After reviewing hundreds of hours of discovery provided by the U.S. Attorney's Office, Nathan's defense attorneys worked to compile names for their witness list, which would include Joy Washburn, the Chakalos neighbor who had contradicted the police timeline of the millionaire's murder, the corrupt bookkeeper William Satti, and Chakalos's blond-haired mistress, who was given the pseudonym "Mistress Y" in court documents. Based on the first six counts in the criminal indictment, Sullivan suspected that most of the witnesses at trial would be asked about the murder of Nathan's grandfather, not Linda Carman. The defense attorneys were also going to ask the judge to sequester the witnesses, especially Nathan's aunts, so that they could not communicate with each other about their testimony.

"We discovered a text from Linda Carman to another family member stating that she was going to, quote, 'blow her father's fucking head off.'

No one took her seriously because they said she never finished anything she started," Minnella claimed. "Before John [Chakalos] was killed, he made his family all sign promissory notes to pay back at least thirty million dollars they had taken out of family trusts."

Nathan worked with Sullivan and Minnella on every aspect of his defense. He read law books in jail and raised astute legal questions on regular phone calls.

"We had a lot of legal discussions, and I remember telling Nathan, 'You would have been a great law student. Maybe not a great lawyer, but a great law student,'" Sullivan recalled. "You're my best investigator."

Nathan called Sullivan on his cell phone from jail just about every day. The lawyer would have to accept the charges, and oftentimes, he had to keep the conversations brief because he had clients in his office or he was home with his children. They spoke on Christmas and on Nathan's birthday. By this time, Nathan had stopped speaking with his father, and Sullivan was his only lifeline to the outside. But Nathan did not seem to care what was happening elsewhere in the world; he was singularly focused on the case.

"I had twenty-four-hour access to Nathan, and he had twenty-four-hour access to me," Sullivan recalled. "I couldn't talk to him every day. It was draining, and I told him that. Sometimes, I needed to be with my own kids. He understood."

The attorney's children, who had normally avoided any discussion about their father's work, all took an interest in this case. "Tell Nathan that I am praying for him," Sullivan's youngest daughter told him.

Sullivan and Minnella were preparing to disclose the witness list for the defense in federal court on June 30 and were working on a new motion in the case to present to the judge a few weeks later.

Sullivan spoke with Nathan by telephone on Wednesday, June 14, 2023, to update him on the case. Over the course of their fifty-six-minute conversation, Sullivan told Nathan that he was going to ask the judge to sequester witnesses and said that he had no doubt that they would win an acquittal on all eight counts including mail fraud, wire fraud, and murder at sea when the case went to trial in October. Sullivan said his client was in fine spirits and that they had action items they were going to address the next day.

At the end of their nearly hour-long phone call, Sullivan said, "Okay, my friend. Sleep well."

The next morning, Sullivan received a text from prosecutor Nathanael Burris asking him if he had time to talk. Sullivan was surprised to receive the text so early in the day and thought perhaps prosecutors had discovered information that would lead to dismissal of the case.

The two opposing attorneys got on the phone, and Burris delivered the tragic news. He told Sullivan that a jail guard was making his early morning rounds and found his client unresponsive in his single cell at 2:45 a.m. Twenty-nine-year-old Nathan Carman was dead.

CHAPTER THIRTY-SIX

Sullivan was thunderstruck. He could not believe what he was hearing. Burris offered no further details other than the fact that Nathan had left a note in his jail cell for his attorneys. Was it a suicide note? Had Nathan taken his own life?

Burris's next call was to Eric Gempp at the Coast Guard Academy in New London. The investigator had just arrived at work and was pulling into his parking space when his cell phone rang. The tone of Burris's voice was sullen, and that led Gempp to believe that something was wrong.

"Nathan Carman is dead," Burris told him.

For a moment, Gempp was speechless. He stared at his cell phone for several seconds, trying to process the reality that Nathan was gone.

"How? Where? Why?" he asked Burris. "Was it another inmate? Was it a medical emergency?"

"Nathan took his own life," the prosecutor replied.

Gempp left his car and walked in a daze toward his office. "I'm thinking to myself, there's no situation that should cause you to take your own life," he recalled. "He was a few months from trial where he would potentially be found not guilty, but if he was convicted, it was life in prison. It was either or. But I have no idea why he did what he did."

News of Nathan's death traveled quickly. His father, Clark, was contacted by a U.S. Marshal's office and was told that Nathan had hanged himself with his own shoelaces. The U.S. Marshal advised Clark to contact the coroner's office in New Hampshire for more details.

"I could not believe it," Clark said. "I still don't believe it. For one, why was he given shoelaces? Why wasn't he monitored in his jail cell? It doesn't make any sense to me. It was not in his mindset. I don't foresee him ever contemplating suicide."

Hours after Nathan's death, Judge Geoffrey Crawford granted a motion from the U.S. Attorney's Office to dismiss all charges against him. Nathan Carman would die an innocent man in the eyes of the law.

That same day, Sullivan and Minnella scrambled to coordinate a brief news conference at a law office in downtown Hartford. Both attorneys appeared distraught when they addressed reporters.

"He became more than a client to us. We were [Nathan's] only contact. We were like part of his family," Minnella said. "So I feel like I lost a member of my family when I lost Nathan Carman."

Sullivan refused to call Nathan's death a suicide. Instead, he told reporters that Nathan had passed away. "We believe that Mr. Carman left us a note that we look forward to receiving to try to make some sense of a very tragic situation… Unfortunately, we will never reach the merits of this case."

Nathan's friend Alicyn Patton could not wrap her head around the idea that Nathan would take his own life. "I'm so confused. He had already done thirteen months, and the fact that this happened four months before his trial doesn't make sense to me. That's if it was a suicide. I feel so sorry for him."

Others were not as kind to Nathan's memory when they received the news of his death. Brian Woods, the original owner of the *Chicken Pox*, expected to be called as a witness in the murder trial.

"I couldn't wait to stare him down in the courtroom. I was looking forward to it," Woods said. "The prick took his own life. He was an asshole. He didn't even have the balls to show up in court."

An autopsy later revealed that Nathan's death was not considered to be "suspicious" and that no one else was involved in his demise. Cheshire County corrections superintendent Douglas Iosue said that his jail had not had a death since 2020 and that it was the first suicide there since 2016.

Sullivan and Minnella received the note that was discovered in Nathan's cell. It made no mention of suicide. Instead, it was a series of notes that Nathan had compiled to push his case forward, as if he was planning to see the trial all the way through to a verdict.

Nathan Carman's remains were cremated and later sent by mail to Marty Minnella, who planned a funeral for his client in Connecticut.

A small group of mourners turned up on a drizzly, humid morning in late June 2023 under the baroque dome at Our Lady of Lourdes Church in Waterbury, Connecticut. An urn carrying Nathan's ashes was brought to the church in a sleek black hearse. Minnella and Sullivan were accompanied by their wives and a few staff members from Minnella's law office. Reporters and news photographers also sat in pews in the nearly empty church. Nathan's ashes were displayed on the altar while the parish priest read from the Book of Lamentations and a choir of four sang from the church balcony accompanied by an organist. Clark Carman was absent because he did not have the money to travel across the country to attend his son's funeral.

Toward the end of the hour-long service, Minnella stood up to deliver a eulogy. At first, he railed against Nathan's aunts for not showing their faces at church to mourn the nephew they had tormented for so long. Then he addressed his fellow mourners and delivered the opening statement that he had planned to present at trial.

"One week ago, at 7:30 in the morning, I received a call that Nathan Carman had passed. I sat there and shook in disbelief. This would be the end of our year-long journey, the end of our search for truth. He was a loving, sensitive, and nonviolent young man," Minnella began. "The two most important people in his life were his grandfather, John Chakalos, whom he idolized, and his mother, Linda Carman, who are now both gone. Nathan worked with his grandfather, ate dinner with his grandfather, dressed like his grandfather, and loved his grandfather more than he loved the air. After a thorough investigation, Nathan was never charged or indicted by either state or federal authorities in Connecticut. But almost ten years later, he was indicted in landlocked Vermont for an alleged crime on the high seas. The grand jury indicted Nathan based on many untruths, calling his behavior a scheme. This was a complete fallacy. We found suspects in his grandfather's death who had both the motive and opportunity, but the grand jury never heard this. As you know, in a grand jury proceeding, there is no defense offered and no one to advocate for the defendant. In all of my forty-eight years in criminal law, I have never seen a more flawed indictment, full of untruths and fiction. It is unfortunate that this trial will never happen. The real story about Nathan Carman may never be told. Why this happened to Nathan, I can never speculate. Nevertheless, I feel that money and political influence and power should never triumph over truth and justice in our country."

Minnella then referenced a note that he had scribbled down after his initial meeting with Nathan in the fall of 2022 and that remained on his kitchen counter at home. *Rejection by one's family can become completely unbearable.*

"I would like to address these final comments to Nathan, because I know that he's listening somewhere, and I know he's saying to me, 'Just one more question, just one more question,'" he continued. "Nathan, you could never have a better advocate or friend than David X. Sullivan, who

Attorney Martin Minnella watches as the urn carrying Nathan Carman's ashes is carried out of church. (Photo by Casey Sherman)

worked hundreds of hours on your case and took your calls day and night and always remained committed and steadfast. All of us on your defense team looked forward to October 10, your trial date, to tell the world your story. I am hopeful that your story will be told. Sleep with the angels, my dear friend."

Minnella gathered his notes and sat back down. Unbeknownst to him, Nathan's aunt Valerie, her husband, Larry, and another family member had slipped into the back of the church just moments before the service began. They made eye contact with no one else in the chapel and left after the service without saying a word to anyone.

A short time later, Clark Carman received a surprise phone call at his home in California. On the other end of the call was Valerie Santilli, whom he had not heard from in several years, since he had picked up Nathan in Boston after his ocean rescue. Valerie made an unusual request of her former brother-in-law. She wanted custody of Nathan's ashes.

"I couldn't believe it," Clark recalled. "At first, I said no way!"

Valerie wanted to bury Nathan's ashes in the Chakalos family plot at Cedar Hill Cemetery in Hartford, right next to his grandfather, whom she had long accused Nathan of murdering in his bed in 2013.

"I finally said yes," Clark said. "I felt that was basically the best place for Nathan because he loved his grandfather."

A decade after John Chakalos's murder, his accused killer, his grandson

Nathan Carman, was laid to rest next to him in the family plot where both men would remain side by side for eternity.

Nathan Carman's gravestone in the family plot next to his grandfather John Chakalos. (photo by Alicyn Patton)

AUTHOR'S NOTE

A probate judge in Connecticut finally declared Linda Carman officially dead on the seventh anniversary of her ill-fated fishing trip with her son. Her estate, worth an estimated $5.7 million, is still being held in a family trust.

Was Nathan Carman a villain or a victim? It is a question that I wrestled with each day while researching and writing this book. Taking an unbiased approach to the story, I focused on all the evidence I had compiled: court documents, U.S. Coast Guard reports, lengthy interviews with key players, and hundreds of stories that had been written about Nathan Carman, his mother, Linda Carman, and his grandfather, John Chakalos. My goal was to present this story as accurately as possible and then let the reader decide whether Nathan was responsible for the brutal murder of his beloved grandfather and the suspected drowning of his mother.

Based on the information that I found, if I had been sitting on the jury of his murder trial, I would likely have voted to acquit Nathan Carman given the legal threshold of reasonable doubt, as so much of the prosecution's case focused on circumstantial evidence. Yet that does not mean that I fully believe that Nathan was innocent of the crimes he was accused of either. Nathan Carman remained an enigma in life and in death. Some days, I think he's the diabolical mastermind that has been depicted by members of his own family and certain members of the media. On other days, I say to myself, "There's no way that he could have possibly committed two murders and got away with them for as long as he did." Nathan went to his death as an innocent man in the eyes of the law, and that could have been motivation enough for him to kill himself in his jail cell, although some people, even his own lawyers, refuse to believe that he died by his own hand.

As an author and investigative journalist, I have covered more than a hundred homicide cases, including the murder of my own aunt, Mary Sullivan, allegedly at the hands of the infamous Boston Strangler in 1964. Yet the Nathan Carman case has confounded me like no other, which is why this journey of discovery has been so memorable to me and will stay with me long after I have typed these words.

I wish to thank all those who answered my questions both on and off the record regarding the Nathan Carman case. The best journalists are good listeners, and I allowed many of the key witnesses in this case to share their own, often conflicting views about Nathan Carman, John Chakalos, Linda Carman, and the Chakalos sisters with minimal interruption. No case is black-and-white, and there are more gray areas here than I ever could have expected. Like many observers of this case, I believe there are only three people who know exactly what happened at 52 Overlook Drive in December 2013 and the area around Block Canyon in 2016, and they are now all dead. As William Shakespeare wrote in *As You Like It*, a play about another murderous plot over a family fortune, "time is the old justice that examines all such offenders, and let time try."

READING GROUP
GUIDE

1. Nathan's closest friend as a child was his horse, Cruise. Did or do you have a pet with whom you're very close? Why are animals so important to us?

2. John and Linda's relationship was not good, even coming to the point of physical altercations. What do you think led to the animosity between them? Were they both to blame?

3. Do you believe the way John and Linda interacted with each other influenced how Nathan acted? How do the actions of our parents and mentors influence our decision-making?

4. John claimed that "Without family, you've got nothing. Family is everything." Do you believe he truly thought this? Do you agree with the statement?

5. How did John attempt to use his money and power to control his family? Do you agree with his decisions? If you had as much money, how would you choose to use it?

6. How does money affect our decisions? Will an excess of money always corrupt, or can it be used responsibly and with care?

7. How did the general public's misunderstanding of autism affect Nathan, especially after Sandy Hook?

8. What do you make of Nathan's buying a boat despite knowing next to nothing about them? Have you ever made an impulsive purchase for the sake of a hobby?

9. Why is it easier to believe that a friendless person committed a crime than a popular, well-liked person? Is this justified?

10. Was the way Nathan was portrayed in the media fair to him? Should you have control over the way you are presented on television, in podcasts, etc.?

11. Do you believe the murder of John Chakalos and the death of Linda Chakalos were related, or were they just a tragic coincidence?

12. Do you believe Nathan deliberately took his mother out on the water to kill her? Did your thoughts change over the course of the book?

ACKNOWLEDGMENTS

Blood in the Water is my eighteenth book over a span of twenty years that began in 2003 with the publication of *A Rose for Mary: The Hunt for the Real Boston Strangler*. Over the course of that time, I have been blessed with an army of supporters who have put up with my moods and all the highs and lows of the writing process and have willed me across the finish line each and every time. My gratitude begins with my beautiful wife, Kristin, who listened patiently as I noodled around with the idea of writing this book and then peppered her with questions and insights about the many unique twists and turns of this fascinating mystery. I love you, my darling. I would also like to thank my brilliant daughters, Bella and Mia Sherman, for their smiles and conversation at the end of a tough day of writing. I would like to thank my mother, Diane Dodd, who continues to show me what grace looks like. A hearty thank you to my uncle Jim Sherman, who proudly still cuts out and saves each newspaper story that I have been featured in. I would also like to thank the Goldsmith-York family for their continued love and support. A big thanks also to my frequent collaborator Dave Wedge.

This book could not have been written without the guidance of my rock star literary agent Peter Steinberg at United Talent Agency or without the incredibly innovative and supportive team at Sourcebooks, especially my editor, Anna Michels, and marketing pros Liz Kelsch, Madeleine Brown, and Kayleigh George. Thanks for making my job so much easier.

Casey Sherman, December 2023

Sources

AUTHOR INTERVIEWS

Richard Arsenault, U.S. Coast Guard

Randall Beach, retired columnist for the *New Haven Register*

Jeannette Brodeur, friend of Linda Carman

Clark Carman, father of Nathan Carman

Kevin Connors, harbormaster, Narragansett, Rhode Island

Tad DiBiase, "no-body" case expert

Brandon Downer, classmate of Nathan Carman's

Eric Gempp, U.S. Coast Guard Investigative Service

Christina Hager, reporter, WBZ-TV News

Michael Iozzi II, witness

Cornelia Jenness, friend of John Chakalos

Don Melanson, chief, Windsor Police Department

Martin Minnella, Nathan Carman's attorney

Alicyn Patton, friend of Nathan Carman's

Shawk Sakaske, witness

David X. Sullivan, Nathan Carman's attorney

Lisa Tutty, FBI (Ret.)

Jed Warner, witness

Joy Washburn, Chakalos family caretaker

W. Russell Webster, U.S. Coast Guard (Ret.)

INVESTIGATIVE DOCUMENTS AND RESOURCES

Charles LaPenna interview, Valerie C. Santilli, Individually and as Executrix of the Estate of John C. Chakalos, Elaine Chakalos, and Charlene Gallagher v. Nathan Carman, State of New Hampshire Sixth Circuit Court, Case Number 313–2017-EQ-00–396, May 5, 2019.

Coast Guard audio with Nathan Carman recorded by Petty Officer Third Class Nicole Groll, United States Coast Guard First District, September 25, 2016.

"Connecticut Police Officer Standards and Training Policy for Handling Missing Persons Investigations," State of Connecticut.

Defendant Nathan Carman's Memorandum in Support of Motion for Leave to Take Three Discovery Depositions, Civil Action No. 17-cv-0038-S-PAS, U.S. District Court for the District of Rhode Island, October 22, 2018.

Limeburner, Richard. "Reverse Drift Analysis of the Path of the *Chicken Pox*'s Life Raft During September 18–25, 2016."

Santilli et al. v. Carman, State of New Hampshire Judicial Branch Notice of Decision, Case Number 313–2017-EQ-00396, May 9, 2019.

Sussex County Sheriff's Department incident report, Nathan Carman, August 15, 2011.

Official Search Warrant for Nathan Carman's home, South Kingstown, Rhode Island, Police Department, September 28, 2016.

United States of America v. Nathan Carman, indictment and public defender appointment, U.S. District Court for the State of Vermont, Criminal No. 5–22-cr-49–1, May 2, 2022.

U.S. Coast Guard Case Report #1022127, April 26, 2016, Sector Southeastern New England.

U.S. Coast Guard First District brief for P/C *Chicken Pox*, September 23, 2016.

Search and Seizure Warrant for Nathan James Carman, State of Connecticut Superior Court, Case Number 2014–1577, July 2014.

U.S. District Court for the District of Rhode Island, National Liability & Fire Insurance Company and Boat Owners Association of the United States v. Nathan Carman, Findings of Fact and Conclusions of Law, November 4, 2019.

U.S. District Court for the District of Rhode Island, National Liability & Fire Insurance Company and Boat Owners Association of the United States v. Nathan Carman, trial transcripts, August 2019.

Notes

CHAPTER ONE

"I hung around with some guys": Richard Arsenault, in discussion with the author, August 29, 2023.

"Hello, this is Nathan Carman": Coast Guard audio with Nathan Carman, recorded by Petty Officer Third Class Nicole Groll, U.S. Coast Guard First District, September 25, 2016.

He doesn't seem lethargic: Arsenault, discussion.

The captain gave it some thought: Dave Altimari and David Owens, "Captain Recalls a Dramatic Day," *Hartford Courant*, October 4, 2016.

CHAPTER TWO

"filled with the rat-a-tats": Randall Beach, "So Long and Thanks, It's Been Good to Know You," *New Haven Register*, November 28, 2020, https://www.nhregister.com/news/article/Randall-Beach-So-long-and-thanks-it-s-been-15759131.php.

"I covered the vigil at Central Park": Randall Beach, in discussion with the author, July 21, 2023.

Hinckley told investigators: United Press International, "2 Calls to Actress Taped by Hinckley," *New York Times*, September 30, 1981, https://www.nytimes.com/1981/09/30/us/2-calls-to-actress-taped-by-hinckley.html.

"He had no other friends": Clark Carman, in discussion with the author, November 9, 2023.

"Nathan and Cruise definitely had a bond": "Mom Tries to Make Sense of Son's Trip to Virginia," *Hartford Courant*, August 25, 2011, https://www.courant.com/2011/08/25 /mom-tries-to-makes-sense-of-sons-trip-to-virginia/.

"He's not pawing": "Mom Tries to Make Sense."

The teen's grandfather continued to pay: Joy Washburn, in discussion with the author, November 19, 2023.

"After the death of his horse": Carman, discussion.

Technically, Nathan was not considered: "Connecticut Police Officer Standards and Training Policy for Handling Missing Persons Investigations," Connecticut Police Officer Standards and Training Council, accessed April 25, 2024, https://portal.ct.gov/ -/media/post/general_notices/missingpersonspolicyfinalcopynov11pdf.pdf?la=en.

"[Nathan] may come off": Mark Spencer and Hillary Federic, "Search for Missing Teen Continues," *Hartford Courant*, August 15, 2011.

Nathan's family members: Washburn, discussion.

"We have a cold trail and no leads": "Search for Missing Teen Continues."

"The special partner he had": Cassandra Day, "Middletown Police: Missing Teen Found Safe in Virginia," Patch, August 16, 2011, https://patch.com/connecticut/northhaven /missing-middletown-teens-family-urges-search-nationwi9108754b23.

"[The Facebook page] is where": Day, "Middletown Police: Missing Teen Found Safe."

"It must be very frightening": Randall Beach, "Family, Volunteers Searching for Nathan Carman in New Haven," *Middletown Press*, August 14, 2011, https://www .middletownpress.com/news/article/Family-volunteers-searching-for-Nathan-Carman -in-11879129.php.

"When you're a mom": Jeannette Brodeur, in discussion with the author, November 30, 2023.

"We're going to find him": Beach, "Family, Volunteers."

"It's like *The Twilight Zone*": Beach, "Family, Volunteers."

CHAPTER THREE

Harrell spoke: Sussex County Sheriff's Department Incident Report (Nathan Carman), August 15, 2011.

"Where did you get all this money?": Sussex County Sheriff's Department Incident Report (Nathan Carman), August 15, 2011.

For much of the day: Day, "Middletown Police: Missing Teen Found Safe."

"Oh, thank goodness": Luther Turmelle, "Missing Middletown Teen Found Safe in Virginia," *New Haven Register*, August 15, 2011, https://www.nhregister.com/news /article/Missing-Middletown-teen-found-safe-in-Virginia-11576900.php.

"He did not want to be found": Randall Beach, "Middletown Parents Just Thankful Runaway Son Is Home Again," *New Haven Register*, August 18, 2011, https://www .nhregister.com/news/article/RANDALL-BEACH-Middletown-parents-just-thankful -11575222.php.

"I don't know what his final plan was": Shawn Beals, "Linda Carman: Grief Led Son to Run Off," *Hartford Courant*, August 25, 2011.

Nathan later told his father: Carman, discussion.

CHAPTER FOUR

"He was intelligent": Brandon Downer, in discussion with the author, September 6, 2023.

"I have Asperger's": Downer, discussion.

One day, during an argument: Shelley Murphy and Evan Allen, "A Son's Hard Times and His Mother's Concern," *Boston Globe*, October 8, 2016, https:// www.bostonglobe.com/metro/2016/10/08/son-hard-times-and-mother-concern /pMv77hgMJXCtYWjgSez1NL/story.html.

CHAPTER FIVE

"Without family, you've got nothing; family is everything": John Chakalos obituary, Carmon Community Funeral Homes, December 20, 2013, https://www .carmonfuneralhome.com/obituaries/obituary-listings?obId=20504391.

"We were both members of a ski club": Carman, discussion.

"When we got to Connecticut, there was nothing": Carman, discussion.

"When he was very young": Carman, discussion.

CHAPTER SIX

"Yes, he is a complicated mess": Murphy and Allen, "Son's Hard Times."

"She always doted on him": Murphy and Allen, "Son's Hard Times."

"His grandfather has insisted": James D. Walsh, "Dead Wake," *New York Magazine*, January 22, 2018, https://nymag.com/intelligencer/2018/01/nathan-carman-linda-carman-death-at-sea.html.

"Nathan was supposed to be there": Carman, discussion.

"They were of the same ilk": Carman, discussion.

"My father is worth $300 million": Walsh, "Dead Wake."

"She was always a bit quiet": Carman, discussion.

CHAPTER SEVEN

"John couldn't really hear anything anymore": Carman, discussion.

"It would be unfair to say": Heidi Evans, "People with Asperger's Rarely Harm Others, So Don't Be So Quick to Link Adam Lanza's Actions with Syndrome: Expert," *New York Daily News*, December 17, 2012, https://www.nydailynews.com/2012/12/17/people-with-aspergers-rarely-harm-others-so-dont-be-so-quick-to-link-adam-lanzas-actions-with-syndrome-expert/.

The backlash against people: Bonnie Rochman, "Troubling Legacy of Sandy Hook May Be Backlash Against Kids with Autism," CNN, December 19, 2012, https://www.cnn.com/2012/12/19/health/shooting-autism/index.html.

"It seems that [the public is] wanting": Rochman, "Troubling Legacy."

"Soon enough, he's gonna slit your throat": Walsh, "Dead Wake."

"Nathan Carman is my only child": Kent Pierce, "Middletown Woman Presumed Lost at Sea Has Been Declared Dead 7 Years Later," WTNH, October 25, 2023, https://www.wtnh.com/news/connecticut/middlesex/middletown-woman-presumed-lost-at-sea-has-been-declared-dead-7-years-later/.

CHAPTER EIGHT

"These are the kind of services for people": Fred Contrada, "Ground Broken for Northampton Assisted-Living Facility at Linda Manor," MassLive.com, September 27, 2013, https://www.masslive.com/news/2013/09/northampton_assisted_living_fa .html.

"John [Chakalos] was very black-and-white": Walsh, "Dead Wake."

"As a monument to himself": Charles LaPenna interview, Valerie C. Santilli, Individually and as Executrix of the Estate of John C. Chakalos, Elaine Chakalos, and Charlene Gallagher v. Nathan James Carman, State of New Hampshire Sixth Circuit Court, Probate Division, Case Number 313–2017-EQ-00–396, May 5, 2019.

"Someday, I'm gonna build me a big mansion": LaPenna interview.

"I became John's right-hand man and woman": Washburn, discussion.

"Fine, I know you all hate me": Washburn, discussion.

"There were maggots crawling": Washburn, discussion.

"I don't know where we went wrong": Washburn, discussion.

"John and Rita used their holiday display": Carter Vanderhoof, "Food Pantry Collects Donations at 'The Farm,'" *Brattleboro Reformer*, December 7, 2011, https://www .reformer.com/local-news/food-pantry-collects-donations-at-the-farm/article _3e4b1ca0-b9a7–543a-8c3a-9d17b8a4228e.html.

"The display was gorgeous": Cornelia Jenness, in discussion with the author, July 21, 2023.

"We're not Jews": Washburn, discussion.

"In all the years": Washburn, discussion.

"It's for our angel": Domenic Poli, "Chesterfield Property Once Again Becomes Winter Wonderland," *Brattleboro Reformer*, December 13, 2013, https://www.reformer.com /local-news/chesterfield-property-once-again-becomes-winter-wonderland/article _9eae6fd0-d123–5c50-be94–82fa1a1ffc57.html.

John Chakalos was especially excited: Ariel Zilber, "Man Accused of Killing His Millionaire Grandfather to Get His Trust Fund Blames 25-Year-Old 'Mistress' Who Was Given $3,500 for Breast Enhancement and Spent the Weekend with Him at a Casino Days before His Murder," *Daily Mail*, October 22, 2018, https://www

.dailymail.co.uk/news/article-6304823/Man-accused-killing-millionaire-grandfather-trust-fund-blames-mistress.html.

He began taking her to lunch: Defendant Nathan Carman's Memorandum in Support of Motion for Leave to Take Three Discovery Depositions, Civil Action No. 17-cv-0038-S-PAS, U.S. District Court for the District of Rhode Island, October 22, 2018, https://www.scribd.com/document/391356567/Nathan-Carman-s-RI-filing.

"[It's] way too big": Defendant Nathan Carman's Memorandum.

CHAPTER NINE

"Nathan's just leaving": Defendant Nathan Carman's Memorandum.

"We were working up there": Washburn, discussion.

An hour later, the same neighbor: Dave Altimari, "New Theory about Millionaire Grandfather's Death in Nathan Carman Case Revolves Around 25-Year-Old 'Mistress Y,'" *Hartford Courant*, October 22, 2018, https://www.courant.com/2018/10/22/new-theory-about-millionaire-grandfathers-death-in-nathan-carman-case-revolves-around-25-year-old-mistress-y/.

The killer then fired two more shots: Donald Melanson, in discussion with the author, September 26, 2023.

"Joy, I just went by John's": Washburn, discussion.

CHAPTER TEN

"One of the daughters": Melanson, discussion.

Valerie had filed for divorce from Rauss: "Man Released on Bail in Harassment Case," *Hartford Courant*, November 2, 2002, https://www.courant.com/2002/11/05/man-released-on-bail-in-harassment-case/.

"That guy deserves a pair of cement shoes!": Washburn, discussion.

"I just want him to leave me alone": "Man Released on Bail."

Interviewing the residents: "Timeline: John Chakalos's Last Day," *Hartford Courant*, October 22, 2018, https://www.courant.com/2018/10/22/timeline-john-chakaloss-last-day/.

"I was home and in my mom's bedroom": Statement of "Neighbor X," December 21, 2013, Defendant Nathan Carman's Memorandum.

"was killed by a bullet to the head": "Police: Windsor Man's Death a Homicide," *Hartford Courant*, December 22, 2013, https://www.newspapers.com/article/hartford-courant -police-windsor-mans-d/102024150/.

"We have many investigators": Dan Crowley, "Developer Shot Dead in Home," *Daily Hampshire Gazette*, January 1, 2014, https://www.newspapers.com/article/daily -hampshire-gazette-developer-shot-d/102024205/.

"He was a dynamic, hard-working": Crowley, "Developer Shot Dead."

"I have bawled all day long": Alyssa Dandrea, "Man Connected with Local Lights Show Found Dead in Connecticut," *Keene Sentinel*, December 21, 2013, https://www .sentinelsource.com/news/local/man-connected-with-local-lights-show-found-dead-in -connecticut/article_61630ebf-8591-5128-8953-08f7d51902d4.html.

"In the end, it's not the years": John Chakalos Tribute Book, December 2013.

"His demeanor was very cool": Carman, discussion.

"had passed away unexpectedly": John Chakalos Obituary, *Hartford Courant*, December 28, 2013, https://www.newspapers.com/article/hartford-courant-obituary-for-john-1 -cha/102024022/.

I wonder if he conducted: Carman, discussion.

"It was a closed casket funeral": Washburn, discussion.

"Nathan killed my father": Washburn, discussion.

CHAPTER ELEVEN

"I would tell you": William Rabbitt police interview, January 7, 2014, Defendant Nathan Carman's Memorandum.

"John had cheated on his wife": Carman, discussion.

"The whole family had lawyers": Melanson, discussion.

"I was never interviewed": Carman, discussion.

"Because the accuracy": Travis Andersen, "Vermont Man Accused of Killing Grandfather Refused Polygraph Test," *Boston Globe*, May 23, 2018, https://www.bostonglobe.com

/metro/2018/05/23/vermont-man-accused-killing-grandfather-refused-polygraph-test
/HJJ9X1RHgGrLB6ppXbVu7M/story.html.

"He was grooming Nathan": Carman, discussion.

"My relationship with my grandfather": Dave Altimari and Mikaela Porter, "Unsealed Records Reveal Where Nathan Carman Says He Was When Grandfather Was Killed," *Hartford Courant*, May 23, 2018, https://www.courant.com/2018/05/23/unsealed -records-reveal-where-nathan-carman-says-he-was-when-grandfather-was-killed/.

The other account contained: United States of America v. Nathan Carman, Indictment, U.S. District Court for the State of Vermont, Criminal No. 5–22-cr-49–1, May 2, 2022, https://www.documentcloud.org/documents/21972497-us-v-nathan-carman-indictment -and-fpd-appointment.

"If any .30 caliber class firearms": Dave Altimari, "Lawyer: Ballistics Report Raises Question about Whether Nathan Carman's Missing Gun Is Murder Weapon," *Hartford Courant*, October 8, 2018, https://www.courant.com/2018/10/08/lawyer-ballistics -report-raises-question-about-whether-nathan-carmans-missing-gun-is-murder -weapon/.

CHAPTER TWELVE

"Detective Wininger's withholding": Steven Goode, "Windsor Officer Demoted, Accused of Withholding Information in Murder Investigation," *Hartford Courant*, July 2, 2014, https://www.courant.com/2014/07/02/windsor-officer-demoted-accused-of-withholding -information-in-murder-investigation/.

"I would never": Goode, "Windsor Officer Demoted."

The bookkeeper was then arraigned: Domenic Poli, "Chakalos' Bookkeeper Facing Larceny Charges," *Brattleboro Reformer*, May 27, 2014, https://www.reformer.com/local -news/chakalos-bookkeeper-facing-larceny-charges/article_8ec50bd2-a576-56c6-a3a7- c2a829fd7605.html.

"I'm sorry": David Owens, "Murdered Man's Bookkeeper Sentenced for Embezzlement," *Hartford Courant*, June 1, 2015, https://www.courant.com/2015/06/01/murdered -mans-bookkeeper-sentenced-for-embezzlement/.

"Part of the greater": Owens, "Murdered Man's Bookkeeper."

"A Sig Sauer is one of the premier": Jed Warner, in discussion with the author, November 12, 2023.

"Show Joy what you just got": Washburn, discussion.

"A person posing [a] risk": Search and Seizure Warrant for Nathan James Carman, State of Connecticut Superior Court, Case Number 2014–1577, July 2014.

"He's a time bomb": "Search Warrants Paint Disturbing Picture of Man Rescued after Weeks Lost at Sea," CBS Boston News, September 28, 2016, https://www.cbsnews.com /boston/news/nathan-carman-linda-carman-missing-boater-rescued-john-chakalos -murder-windsor-connecticut-vernon-vermont/.

Nathan claimed that no one: Dave Altimari, David Owens, Mikaela Porter, and Shawn R. Beals, "Nathan Carman: Grandfather Was 'Like a Father to Me,'" *Hartford Courant*, September 28, 2016, https://www.courant.com/2016/09/28/nathan-carman -grandfather-was-like-a-father-to-me/.

"Before invoking his Fifth Amendment rights": Melanson, discussion.

Nathan also destroyed: Lisa Backus, "Prosecutors: Former CT Resident Nathan Carman Hid Evidence in Grandfather's Homicide," CT Insider, July 25, 2022, https://www .ctinsider.com/news/article/Prosecutors-Former-CT-resident-Nathan-Carman-hid -17327657.php.

"If they [Windsor Police] had asked me": *20/20*, season 40, episode 25, "Lost at Sea," featuring interview of Nathan Carman by Linzie Janis, aired February 3, 2017, on CBS, https://www.youtube.com/watch?v=-GHRWC9jY3M.

"It's not like Wininger could tamper": Melanson, discussion.

"You know your son": Carman, discussion.

"A risk of imminent personal injury": Liz Hardaway and Derek Turner, "Timeline: Nathan Carman, Accused of Killing Mother at Sea, Dies," CT Insider, June 22, 2023, https://www.ctinsider.com/projects/2023/nathan-carman-update-death-timeline/.

CHAPTER THIRTEEN

Nathan got to work right away: Kevin Cullen, "In Vermont, a House That, Like the Owner's

Story, No One Would Buy," *Boston Globe*, May 12, 2022, https://www.bostonglobe.com/2022/05/12/metro/vermont-house-that-like-owners-story-no-one-would-buy/.

"I'd hear him pounding nails": Andy Rosen, Evan Allen, and Shelley Murphy, "Safety of Vessel Under Question," *Boston Globe*, October 6, 2016, https://epaper.bostonglobe.com/BostonGlobe/article_popover.aspx?guid=7923e8dc-955c-4185-9799-adca5eb0f94f&source=next.

"The first thing that come to mind": Sasha Goldstein, "Vermont Man Under Investigation after Rescue at Sea," *Seven Days* (Burlington, VT), September 27, 2016, https://www.sevendaysvt.com/OffMessage/archives/2016/09/27/vermont-man-under-investigation-after-rescue-at-sea.

"He told me he was a big boy": Goldstein, "Vermont Man Under Investigation."

"Fabulous outposts for some": Linda Carman Facebook post, December 8, 2015.

"This person killed at least once": "Sisters Want Nephew Named Murderer of John Chakalos; Linda Carman Presumed Dead," True Crime Daily, September 21, 2017, https://truecrimedaily.com/2017/09/21/sisters-want-nephew-named-murderer-of-john-chakalos-linda-carman-presumed-dead/.

"Maybe it will lead to something": Catalina Trivino, "Family Offers Reward on I-91 Billboard for Cold Case Murder," NBC Connecticut, May 24, 2016, https://www.nbcconnecticut.com/news/local/family-offers-reward-on-i-91-billboard-for-cold-murder-case/53063/.

CHAPTER FOURTEEN

"My first impression": Brian Woods, in discussion with the author, November 12, 2023.

CHAPTER FIFTEEN

Nathan radioed the Coast Guard: U.S. Coast Guard Case Report #1022127, Sector Southeastern New England, April 26, 2016.

"During the incident": W. Russell Webster, in discussion with the author, July 6, 2023.

"I'm above Northampton": Shawn Sakaske, in discussion with the author, November 24, 2023.

"The fragile deep-sea ecosystems": Tanya Somanader, "Watch: President Obama Creates the First Marine National Monument in the Atlantic Ocean," Obama White House Archives, September 15, 2016, https://obamawhitehouse.archives.gov/blog/2016/09 /15/watch-president-obama-creates-first-marine-national-monument-atlantic-ocean.

"I saw the boat passing": Kevin Connors, in discussion with the author, August 1, 2023.

"Uncomfortable with [Nathan's] demeanor": "Lost at Sea."

The trip added to the growing tension: Dave Altimari, "Lawyers Differ on Carmans' Planned Christmas Trip," *Hartford Courant*, December 16, 2016, https://www.courant .com/2016/12/16/lawyers-differ-on-carmans-planned-christmas-trip/.

"She wasn't interested in fishing": Brodeur, discussion.

CHAPTER SIXTEEN

At some point before he left: United States of America v. Nathan Carman, Indictment.

"What are you doing?": Mike Iozzi, in discussion with the author, November 25, 2023.

Without the fiberglass backing: National Liability & Fire Insurance Company and Boat Owners Association of the United States v. Nathan Carman, 419 F. Supp. 3d 336 (D.R.I. 2019), https://casetext.com/case/natl-liab-fire-ins-co-v-carman-2.

The U.S. Coast Guard gave: Dave Altimari and David Owens, "Drinking Water Key to Carman's Survival on Raft, Experts Say," *Hartford Courant*, October 21, 2016, https:// www.courant.com/2016/10/21/drinking-water-key-to-carmans-survival-on-raft -experts-say/.

"My mom and I had an agreement": Katie Mulvaney, "Carman: As Boat Foundered, Mom Became 'Problem,'" *Providence Journal*, August 23, 2019, https://www .providencejournal.com/story/news/courts/2019/08/23/nathan-carman-as-boat-took -on-water-mom-was-more-of-problem-than-solution/986618007/.

"Heading out to Striper Rock": Tony Gugliotta, "Neighbors Await Word on Woman Reported Missing," NBC10 News, September 26, 2016, https://turnto10.com/news /local/neighbors-await-word-on-woman-reported-missing.

"Where was she going": Cassandra Day, "Merchant Vessel Rescues Connecticut Boater 100 Miles East of Martha's Vineyard After 8 Days at Sea," *New Haven Register*,

September 26, 2016, https://www.nhregister.com/connecticut/article/Merchant-vessel
-rescues-Connecticut-boater-100–11321572.php.

Linda then texted Jeannette Brodeur: Brodeur, discussion.

"I couldn't really see anybody on board": Altimari and Owens, "Drinking Water Key."

"It came in as a search and rescue case": Arsenault, discussion.

"The Coast Guard always looked": Webster, discussion.

After identifying the search radius: U.S. Coast Guard First District brief for P/C *Chicken Pox*, September 23, 2016.

"We did our planning module": Arsenault, discussion.

CHAPTER SEVENTEEN

"I almost felt like": Mulvaney, "Carman: As Boat Foundered."

"I heard a noise": "Lost at Sea."

"I treated my mother like a passenger": Mulvaney, "Carman: As Boat Foundered."

"I was walking on the deck": "Lost at Sea."

"I don't know if she got hit": Mulvaney, "Carman: As Boat Foundered."

"I assumed that": "Lost at Sea."

Richard Arsenault and his search and rescue: U.S. Coast Guard First District brief.

"What happens to folks": Arsenault, discussion.

There were several examples: "Longest Time Adrift at Sea," Guinness World Records, accessed April 26, 2024, https://www.guinnessworldrecords.com/world-records/longest
-time-adrift-at-sea.

"The Coast Guard had": Eric Gempp, in discussion with the author, January 3, 2024.

Investigators quickly determined: U.S. Coast Guard First District brief.

"Wait a minute": Sakaske, discussion.

"You'd better make your": Woods, discussion.

"I know she would never decide": Shawn R. Beals, "Coast Guard Continues Search for Missing Boaters from Middletown," *Hartford Courant*, September 21, 2016, https://
www.courant.com/2016/09/21/coast-guard-continues-search-for-missing-boaters-from
-middletown/.

Since he was alone: "Lost at Sea."

"There are always lessons": Arsenault, discussion.

CHAPTER EIGHTEEN

"Town freak": Dave Altimari, "Records Provide New Insight into Coast Guard Search for Nathan, Linda Carman," *Hartford Courant*, April 29, 2018, https://www.courant.com /2018/04/29/records-provide-new-insight-into-coast-guard-search-for-nathan-linda -carman/.

"When you deliver": Evan Lubofsky, "A Son Is Rescued at Sea. But What Happened to His Mother?," *Wired*, July 13, 2021, https://www.wired.com/story/a-son-is-rescued-at-sea -but-what-happened-to-his-mother/.

"To sit in a raft": Arsenault, discussion.

"If my mom is lost": Dave Altimari, "In Letters to Captain, Nathan Carman Laments Likely Loss of Mother," *Hartford Courant*, October 5, 2016, https://www.courant.com/2016 /10/05/in-letters-to-captain-nathan-carman-laments-likely-loss-of-mother/.

"I immediately flew": Carman, discussion.

"Working the boats": Gempp, discussion.

"I don't know how one": Day, "Merchant Vessel Rescues Connecticut Boater."

"I was at work": Brodeur, discussion.

"They spotted what they thought": Day, "Merchant Vessel Rescues Connecticut Boater."

"He's coming in": Christina Hager, in discussion with the author, April 28, 2023.

"If he had been in a raft": Webster, discussion.

"I began questioning": Gempp, discussion.

"We cooperated fully": "Man Who Survived Boat Sinking, But Lost His Mother, Arrives in Boston," *Boston Globe*, September 27, 2016, https://www.bostonglobe.com/metro /2016/09/27/man-who-survived-boat-sinking-but-lost-his-mother-expected-boston /p63AgDztT7WDy2485AmY8L/story.html.

"I just want to thank": John Atwater, "'I Feel Healthy. Emotionally, I've Been through a Huge Amount,'" WCVB News, September 27, 2016, https://www.wcvb.com/article/i -feel-healthy-emotionally-ive-been-through-a-huge-amount-2/8110658.

"Some people didn't know": Hager, discussion.

"Believe that evidence": Search warrant for Nathan Carman's home, South Kingstown, Rhode Island, Police Department, September 28, 2016.

"She filled the first jar": Allen and Murphy, "Son's Hard Times."

CHAPTER NINETEEN

"Nathan has not given up hope": Dave Altimari, "Man Rescued at Sea Plans Memorial for Presumed-Dead Mother, Upsetting Her Sisters," *New Hampshire Union Leader*, October 24, 2016, https://www.unionleader.com/news/safety/man-rescued-at-sea-plans-memorial-for-presumed-dead-mother-upsetting-her-sisters/article_08f77aab-07d4–585b-a7c0–6666ad62ae1e.html.

"I hope beyond words": Dave Altimari, "After Service for His Mother, Nathan Carman Says 'I Hope She Will Be Found,'" *Hartford Courant*, October 26, 2016, https://www.courant.com/2016/10/26/after-service-for-his-mother-nathan-carman-says-i-hope-she-will-be-found/.

"Linda's family and friends": Altimari, "Man Rescued at Sea Plans Memorial."

"I met him": Brodeur, discussion.

"I'm very grateful": Altimari, "After Service for His Mother."

"It just reminded us": Brodeur, discussion.

"Linda's family fully supports": Dave Altimari, "Linda Carman's Friend Moves to Become Trustee of Financial Affairs," *Hartford Courant*, November 10, 2016, https://www.courant.com/2016/11/10/linda-carmans-friend-moves-to-become-trustee-of-financial-affairs/.

"We would ask questions": Gempp, discussion.

"It was a circumstantial case": Melanson, discussion.

"Why is the FBI calling me?": Sakaske, discussion.

CHAPTER TWENTY

"You began moving": Dave Altimari and David Owens, "Insurance Companies Say Nathan Carman's Boat Was Not Seaworthy When It Sank, Deny Coverage," *Hartford*

Courant, January 30, 2017, https://www.courant.com/2017/01/30/insurance-companies-say-nathan-carmans-boat-was-not-seaworthy-when-it-sank-deny-coverage/.

"Your boat's sinking": Andy Rosen, "Insurer Won't Pay Claim on Boat That Sank, Killing Woman," *Boston Globe*, January 31, 2017, https://www.bostonglobe.com/metro/2017/01/30/insurance-company-refuses-pay-claim-boat-that-sank-off-rhode-island-with-woman-aboard/VDTEH0JtxaBcY7SjAd2LkK/story.html.

"Why would anyone sabotage": Linzie Janis, "Reporter's Notebook: What It Was Like to Interview Rescued Boater Nathan Carman," ABC News, February 2, 2017, https://abcnews.go.com/US/reporters-notebook-interview-rescued-boater-nathan-carman/story?id=45201525.

"I'm not sure": "Lost at Sea."

"Wasn't Nathan's motivation": Janis, "Reporter's Notebook."

"It makes me feel": "Lost at Sea."

CHAPTER TWENTY-ONE

"Was it missing at sea": "Lost at Sea."

"I thought it was bullshit": Sakaske, discussion.

"I love it when the bad guy": Anonymous user, comment on "Did Nathan kill his wealthy grandfather John Charles Carman in 2013, and then sink his very own mother Linda out at sea in 2016...for an attempt at his pending inheritance of millions?," Reddit, June 26, 2023, https://www.reddit.com/r/TrueCrimeDiscussion/comments/14j6ayz/did_nathan_kill_his_wealthy_grandfather_john/; Gerealtor, comment on "Did Nathan kill his wealthy grandfather John Charles Carman in 2013, and then sink his very own mother Linda out at sea in 2016...for an attempt at his pending inheritance of millions?," Reddit, June 26, 2023, https://www.reddit.com/r/TrueCrimeDiscussion/comments/14j6ayz/did_nathan_kill_his_wealthy_grandfather_john/; AnastasiaBeavrhausn, comment on "Boat accident or murder?," Reddit, April 12, 2020, https://www.reddit.com/r/UnresolvedMysteries/comments/fzzocv/boat_accident_or_murder/.

"Not good that he": scarab63, comment on "Two Missing off Block Island," Boating & Fishing Forum, Hull Truth, September 27, 2016, https://www.thehulltruth.com /northeast/789398-two-missing-off-block-island-5.html.

"The question raised": Charles Doane, "Nathan Carman: Suspicious Circumstances Surrounding His Week Adrift in a Liferaft [sic]," WaveTrain, October 4, 2016, https:// wavetrain.net/2016/10/04/nathan-carman-suspicious-circumstances-surrounding-his -week-adrift-in-a-liferaft/.

"People with Asperger's": "Lost at Sea."

"His recollection of events": Gempp, discussion.

During the course: Search and Seizure Warrant for Nathan James Carman.

"The facts contained": Dave Altimari, "Carman Wants Warrant Sealed," *Hartford Courant*, April 11, 2017, https://www.newspapers.com/article/hartford-courant -carman-wants-warrant-se/102030014/.

"The warrant has been public": "Man Rescued at Sea Denied Request for Sealing of Warrant," *Boston Globe*, April 20, 2017, https://www.bostonglobe .com/metro/2017/04/20/man-rescued-sea-denied-request-sealing-warrant /qRhmMMs982KWfMzOqB9tLL/story.html.

CHAPTER TWENTY-TWO

"In 2013, four sisters": Dave Altimari, "Sisters Connect Carman to Death," *Hartford Courant*, July 18, 2017, https://www.newspapers.com/article/hartford-courant-sister -connect-carman-t/102030139/.

"[The Chakalos sisters]": Altimari, "Sisters Connect Carman to Death."

critics in the legal community: Nili Cohen, "The Slayer Rule," *Boston University Legal Review* 92 (2012): 793–810, https://dx.doi.org/10.2139/ssrn.2141336.

"His actions/inactions": Dave Altimari, "Boat Insurers Fight Payout," *Hartford Courant*, August 4, 2017, https://www.newspapers.com/article/hartford-courant-boat-insurers -fight-pay/102030582/.

"[Nathan's] brain works": Travis Andersen, "Lawyers for Nathan Carman Push Back on Information Request from Boat Insurer," *Boston Globe*, October 3, 2017, https://

www.bostonglobe.com/metro/2017/10/03/lawyers-for-nathan-carman-push-back
-information-request-from-boat-insurer/hHrfalTTcbhj5Mal3TGdVO/story.html.

"I told you that": Michelle R. Smith, "Court Hearing for Boater Whose Relatives Died
Mysteriously," Associated Press, August 9, 2017, https://apnews.com/general-news
-d5256c4b9dd74cca9be7a586b80d5db0.

CHAPTER TWENTY-THREE

"well-known, active member": Dave Altimari, "Carman's Lawyer Asks Court to Toss
Aunts' Petition," *Hartford Courant*, December 7, 2017, https://www.newspapers.com
/article/hartford-courant-carmans-lawyer-asks-co/102032816/.

"The sisters brought this case": Matthew Kauffman, "Mother's Status Key in Carman
Case," *Hartford Courant*, December 16, 2017, https://www.newspapers.com/article
/hartford-courant-mothers-status-key-in/102033260/.

"I did not kill": Dave Altimari, "Nathan Carman Fires His Attorneys, Calls Aunts
'Greedy,'" *Hartford Courant*, February 7, 2018, https://www.courant.com/2018/02/07
/nathan-carman-fires-his-attorneys-calls-aunts-greedy/.

CHAPTER TWENTY-FOUR

"I'm a bit concerned": Nathan Carman Slayer Rule Hearing, aired on Law & Crime Trial
Network, April 3, 2018.

"It's completely outrageous": Travis Andersen, "Nathan Carman Says Aunts Had
'Substantial Motive' to Murder His Grandfather," *Boston Globe*, April 3, 2018, https://
www.bostonglobe.com/metro/2018/04/03/nathan-carman-says-aunts-had-substantial
-motive-murder-his-grandfather/hKHR0P3cLQ3wZwog4BgeTO/story.html.

CHAPTER TWENTY-FIVE

"At least two of my aunts": Dave Altimari, "Nathan Carman Pushes Back Against Aunts'
Allegations He Killed Grandfather," *Hartford Courant*, May 21, 2018, https://www
.courant.com/2018/05/21/nathan-carman-pushes-back-against-aunts-allegations-he
-killed-grandfather/.

"I expect to prevail": "Judge Schedules 10-Day Trial in Mystery Deaths Case," WBZ News Boston, June 5, 2018, https://www.cbsnews.com/boston/news/nathan-carman-judge -schedules-10-day-trial-mystery-deaths-case/.

"My fam is only alive cuz": Dave Altimari, "Facebook Page with Threat to Family, Possibly Belonging to Nathan Carman, Subject of Court Motion," *Hartford Courant*, July 30, 2018, https://www.courant.com/2018/07/30/facebook-page-with-threat-to-family -possibly-belonging-to-nathan-carman-subject-of-court-motion/.

"He's hiding assets": Dave Altimari, "Legal Fight between Nathan Carman and His Family Comes to West Hartford," *Hartford Courant*, August 7, 2018, https://www.courant.com /2018/08/07/legal-fight-between-nathan-carman-and-his-family-comes-to-west-hartford/.

"How do you lose a gun like that?": Bob Ward, "Murder, Mystery and Money: The Accusations Swirling around Nathan Carman," Boston 25 News, October 8, 2018, https://www.boston25news.com/news/murder-mystery-and-money-the-accusations -swirling-around-nathan-carman/637186549/.

"A savvy businessman": Valerie C. Santilli, Individually and as Executrix of the Estate of John C. Chakalos, Elaine Chakalos, and Charlene Gallagher v. Nathan James Carman, State of New Hampshire Sixth Circuit Court, Probate Division, Case Number 313–2017-EQ-00–396, Order on Motion to Reconsider, May 9, 2019, https://www .shaheengordon.com/documents/5-9-19-Santilli-v-Carman-Order-on-Motion-to -Reconsider.pdf.

"Object to the word 'home'": Santilli et al. v. Carman, Order on Motion to Reconsider.

"We didn't want John and Rita": Santilli et al. v. Carman, Order on Motion to Reconsider.

"Did you believe I was guilty": Dave Altimari, "Nathan Carman Tells Judge Aunt Wants to Punish Him for Grandfather's Death," *Hartford Courant*, September 27, 2018, https://www.courant.com/2018/09/27/nathan-carman-tells-judge-aunt-wants -to-punish-him-for-grandfathers-death/.

CHAPTER TWENTY-SIX

"Lawyer: Evidence Could": "Lawyer: Evidence Could Exonerate Man in Windsor Grandfather's Death," *Meriden Record-Journal*, September 19, 2018.

"Testimony from 'Mistress Y'": Defendant Nathan Carman's Memorandum.

"While they were at the casino": Laurel J. Sweet, "Nathan Carman Lawyer Airs Dirty Laundry," *Boston Herald*, November 14, 2018, https://www.bostonherald.com/2018 /10/26/nathan-carman-lawyer-airs-dirty-laundry/.

"Nathan's shameful attack": Sweet, "Nathan Carman Lawyer."

"Courts are presumptively open": Cassandra Day, "1st Amendment Advocates Seek Transparency in Nathan Carman Case," *Middletown Press*, April 20, 2018, https:// www.middletownpress.com/middletown/article/1st-Amendment-advocates-seek -transparency-in-12852223.php.

"On 12/20/13": Defendant Nathan Carman's Memorandum.

"Doesn't indicate that the murder weapon": Altimari, "Lawyer: Ballistics Report Raises."

"If any .30 class firearms": Altimari, "Lawyer: Ballistics Report Raises."

"Uncivilized, bordering on unethical": Dave Altimari, "New Hampshire Judge in Nathan Carman Case Rebukes Attorneys, Accusing Them of Trying to Take Advantage of Him," *Hartford Courant*, December 21, 2018, https://www.courant.com/2018/12 /21/new-hampshire-judge-in-nathan-carman-case-rebukes-attorneys-accusing-them -of-trying-to-take-advantage-of-him/.

"I did that": Dave Altimari, "New Hampshire Judge Sets January Trial Date in Nathan Carman Case," *Hartford Courant*, October 4, 2018, https://www.courant.com/2018/10 /04/new-hampshire-judge-sets-january-trial-date-in-nathan-carman-case/.

"We are going to move forward": Altimari, "New Hampshire Judge Sets."

CHAPTER TWENTY-SEVEN

"The Sig Sauer": Travis Andersen, "Nathan Carman Tossed Alleged Murder Weapon in the Ocean after Grandpa Slain, Insurer Says," *Boston Globe*, December 31, 2018, https:// www.bostonglobe.com/metro/2018/12/31/nathan-carman-tossed-alleged-murder -weapon-ocean-after-grandpa-slain-insurer-says/ogX04MP0FDWHGGxEbkEMqM /story.html.

"Striking, chilling, parallel losses": Andersen, "Nathan Carman Tossed."

"Nathan had been given": Carman, discussion.

"unlimited resources": Travis Andersen, "Insurer Trying to 'Wear Down' Nathan Carman, Lawyer Says in Court Filing," *Boston Globe*, January 11, 2019, https://www .bostonglobe.com/metro/2019/01/11/insurer-trying-wear-down-nathan-carman -lawyer-says-blasts-false-murder-allegations/XLaVtPwvHCrVBPvcfJOzgP/story .html.

"This has taken up": Dave Altimari, "Judge Postpones Start of Carman Trial," *Hartford Courant*, January 12, 2019, https://www.newspapers.com/article/hartford-courant -judge-postpones-start-o/102039961/.

"The records show": "Judge to Reconsider Home of Late Grandfather in Boater Case," Associated Press, April 23, 2019, https://apnews.com/general-news -e34ee5dc042e4db3b73e796c1bb52b95.

"The court determines": Santilli et al. v. Carman, Order on Motion to Reconsider.

"I want to make clear": Dave Altimari, "Judge Tosses 'Slayer Petition,'" *Hartford Courant*, May 11, 2019, https://www.newspapers.com/article/hartford-courant-judge-tosses -slayer-pe/102040483/.

"John immersed himself": Altimari, "Judge Tosses 'Slayer Petition.'"

CHAPTER TWENTY-EIGHT

"On the very day": Josh Kovner, "Report Defies Carman's Story," *Hartford Courant*, July 19, 2019, https://www.newspapers.com/article/hartford-courant-report-defies -carmans/102041683/.

The insurance companies' attorneys: Richard Limeburner, "Reverse Drift Analysis of the Path of the *Chicken Pox*'s Life Raft During September 18–25, 2016," Supplemental Expert Report, April 19, 2019, https://www.whoi.edu/science/PO /coastal/RL2007/pdfs/R.%20Limeburner%20Life%20Raft%20Path%20Report %202022revised.pdf.

"If I were Nathan": Webster, discussion.

"Because the issues": Dave Altimari, "With Trial Near, a Narrowed Focus," *Hartford Courant*, August 11, 2019, https://www.newspapers.com/article/hartford-courant-with -trial-near-a-narr/102041817/.

"The evidence will show": Opening Statements of Counsel, National Liability & Fire Insurance Company and Boat Owners Association of the United States v. Nathan Carman, August 13, 2019.

"He [Nathan] wouldn't look at me": Woods, discussion.

"I was concerned about": Testimony of Brian Woods, National Liability & Fire Insurance Company and Boat Owners Association of the United States v. Nathan Carman, August 13, 2019.

"He was purchasing repair items": Gempp, discussion.

"It informed the investigation": Lisa Tutty, in discussion with the author, January 30, 2024.

"They had their reason": Gempp, discussion.

"It was in good, serviceable condition": Testimony of Bernard Feeney, National Liability & Fire Insurance Company and Boat Owners Association of the United States v. Nathan Carman, August 14, 2019.

"I don't see how this boat": Testimony of Eric Greene, National Liability & Fire Insurance Company and Boat Owners Association of the United States v. Nathan Carman, August 14, 2019.

"I don't see how a drifting": Testimony of Richard Limeburner, National Liability & Fire Insurance Company and Boat Owners Association of the United States v. Nathan Carman, August 14, 2019.

CHAPTER TWENTY-NINE

"Mr. Carman did say": Testimony of Martha Charlesworth, National Liability & Fire Insurance Company and Boat Owners Association of the United States v. Nathan Carman, August 15, 2019.

"I know for a fact": Testimony of Nathan Carman, National Liability & Fire Insurance Company and Boat Owners Association of the United States v. Nathan Carman, August 22, 2019.

"This is one creepy dude": Comments on Shelley Murphy, "Nathan Carman Says His Mother Was 'Kind of a Problem' While Boat Was Sinking," *Boston Globe*, August

23, 2019, https://www.bostonglobe.com/2019/08/23/metro/nathan-carman-says-his-mother-was-kind-problem-boat-was-sinking/.

CHAPTER THIRTY

"Look at Mr. Carman's": Closing arguments, National Liability & Fire Insurance Company and Boat Owners Association of the United States v. Nathan Carman, September 4, 2019.

"I almost feel like": Ashley Afonso, "Nathan Carman Speaks Outside Court after Closing Arguments Heard in Insurance Case," FOX61 News, September 4, 2019, https://www.fox61.com/article/news/local/outreach/awareness-months/closing-arguments-begin-wednesday-in-nathan-carman-insurance-case/520-bf7b31de-23f9–48ba-853c-6f2496a98405.

"Based on the evidence": *National Liability v. Carman*, 419 F. Supp. 3d 336.

"Nothing raised by": Mark Pratt, "Judge Denies Motion for New Trial in Boat Sinking Case," Associated Press, December 30, 2019, https://apnews.com/regional-us-general-news-national-national-d8fa44c67d2e003a3b08999f4c290861.

CHAPTER THIRTY-ONE

"I heard about the case": Alicyn Patton, in discussion with the author, November 30, 2023.

"I don't mean this in a bad way": Text messages between Nathan Carman and Alicyn Patton, February 2021.

CHAPTER THIRTY-TWO

"At this point": Gempp, discussion.

"Kolo is an exemplary": Alan J. Keays, "Shelburne Attorney Takes Oath as Top Federal Prosecutor in Vermont," VTDigger, December 10, 2021, https://vtdigger.org/2021/12/10/shelburne-attorney-takes-oath-as-top-federal-prosecutor-in-vermont/.

"Beginning in or about 2013": United States of America v. Nathan Carman, Indictment.

"When I heard that Nathan had been arrested": Carman, discussion.

"Do you have anything to say": "Nathan Carman Pleads Not Guilty During

Arraignment," Local 22 ABC News, May 11, 2022, YouTube video, 1:42, https://www
.youtube.com/watch?v=AAoOd9EGifE.

CHAPTER THIRTY-THREE

"For an individual": Bob Audette, "'A Highly Unconventional Problem Solving Style': US
Attorney Calls for Pretrial Detention for Nathan Carman," *Brattleboro Reformer*, May
11, 2022, https://www.reformer.com/local-news/a-highly-unconventional-problem
-solving-style-us-attorney-calls-for-pretrial-detention-for-nathan-carman/article
_2de7b09e-d140–11ec-9754–033f10797863.html.

"If anyone could have survived prison": Carman, discussion.

"At no time during that lengthy period": "Man Charged with Killing Mother at Sea
Seeks Freedom," Associated Press, July 6, 2022, https://apnews.com/article/vermont
-burlington-cbacdcf1cd2006ae61771f6467cff85b.

"He came to our church": Lisa Backus, "Former CT Resident Nathan Carman,
Accused of Killing Mom for Inheritance, Seeks Release with Friends' Help," CT Insider,
July 20, 2022, https://www.ctinsider.com/news/article/Former-CT-resident-Nathan
-Carman-accused-of-17317233.php.

"I see no financial motive": Backus, "Former CT Resident."

"Unfortunately, I don't have a house": Alicyn Patton, character reference letter in
regard for Nathan Carman, June 27, 2022.

"We are very concerned": Christine Dempsey, "Accused of Killing Mom and
Grandfather, Former CT Resident Nathan Carman Is 'a Danger to This Family,'
Letter States," *Middletown Press*, August 1, 2022, https://www.middletownpress
.com/news/article/Accused-of-killing-mom-and-grandfather-former-CT-17343009
.php.

"Two days after Carman got his grades": Kevin Cullen, "Is Nathan Carman a Horrible
Monster, or Just Horribly Misunderstood?," *Boston Globe*, August 2, 2022, https://
www.bostonglobe.com/2022/08/02/metro/is-nathan-carman-horrible-monster-or-just
-horribly-misunderstood/.

"The seriousness of the charges": "Man Charged with Killing His Mother at Sea to Remain Detained," Associated Press, August 2, 2022, https://apnews.com/article/connecticut-vermont-burlington-84c08abf90486664f97359cc445b27cd.

DiBiase found that: Thomas A. (Tad) DiBiase, "'No-body' Murder Trials in the United States," No-body Murder Cases, January 2023, https://www.nobodycases.com/wp-content/uploads/2023/01/Nobodytable-Jan-2023.pdf.

"What you find in these cases": Tad DiBiase, in discussion with the author, December 16, 2023.

"Klowitonski picked up a tar stick": "A Murder at Sea," *New York Times*, January 16, 1880, https://www.nytimes.com/1880/01/16/archives/a-murder-at-sea.html.

"Kill me once": Anonymous user, comment on "Boat accident or murder?," Reddit, April 12, 2020, https://www.reddit.com/r/UnresolvedMysteries/comments/fzzocv/boat_accident_or_murder/.

"An elaborate, almost Shakespearean conspiracy": Cullen, "In Vermont."

"I can't really talk": Patton, discussion.

CHAPTER THIRTY-FOUR

"Come into me. I'll fight you": Julie Stagis, "Killer's Defense: He Was Possessed," *Hartford Courant*, April 22, 2014.

"irrelevant, unprovable and needlessly confusing": Stagis, "Killer's Defense."

"And what I saw in Arne as a young guy": Stagis, "Killer's Defense."

"You're the real victim here": Martin Minnella, in discussion with the author, December 17, 2023.

"I read the indictment": David X. Sullivan, in discussion with the author, December 16, 2023.

"She was very cooperative": Gempp, discussion.

"I drove up to see him": Patton, discussion.

"[The indictment includes] matter-of-fact": Lisa Rathke, "Man Charged with Killing Mom at Sea Seeks Grand Jury Minutes," Associated Press, January 30, 2023, https://apnews.com/article/indictments-fraud-844517d8cb554f04189bb95adb2b4030.

CHAPTER THIRTY-FIVE

Although the jail promoted: Christopher Cartwright, "Former Keene Inmate Alleges Treatment Violated Constitutional Rights," *Keene Sentinel*, August 31, 2023, https://www.sentinelsource.com/news/local/public_safety/former-keene-jail-inmate-alleges-treatment-violated-constitutional-rights/article_b9812015-1275-519c-859f-8a3e739096ed.html.

"Nathan did all the repairs to that boat": Minnella, discussion.

"He wasn't a skilled mariner": Sullivan, discussion.

"Athena was aware": "AG Healey Secures $1.75 Million Resolution with Nursing Home Chain over Failure to Meet the Needs of Residents with Substance Abuse Disorder," press release, Massachusetts Office of the Attorney General, December 21, 2022, https://www.mass.gov/news/ag-healey-secures-175-million-resolution-with-nursing-home-chain-over-failure-to-meet-the-needs-of-residents-with-substance-use-disorder.

Santilli's company was also facing: Dave Altimari and Jenna Carlesso, "Lawsuits, Fines, Complaints Put Pressure on Athena Nursing Homes," CT Mirror, January 15, 2023, https://ctmirror.org/2023/01/15/ct-athena-health-systems-nursing-home-lawsuit-massachusetts-rhode-island-connecticut/.

"We had experts ready to testify": Minnella, discussion.

"We discovered a text": Minnella, discussion.

"We had a lot of legal discussions": Sullivan, discussion.

CHAPTER THIRTY-SIX

"Nathan Carman is dead": Gempp, discussion.

"I could not believe it": Carman, discussion.

"He became more than a client": Tim Callery, "Nathan Carman, Who Faced Murder-on-the-High-Seas Trial in Mother's Death, Found Dead in New Hampshire Jail Cell," WMUR-TV, June 15, 2023, https://www.wmur.com/article/nathan-carman-dead/44210855 (includes video of attorneys' remarks).

"I'm so confused": Patton, discussion.

"I couldn't wait to stare him down": Woods, discussion.

"Nathan's death was not considered": Lisa Backus, "Nathan Carman, Accused of Killing

His CT Mom, Left Note in Cell, Death Not Suspicious, Officials Say," CT Insider, June 16, 2023, https://www.ctinsider.com/connecticut/article/nathan-carman-ct-cause -of-death-note-jail-cell-18156065.php.

"One week ago": Author's notes from Nathan Carman's funeral, June 22, 2023.

"I couldn't believe it": Carman, discussion.

"time is the old justice": Shakespeare, *As You Like It*, act 4, sc. 1.

ABOUT THE AUTHOR

Casey Sherman is a *New York Times, Wall Street Journal, USA Today, Los Angeles Times* and *Boston Globe* bestselling author of eighteen books, including *The Finest Hours* (now a major Walt Disney Studios motion picture starring Chris Pine and Casey Affleck) and *Patriots Day* (now an acclaimed motion picture from CBS Films starring Mark Wahlberg and Kevin Bacon). Sherman's true-crime bestseller, *Helltown*, is now in development as a limited television series for Amazon Studios. Sherman will serve as executive producer on the project, which is slated to star Oscar Isaac (*Dune*), with director Edward Berger (Netflix, *All Quiet on the Western Front*) and producers Robert Downey Jr. and Susan Downey (HBO's *Perry Mason*). Sherman's other books include *A Murder in Hollywood*, a USA Today #1 true-crime bestseller; James Patterson's *The Last Days of John Lennon*, which spent more than twenty-three weeks on the *New York Times* bestsellers list; *12: The Inside Story of Tom Brady's Fight for Redemption*; and *Hunting Whitey: The Inside Story of the Capture and Killing of America's Most Wanted Crime*

Boss. Sherman has appeared on more than one hundred television and radio programs and is a contributing writer for *TIME* magazine, *Esquire*, the *Washington Post*, the *Daily Beast*, *Boston Magazine*, and the *Boston Herald*.

CHECK OUT THE LATEST BOOKS FROM TRUE CRIME MASTER CASEY SHERMAN!

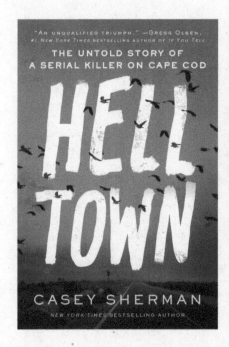

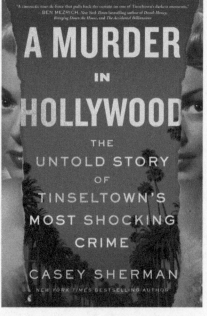